ADVANCE PRAISE

This is both a compelling personal story and a shatteringly painful account of the internal politics and lies that fueled the anti-gay movement.

Mathew Shurka, Co-Founder, Born Perfect
Shannon Minter, Legal Director, NCLR

Randy's book *WHY* is another important opportunity for people to learn about the enormous harm misguided and ill-informed religious teachings cause to innocent, vulnerable people—especially LGBTQ+ youth. Randy writes his difficult life story in a spirited way keeping your attention page after page. Now, he shares a certain joyfulness about his life, making this a compelling book. Please think about buying this book and giving it to people who, unknowingly, are causing the kind of harm that too often leads to LGBTQ+ people taking their lives, using drugs or alcohol dangerously, or suffering severe emotional distress.

Mitchell Gold, Philanthropist and Co-Founder
Mitchell Gold + Bob Williams Home Furnishings

At once both wrenching and laugh-out-loud hilarious, Randy Scobey's new memoir, *WHY*, is a joy to read. From surviving abuse to wrestling with his own demons to literally being saved by an angel, his in and out and then back in and then back out again story is inspiring on so many levels. Indeed, Scobey's greatest triumph and lesson, from which we can all learn, is that living an authentic life is our greatest blessing. Five stars!

Daniel Karslake, Director/Producer:
For the Bible Tells Me So
For They Know Not What They Do

WHY is a meaningful memoir of death and resurrection. Death wasn't the final chapter in Jesus' story, and it isn't in Randy's either. The death of Exodus and Randy's journey out of the stained-glass closet brought him new life along with others who overcame the shame and harm of conversion therapy and religious stigma. He survived the wilderness wanderings and came out of it refined by the fire. That's how God works. God can use the most unexpected people to set things right. Rightly gay at that!

Rev. Terri Steed Pierce, Lead Pastor
Joy Metropolitan Community Church, Orlando, Florida

Randy Scobey's *WHY* reminds us that to be authentic takes courage. To share your story with the world is brave. Randy's journey is the story of a man who goes to hell so that he can come out the other side and find personal peace. This is more than a coming out story; this is a personal love story to self and freedom that we can all learn from. *WHY* is about finding your own God and living life one blink at a time. It is a celebration of the human spirit. Take Randy's lead and ask yourself "WHY"… you may find the courage to finally be free.

Gregory Zarian
Emmy-nominated actor/Anti-bullying activist

Randy and I were once bitter enemies. I was an LGBTQ activist and he was an ex-gay leader. We sparred in green rooms, on talk radio shows, and in dueling press releases. To my pleasant surprise, we are friends today, both fighting for LGBTQ equality.

WHY is a powerful, fully engaging book that chronicles Randy's harrowing journey from darkness into the light. I highly recommend this page-turner, which I found enlightening, eye-opening and entertaining. This is a must-read memoir.

Wayne Besen, Author
Lies with a Straight Face: Exposing the Creeps and Cons Inside the 'Ex-Gay' Industry

Randy Scobey's memoir, *WHY*, leaves no room for lingering questions. It unravels the intricacies of one man's extraordinary life and his journey from being a global "ex-gay" leader to an out, proud, married, gay man… again. It's honest, heartfelt and, at times, raw. This work is intensely relevant to a variety of audiences: religious conservatives, the queer community, families and allies, and ex-gay/reparative/conversion "therapy" survivors.

Anthony Venn-Brown, OAM
Author of the bestseller *A Life of Unlearning: A Preacher's Struggle with His Homosexuality, Church and Faith*
Founder and CEO, Ambassadors & Bridge Builders International (ABBI)

WHY: A Memoir is a true testament that turning away from false misinformation and dogma is possible if we simply allow ourselves to not conform to the status quo of the past's misguided ideas of stigma and shame, and allow our hearts and minds to be transformed by the wisdom and knowledge God continues to show us today through research and personal stories. Randy Scobey is a delightful storyteller of a very poignant and important tale that must be shared to save others from the same emotional, psychological, physical, and spiritual harms and abuses caused by conversion therapy. I am so grateful for his courage and boldness to share his journey and the hard-learned lessons he needed to discover to fully accept the truth: that he is fully loved by God as a gay man of faith… perfect just as he is!

Jane Clementi
Co-Founder & CEO, Tyler Clementi Foundation

Randy Scobey has been asking the question "why?" for a while. Why did God make me gay? Why am I feeling so much incongruence between who I am and the community around me? Why do I fear the reactions of others? Why can't I be accepted for who I am? These questions help us understand the pressures that can drive someone into the throes of ex-LGBTQ programming. In this book, you'll get a behind-the-scenes look at what drives so-called conversion therapy programs. Scobey has been both at the heights of power and the bottom of the social scale, and he will give you an honest and reflective review of his life. More important than learning what he did, is WHY he did it. He is unflinching and honest, and the rest of us have a lot to learn from his experience.

Deacon Ross Murray
GLAAD & The Naming Project

WHY is not just the memoir of Randy Scobey, one-time Executive Vice President of the now defunct Exodus International, which was well known for their "Pray Away the Gay" antics. No, *WHY* is also representative of the stories so commonly heard, even today, about the deep struggle of living a peaceful, loving, and happy life being gay while still holding on to your beliefs in your religion.

Human nature combines both good and evil living in the same soul. Scobey takes us on the long struggle of his sound, loving soul's fight to escape the evil who did everything it could to control him. Sadly, this kind of story needs to be told to give hope to those who still struggle even today.

Alan R. Warren
Best-Selling author of 30 books
NBC News Radio Host
KCAA 106.5 F.M. Los Angeles/1050 A.M. Palm Springs
KKNW 1150 A.M. Seattle

Why does someone self-abuse? Why does someone enter a toxic religion? Why does someone end up in serial harmful relationships? Why does someone determine to close a huge organization? Why do people remain in unhealthy closeted homosexuality? Why? In *WHY*, Randy answers this question over and over, and over again.

"Why" is the question we all ask when we are at the deepest level of despair and pain, seeking answers to life's questions. But Randy didn't stop with just screaming the question with tight fists—he pursued until the answers were found. In his memoir, Randy has completely exposed himself vulnerably and humbly. His writing is something that will allow anyone to see themselves within his words.

This appropriately-named book is an entire encyclopedia of information for anyone going through the transition from a toxic anti-gay theological and life experience. It's not a book that can just be read, it must be digested, processed, and maybe even needs to be done with a group of trusted friends. Each sentence, each paragraph has far too much in it to just go on to the next one. I can imagine spending days or weeks just pondering many of Randy's personal life experiences. It's a study guide that will help anyone evaluate their own transition alongside someone who has deeply revealed their own life experiences.

Family abuse, toxic religion, personal addictions, closeted homosexuality, self-abuse… Randy has vulnerably exposed his own life so that you will know you are not alone.

John Smid
Former ex-gay leader for 22 years, 18 years Executive Director for Love in Action and 11 years as a board member of Exodus International

Randy's memoir is an honest look at the growth of a soul here on planet earth. He's come here to do the work of the Divine and along the way, had to learn some valuable lessons that he can now apply to his own life and share with others. His authenticity, heart, and sense of humor shine through as he details some very tormenting and troubling times he experienced throughout his life. If I had known all of this about Randy prior to meeting and getting to know him, I would have never imagined much of what was shared in his book. It just goes to show we must not judge one another, and that is perhaps one of the greatest messages of this book. Judgment doesn't serve any of us and we certainly never know someone's most intimate perspective, experiences, and/or potential outcomes. In *WHY*, Randy tells us who he is—then and now—and who he has the intention to be. He shares this with a genuineness that allows us to feel into his pain, his healing, and his ever-evolving journey of transformation, love, growth, and up-leveling of consciousness.

Jennifer Foster
Co-Founder of One Orlando Alliance, Writer/Producer/Director at Foster Productions, Inc.

WHY

A MEMOIR

RANDY SCOBEY

INSPIREBYTES OMNI MEDIA

This publication is distributed worldwide in the English language in the following formats:

ISBN Hardcover: 978-1-953445-62-9
ISBN Paperback: 978-1-953445-56-8
ISBN E-Book: 978-1-953445-57-5

Library of Congress Control Number: 2024933435

INSPIREBYTES OMNI MEDIA

Inspirebytes Omni Media LLC
PO Box 988
Wilmette, IL 60091

For more information, please visit www.inspirebytes.com.

I dedicate this book to:

Dan & Autumn, you are my husband and daughter, my family. I would do anything for you. Thank you for your love and showing me what family, love, commitment, and laughter look like.

All LGBTQ+ youth and young adults trying to find their way. If you need help, we are here.

To ex-gay survivors, your courage caused the crescendo that led to the closing of Exodus. Even when you were ignored and disrespected (by others and me), your tenacity saved lives, is saving lives, and changed hardened hearts like mine.

This book is also to honor the legacy of:

My Beautiful Michael
Momma Mella
Anne Heche

ACKNOWLEDGMENTS

Thank you Dr. Buddha who helped me with PTSD and started my true path toward authenticity. To Alan & Leslie Chambers for being a chosen family before I knew what that even meant. To all the asshole gay bloggers (you know who you are) who never relented and eventually became friends. Rev. Terri Steed Pierce, your pastoral heart set this book in motion.

Maggie H., Mike A., Ken M., and Steve S. with the Bridges Across project in the '90s, you all tried. I didn't listen at the time, but I never forgot that when you told me you loved and/or cared for me, I believed you.

Amira, you're everything! I love you, AmooBoo.

To Rik, Allen, Anthony, Victoria, Valerie, Brian, Scooby, Cece, Momma B, Papa Dan, Bruce and Dale; along with Loren, Aly, Eli, Simon, Silas, and Rose T. and the rest of The Family I married into, you didn't have to accept me, but you did, unconditionally. Words can't express how safe and empowering you have been. Our potlucks, birthday soirees, holidays, and pool parties are the stuff of legends. You're life-giving, and your love empowers. I love y'all.

And special thanks to Carrie Duncan Newman. This book didn't start until you gave it its first big push.

And to Martina, you have been my editor, cheerleader, teacher and sounding board. You let me ugly cry when I needed to and have been a clarifying light throughout the process. I still find your ability to read my mind unnerving but am glad you know how to use that ability with care and integrity for my continued growth and wellbeing.

TABLE OF CONTENTS

FOREWORD

by Anne Heche

A note from Anne's best friend, Heather Duffy:

"Anne and I met Randy on our podcast, *Better Together with Anne & Heather*, and we were both so moved by his story. Anne was honored to write the foreword to this book. His story encompasses so much of what Anne and I have stood for in our lives—acceptance, growth, equality, and understanding. Randy's story shows us that life is a journey. The path to where we are meant to be is not always easy, but it's there waiting for us, and living in honesty, acceptance, and kindness is the fastest road to get us there."

"For you created my inmost being; you knit me together in my mother's womb. I praise you because I am fearfully and wonderfully made; your works are wonderful, I know that full well." Psalm 139:13-14, NIV

I have met many interesting people in the more than 30 years I have been in the entertainment industry. I have worked alongside fascinating and talented actors like Harrison Ford, Johnny Depp, Sharon Stone, and Robert De Niro. But I must say, I am particularly inspired by the stories of the people I have met on my podcast. And that is how I got to know Randy and his incredible life story.

Randy came on *Better Together with Anne & Heather* to share his life's twists and turns. The story you are about to read is honest, brave, and close to home to me in many ways. For one, I also came from a family that did not embrace honesty and openness with sexuality. My father was a gay man who hid that fact his entire life and was only outed through his death from AIDS in the 1980s. So, when I met Ellen DeGeneres in 1997 and was given the opportunity to stand up for gender-free love, I did. My mother's response was to reject me and embrace the teachings of conversion therapy. Just like Randy, she toured the country speaking about the efficacy of conversion therapy and wrote books on the topic. Ironically, she and Randy even crossed paths at various events.

Randy's story would have been very different had he been accepted, loved, and celebrated from the beginning for who he is, and this point emphasizes how important allies are in our world. His journey also reminds us that life is long, and we all grow and evolve. I am inspired by his story of the kind human being that took him into their home when he had nowhere to go—highlighting the impact that one person can have on a life and reminding us that we should always have an extra seat at our table for those who need us.

Randy did two complete 180-degree turns in life to end up right where he began—because his true self is beautiful and exactly how he was supposed to be. The practice of conversion therapy is rejected by main-stream medical and mental health organizations, and there are regulations protecting youth from this practice in many states. There is clear evidence that conversion therapy not only does not work but is harmful. There is also valid evidence that societal prejudice causes significant medical, psychological, and other harm to LGBTQ+ people.

It has taken many decades and a lot of pain that Randy openly discusses in this book to understand that you can't pray away your sexual orientation or gender identity. So rather than trying to pray away the gay, let's pray away the judgment, hatred, selfishness, unkindness, prejudice, and closed-mind-edness. That is what we need less of in this world!

INTRODUCTION

A Tale of Two Closets

I have two "coming out" stories. I don't recommend it. Coming out once is difficult enough, but twice is #NotFun. Once you are out, please stay out. You're good. God's good. It's all good.

The first time I came out, my mom forced me out of the house. Unfortunately, her culturally-derived conservative Christianity told her that it was okay for a mother to stigmatize and abandon her child. So, she threw me out of the house at 19. It was 1987, and I was homeless, afraid, and alone when a Christian drag queen took me in. I credit God for using the fantastic Momma Mella to save my life.

However, even though I was "out" and seemingly safe, I didn't yet feel that I "belonged" anywhere. Momma Mella gave me a roof over my head, warm meals, and showed me unconditional love... and I was still a mess. As a naive 19-year-old, I had not yet developed social/coping/survival skills. As a result, I got involved in the dark side of club life—including substance abuse—in spite of Momma Mella's love and support.

For the next five years, I spiraled into a living nightmare... though I was barely living. I got involved in an incredibly abusive relationship that left me even more hollow as a person, if that was possible. I engaged in increasing drug and alcohol abuse while living on a couch for $40 a week. In only five years, my life had gotten further and further away from my understanding of who I was—who I *am*. A sober understanding that was nowhere to be found.

Taking a moment to understand this period of time, I can look back and see that it played a significant role in what was to come. The ex-gay movement preys on the darkness of people's pasts and turns traumatic experiences into fodder for conversion therapy. By attaching stigma to being gay and making sexuality the root cause of trauma—instead of the actual trauma and mental health issues themselves—they are able to "scapegoat" being gay in order to serve their narrative. For me, this meant that I had accumulated a lot of dark experiences that left me feeling desperate with no hope.

Then, one night, I went back to my rented couch after yet another party, and I looked around me and realized that I was going to die if things didn't change. At age 24, I sought a way to become healthy and responsible, and I became a "born-again" Christian. (Today, I am of the Universalist persuasion.) This was the best way I knew how to make a complete shift at that time.

However, owing to where I was emotionally, I was a prime target for the ex-gay community as I was gullible and desperate, ready to buy into a worldview and culturally-derived gospel that served as a beacon of hope for me. This opened the door for me to enter a new closet: the church closet of "ex-gay brokenness." If you don't know, ex-gay brokenness is code for shame, condemnation, and negative behavior modification. It is the "pastoral" form of conversion therapy—which is what makes it look palatable on the outside.

I stayed in that stained-glass closet for 23 years. I went from a shut-down, neurotic, substance-abusing gay man to becoming an upper-echelon leader in the ex-gay conversion therapy movement—and I was *still* searching for belonging. After several heartbreaking years of conflict with hardliners in the ex-gay world and the death of a friend to suicide, I couldn't ignore the truth. The blinders were ripped off. I allowed myself to finally read much of the mountains of literature produced by every reputable professional counseling organization condemning efforts to change sexual orientation and gender identity. I finally had to admit they were correct in their findings that ex-gay ministry, also known as conversion therapy, didn't work. More importantly, it was also found to be incredibly harmful. Humbled and grieving, I came out again on January 12, 2015. Now? I am married to a dude.

Yeah, quite the rollercoaster.

After coming out the second time, culturally-derived Christianity taught almost all my conservative friends that it was okay to ignore, ghost, or publicly condemn me. The same ones who watched me find my voice and gifts and use my superpowers to promote the lie that "freedom from homosexuality" was possible now had no use for me. A few were loud and boisterous about disowning me, but most silently walked away to gossip with others instead of talking to me. Yet, as heartbreaking as that was, it was juxtaposed by all of the other LGBTQ+ people of faith in my life who rallied around me, just as Mella did in the '80s. I had finally found belonging in being who I am—being me—and I was home.

Most importantly (to me, at least), God affirms and loves me. They always have, always will. He loves all of me. She created my relational state of being as a man who adores my now-husband and my life. Like the Good Shepherd Jesus is, He is with me to guide and protect me every step along the way, no matter how much I sometimes behave like an asshole.

Over the years, I have learned that culturally-derived Christianity stigmatizes and abandons. Its teaching is far removed from grace and love. True grace and love run to and embrace their LGBTQ+ brothers and sisters, to help them and support them.

When people come out, we *must* help them find their resources. Unlike the '80s, we have many organizations—like Zebra Youth and the Trevor Project—that help support homeless and desperate LGBTQ+ youth. In addition, we have mental health counselors, substance abuse programs, issue-specific resources, affirming faith communities, and more resources that we can plug newly "out" people into if they need and want them. I've included an appendix at the end of this book with a list of helpful resources. My hope is that it can serve as a starting point for someone who needs it.

Helping doesn't stop there, though. We need to create opportunities for empathy and connection. We need to remember how to listen to each other, and we need to find the courage and strength to share our stories and experiences. I know that some people will never want to hear or read my story because of my past work with Exodus. I truly understand their reluctance and those who have expressed anger. The anger comes from a genuine place I empathize with and know is valid.

I believe their decision to not engage with my story is an act of self-protection from triggers, and I am glad they know to draw that boundary for themself and think it's brave. When their decision to not engage is inspired by their bottled-up rage directed at the self-loathing version of me as a symbol of what they went through, I genuinely apologize. While I hope they would be open to seeing the whole of my journey written in this book, I don't know that I would feel differently if I were in their shoes. I wish them all the love and encouragement I can send as they gather the courage to share their own stories to heal and defeat conversion therapy.

Ultimately, we need all of our stories to get out there. As a survivor of multiple traumas and a lifetime of abuse, as well as being a former ex-gay leader at the top of Exodus International, this is my story. I share it in the hope that it can help.

Author and all-round diva Jackie Collins once said, "Everyone has a book to write because everyone has a story within them." I agree and want to add my story to the myriads testifying to the fact that "coming out" is in and of itself a miracle. It took far too long, but I know now that being a healthy and thriving LGBTQ+ person is a lifelong opportunity and gift. To say it is a state of brokenness is systemic and generational religious bigotry at its mainstream evangelical finest. I know because I have lived on both sides of that argument.

I hope you find this book challenging, encouraging, and entertaining. (I mean, I cuss in it and everything!) My somewhat bizarre life isn't any better or worse than anyone else's, but it was and is not dull. The following pages will reveal quite a cast of characters that I hope will humanize the issues from the dramatically different viewpoints I have lived out. Of course, I would love it if, after reading this book, you would say, "That was the most awesome memoir EVER!" and make bumper stickers out of quotes in it or something.

More importantly, I hope you walk away with a deeper understanding and compassion for the LGBTQ+ community, including an understanding of both why and how some of us get trapped by ex-gay/conversion ideology… and if that's you, how to escape it. If your perspective is changed even a little bit for the better, I will have accomplished my reason for writing this book.

Being free is a good thing. You are already the miracle you have been longing for. We can live and know that it is true; love always wins.

PART ONE

"Memories demand attention, and these memories will have teeth."
–C. Kennedy, *Slaying Isidore's Dragons*

"Be a pain transformer, not a pain transmitter.
This is the only way the world will heal."
–John Mark Green

"A child is a beam of sunlight from the Infinite and Eternal, with
possibilities of virtue and vice, but as yet unstained."
–Lyman Abbott

CHAPTER 1

Like Billions Before, I Arrived

Right off the bat, I say on social media from time to time that being raised by a pack of drag queens made me what I am today. Today, I will confess something: All *this* (gestures all around me) can't be blamed on drag queens.

No, I wasn't raised at the end of a rainbow filled with glitter, riding a unicorn in my baby jumper covered with rhinestones, lycra, and pancake makeup. I did not take my first toddling steps in toddler-sensible three-inch heels. Indeed, the default language I've had to learn to control among mature adults is "snark," but my upbringing did not consist of an environment filled with foam rubber hips, fake talons (nails), rubber boobs, and wigs/weaves for days. I wish I could say that a pack of drag queens raised me because that would have been a fascinating upbringing.

I have always found drag queens fascinating, and as I mentioned in the introduction, God used one to help save my life. That story comes later in the book. But still, no, I was raised by a single, temperamental Gemini of a mom who drove an excellent, vibrant yellow Chevy Charger and fed us Coke and Little Debbie for breakfast.

Well, come to think of it, that may be, in some ways, very similar to what one might experience when raised by drag queens. At the least, it was certainly very colorful at times!

The Early Days Were Foreboding, Except for Teddy Bear

The first memory I have, and it might have been a dream when I was a kid, was being a baby in the new baby ward of the hospital. It was nighttime, and I remember hearing some other babies gurgling in their sleep. Then, with my blurry, half-open baby eyes, I looked up at the ceiling and thought, "I have a feeling this is going to get fucked up real quick." *(See, snarky English is a language I come by naturally, even in the dream version of infant Randy.)*

What do I mean by "fucked up?" Well, let me tell you a few stories from the first couple of years of my life.

Ever since I was born, one of my birthday gifts from my mother has been the reminder that she was in labor with me for 36 hours. As I write this book at 55 years old, this has not changed. My mother *still* reminds me every year, without fail, about her laborious process of giving me life. Apparently, my big head got lodged in her hip, and they had to do an emergency C-section to get me out. It seems I have been a pain in her side since day one! Thankfully, I had more than a little help in those early days.

Mom told me that the night they brought me home from the hospital, our black Pomeranian named Teddy Bear stood guard over me. He took up a protective posture under my crib all night long. So my very earliest Guardian Angel Squad included a Pomeranian named Teddy Bear. I guess that fluffy puppy knew that I would probably need all the help I could get in that household, and that was just the first day.

Then, when I was a six-month-old baby, I developed a leg infection that quickly grew out of control. So much so that if they didn't get it under control, I could have lost my leg. I immediately underwent surgery to remove the infection, and once again had to stay in the hospital for a few days, just like when I was born. They went in through my buttocks and brought the infection under control and killed it. The surgery was successful, and I still have a large scar on my ass to prove it. I also still have my leg.

Finally, sometime when I was still young enough to nap in a bassinet (a vintage version of a baby carrier or car seat), my mom realized that she had left me on the edge of the breakfast table and locked herself out of the house. I get it, young mothers are stressed, tired, and overwhelmed with all the things—but to me, this felt like a foreshadowing of what was to come and also became my "normal" childhood. One in which I often felt forgotten, abandoned, and overlooked. My mom had to call the neighbors to get help to open up the house again and rescue me before I plummeted off the table to the floor. Thankfully, they got inside the house quickly enough that nobody (me) was hurt—at least not physically.

The Emergence of a Fear-Centric Life, Destroying the Water Sprinkler System, and My First Experience with the Divine in Nature

When I was seven, before moving back to Tennessee to be with our "kin," we lived in Carrollton, Texas. It was in that townhome that I first learned about the concept of death by a serial killer. I remember seeing something about the Charles Manson Helter Skelter murders on television. As a result, I was terrified—and convinced—that there were horrible serial killers in the neighborhood. I obsessively kept looking out the window into the deepening evening shadows, where every movement was full of maniacal eyes, blood, and long knives. At least in my mind.

I remember it very clearly. It was such a rush, and I hated it. As I became aware of danger for the first time, it seemed that there was always danger in that townhome every time I turned around:

- My war with Big Ass Spiders started there.
- Humongous snakes, poisonous and not.
- Big ol' bats hung from the tree on a chilly gray evening.
- Mom's anger—Mom also has nosebleeds that wouldn't stop (she had to have surgery to finally eliminate them).
- Drunk Bio Dad showed up a few times.
- Plus, the townhome had ghosts. I'm convinced of it.

But there was also the community swimming pool where my little brother, at the age of two, ran straight toward the deep end of the adult pool and jumped in. Mom hated water and didn't know how to swim. Thankfully, a teenage boy pulled him out. Ben (my brother) was scared, and I was jealous of the attention. Mom was both terrified and furious. I remember her telling me that he did what I had done at his age, albeit at a different pool. Apparently, I kicked up my two-year-old heels, cannonballed into the deep end of the pool, and nearly drowned. I don't remember doing it, but I remember being jealous of two-year-old me when I heard about it.

Speaking of little boys doing bad things, we once destroyed the sprinkler system around our townhome. Of course, we didn't know that it was a sprinkler system at the time. They were just long metal rods sticking up out of the ground (this was before they had automated sprinkler heads that popped up and retreated back into the ground).

No, these were foot-long, skinny metal pipes, and 100% enticing to play with. I remember seeing one and naturally wanting to own and destroy it. So I went to yank on the pipe, only to discover that it wouldn't budge. It was connected underneath, though I had no idea why it would be connected. It was tough to pull out of the ground, so I worked and worked it, and eventually, it broke. I had my pipe! My brother was now, of course, demanding he get one too. Then all the little boys in the neighborhood wanted their own, which is how we destroyed the water sprinkler system. There was no immediate damage—meaning there wasn't any flooding water from the broken pipes underground—so our actions initially went unnoticed

However, when one of the teenage girls came by and saw what we had done, she casually said, "Oh, you're going to get it now." She then explained what those pipes were, and the growing horror on my face told the story. The other boys dropped their pipes and ran. My brother and I picked them up and took all the pipes to the little square brick water fountain in the yard to the east of our corner townhome, and I dropped the pipes into the fountain, warning my brother never to tell anyone.

Of course, I couldn't live with myself. (As an aside, I think I always confessed to everything when I was little, and I have a vast, unrelenting conscience on just about everything still.) I don't think I ratted out my brother Ben, but I ended up telling my mom what I had done. She was furious, absolutely beside herself. I got a whipping before she stormed out of the house, saying she would run away and never come back.

My mom was angry and hyperbolic, but at the time, I thought she was serious. As I saw her storm down the street, I knew I couldn't take care of my brother in a house that was infested with serial killers, snakes, bats, and Big Ass Spiders! Crying, I went to the elderly couple that lived next door. My brother was behind me, also crying. I knocked on the door, and they answered, looking very pensive. I was their version of 'Dennis the Menace' by the looks on their faces. The older gentleman said, "What's the matter?"

Looking up with my blond head (I was blond when I was a child) and big, fearful brown eyes, I sobbed, "My mom just ran away."

His wrinkles furrowed even more. "She ran away? Now, why would she do that?"

"Because I destroyed the water sprinklers."

Anger joined worry in his eyes. "You did what? You go back to your home right now and close the door. I am sure she went for a walk and will be back."

Sure enough, as we turned to go back to the house, she was coming back. She saw us at the neighbor's house and said, "What were you doing?"

I replied, "I thought you were running away!" All I remember is that she looked exasperated and marched us back inside our townhome, where fear still reigned, but it was the only version of "home" I knew.

A Moment of Beauty in the Midst of the Fear

Though we still lived in the scary townhome, life had its better moments. It was almost as if I was being rewarded for all the struggles and pain. I specifically remember this one time when our babysitter Jonathan let us play outside in the rain.

Jonathan stood in the doorway as my brother and I ran around, squealing with delight. We would try to do cartwheels, jump in all the puddles, and twirl around in place, all while millions of drops of water cascaded over us. I loved being drenched, feeling the rain hitting my head and body. I loved trying to cup it in my hand or opening my upturned mouth to "take a drink" from God's goblet.

This scene may have been one of the happiest moments of my childhood. Though we would play in the rain with other babysitters over the years, none of them seemed to enjoy it as much as Jonathan watching over us from the doorway.

I loved playing in the rain. I still do it from time to time. But it was that particular inaugural rain-playing moment when an inner sense of wonder awakened within me. I can almost remember the exact moment I was struck by awe for the first time. It was when the soft rain punched through brilliant sunlight coming in from the south. The clouds above turned gorgeous shades of pink and orange, and I remember stopping, transfixed in my tracks.

The word "brilliant" means "(of light or color) very bright and radiant."[1] So, when I say that the clouds turned pink and orange, I'm not referring to just a pastel-colored sky. No, the clouds lit up in brilliant, vibrant shades of

---

1 Google. (n.d.). "*Brilliant*." Google search. https://www.google.com/search?q=brilliant+definition&sca_esv=

pink and orange. It wasn't simply gorgeous, it was stunning to my young eyes, and the memory brings a tear to the same 55-year-old eyes all these years later. At that moment, the world had a different hue. The light had made something beautiful into something transcendent, and my soul was delighted.

The exciting thing is that it is raining outside as I write this. I am not lying for dramatic purposes, either. You can ask Jesus; He'll back me up on this one. I might need to go jump in a puddle, get drenched, and watch the sky.

Befuddling the Baptists

You'd think that single moment of awe would have prompted me to seek out opportunities to explore faith, but after moving to Tennessee in 1976, we only went to church for around six months while I was growing up. My brother and I would climb on the church bus and sing, "three little angels all dressed in white, tried to get to heaven on the end of a kite, but the kite broke and down they all fell, instead of going to heaven, they all went to… two little angels all dressed in white…" Kind of macabre, but we didn't care. We would get to church and go to our respective Sunday school classes. I liked mine because if I memorized the Bible books in order, I would get a nickel for each book. I never got very far, but one Sunday, I walked out of the class in my little kid's light green polyester suit with "stacked" shoes (see, I was drawn to heels even then) with 75 cents after reciting the names of the first 15 books of the Bible in order!

I wasn't always "good" at Sunday school, however. I remember there was a construction project going on at the church, and my brother and I would find each other and convince our friends to go with us and hide in the construction area for the sanctuary expansion.

Little kids hiding in a construction zone of a large building is a dangerous problem for obvious reasons. The Sunday school teacher's responsibility was to make sure all the kids there without their parents made it to the sanctuary. Almost every Sunday, the teachers and deacons would get a good workout finding and chasing us through the construction area. To their credit, they didn't take after the pastor and shame or condemn us. I remember threats of paddling but never remember seeing anyone, especially those of us who deserved it, getting paddled. Of course, my mother never knew. But, since she was working three jobs, sticking us on a bus meant she could have a few hours of the week to herself to sleep and be quiet.

However, after driving the deacons crazy one Sunday, my brother and I decided to pretend like we were farting during the sermon. We did that whole thing with your mouth making just *awful* fart sounds. We timed it perfectly with the preacher's accentuated moments. Now, mind you, this was a huge congregation. Easily 2,000 or more. I don't know what we were thinking, but we definitely thought it was funny. The chuckling from the congregation seemed to confirm this fact, too. Of course, there was a lot of scowling as well, but we didn't care.

The preacher played it cool until he figured out the origin of the coarse noises. Then, "Boys!" as he looked in our direction, "BOYS! Come up here, please." I was terrified. Ben seemed to think it was fun. I can't remember what the preacher said, but we were invited to sit in the big chairs he and his associate pastor usually occupied. They were like thrones, and they were *right* behind him. We sat there for the rest of his sermon.

We didn't make any more noises, and while I was fascinated seeing 2,000 people from that perspective, Ben was the one having the most fun. He loved attention, and with those doe eyes, beaming grin, and inability to hold still, he kept entertaining the congregation with weird looks as he squirmed continually in his chair. Basically, Ben stole the show that Sunday.

We Drove Dierdre Out of Her Mind, Determined Pam Was an Asshole, and I Nearly Shot Her Friend

Being rambunctious boys wasn't limited to scaring church elders, though.

Dierdre looked like Marcia from *The Brady Bunch*. Same style, but much cuter. She was our first babysitter after moving to Nashville. Dierdre was sweet, but she had NO clue how to rein us in. I don't even remember her trying. Three out of the maybe five times she babysat us, my brother ended up in the emergency room getting stitches. Twice to his head and one underneath his chin. We were very serious about playing indoor volleyball (with a balloon), and one time he fell in the bathroom and hit his chin on the tub.

After that, I remember my mom trying to get her to babysit for us, but her mom must have told my mother that Dierdre wouldn't ever babysit for us again. My mom looked at me with the sunset coming through the window, hung up the phone, and said, "Well, are you happy? You drove Dierdre out of her mind." She wasn't the only babysitter we struggled with. Or who struggled with us.

WHY

When I was 11 or 12, my mother decided that we needed a babysitter during the summer months. So, she hired Pam, who lived down the street.

My brother and I loved Pam because she was a psycho party animal and couldn't care less what my brother and I did. As a result, we didn't take pleasure in breaking the rules in front of her because she always broke the rules herself. In fact, we worried about her and ended up babysitting the babysitter more often than not! Every day the house would fill up with her friends. Every day they were having sex all over the place. Every day they smoked pot and taught me how to smoke cigarettes. And just in case that wasn't enough, she tried to hide her stash of marijuana in the intake vent of our air conditioner. Marijuana, with its powerful smell, hidden in the *intake* vent of the air conditioner! She was literally blowing that strong smell throughout the house. Dumb dumb dumb, and yes, that's what eventually got her fired. Well, that and the fact I nearly shot her boyfriend, Shane.

After having sex, Pam tried to get Shane to leave the downstairs half bath where the sexual activity occurred because my mom was due home at any moment. He wouldn't. Shane must have been high or something. He also threatened to kill my little brother, who loved taunting him. I knew if my mom came home and found Shane there, it would be a very long, wrath-filled evening. I also hated him pushing Pam around and threatening my brother. So, while he was refusing to leave and pestering Pam as she begged him to go, I went upstairs to my mom's bedside table, pulled the gun out of the drawer, and stood at the top of the stairs. The foot of the stairs was directly in front of the front door in a straight line. "Hey Shane, you asshole, I've got something for you." He was probably mad that I called him an asshole and came around at a clip to jog up the stairs. But when his mind registered a pistol pointed right at him, he screamed, hurtled backward, and awkwardly tumbled out the front door, into and through the front thorn bushes, yelling for me not to shoot.

To be clear, I was not calm, cool, and collected. I was crying and upset. I remember Pam crying and telling me to put the gun back, which I was already doing.

I don't remember what I told my mother, but I told her that I didn't like Pam's friends and that they had threatened Ben. I know I didn't tell her about the gun. Shortly after that and the discovery of the weed in the intake vent, we didn't see Pam anymore, and we were left to take care of ourselves.

That worked out well; I thought I was a little old for a babysitter anyway. You might have agreed, until the incident where I accidentally set the carpet on fire with my makeshift hillbilly flame thrower. What's that? Well, it's a can of Aqua Net hairspray and a lighter. We've all seen it in the movies, but it's very different in real life. We put the fire out quickly, but the remaining body-sized oval of melted carpet was hard to hide. I tried plucking it out with a fork, but it was like concrete. I got in a lot of trouble for that.

Of Granny Grunt, Elvis Presley, Alice Cooper, and Eating Pig Brains

When my grandmother was alive, we would visit her once or twice a month. She lived in a small house in a small town called Shelbyville, Tennessee. I loved going to Granny Grunt's house. She would always have an ice cream sandwich and a "Cokey Coley" ready for me when I arrived. I can remember the sweet taste of the ice cream treat and the feel of the cool glass Coke bottle in my hand. When I was done, I would dutifully wash it out and return it to the little crate it came in so she could return the bottles to the grocery store for some pocket change.

We called her our "Granny Grunt" because she grunted and grumbled a lot. No kidding. My youngest of three maternal cousins gave her that name. I love that she never sought to correct us or keep us from calling her that. Well, I don't remember if she did, and regardless, we didn't stop. I remember my cute, blond-headed little cousin saying, "Ganny Gunt!" because she couldn't pronounce the "r" in the words. Who had the nerve to try and make that cuteness stop? Nobody, that's who.

Granny Grunt's house had been her home for most of her adult life. It is where my mom survived rheumatic fever and where their father abandoned my mom and her two sisters. He was a hell of a man who was sexist and cruel. Nevertheless, those three daughters were the beauties of Shelbyville and all of middle Tennessee, and they experienced all the drama that small-town beauties—also the valedictorians or salutatorians of their classes—might encounter.

To give you an idea of how small this town was when my mom was growing up, all the kids were in one school. *All* of them. My mom was the valedictorian out of 12 senior students. She was and is brilliant. She earned her place with perfect grades. The one time she got an A-, her mother, Granny Grunt, severely shamed her. She and my bio dad were both brilliant and good looking, and big-time small-town drama has followed them most of their lives.

Granny Grunt's house had two bedrooms and one bath, and it was falling apart when I moved into it for six months in 1996 at the age of 28. It had cracked and warped linoleum in the kitchen. I don't remember the design on the floor because I would be more fascinated by the distortions of what once was and should have been. While Granny Grunt kept a clean home, it was very old, and she hated spending money on many things, including the linoleum. So, if it was something that couldn't be replaced easily or inexpensively, it didn't get done.

Granny Grunt's house also had a furnace under the floor (in the crawl space) right at the entrance into the living room from the dining room where the floors were wood. It only took one time placing one part of one bare foot on it when it fired up, and you would surely remember never to do it again. That was an exquisite kind of hurt that led to a different kind of pain as I was punished for not being careful. In time my brother and I made a game out of it, as we often did, and we would run and jump over it when no one was looking. Which, of course, rattled the whole tiny house, and was always followed with, "Boys! Stop that right now!"

I thought that thing would kill us one day. My mom often fretted to me about the gas and it being a fire hazard. I didn't ever want to look down into it, afraid that some Stephen King demonic presence inhabited the gears and turned the pilot light into its only evil eye that would stare me to death, roast me, and feed me to Sasquatch.

I was a little obsessed with being afraid of Sasquatch at that point. Charles Manson, Sasquatch, and punishing floor furnaces. To name a few fears.

See a pattern yet?

Granny's house always smelled of pinto beans, cornbread, and old house smell. While it hadn't aged perfectly, it was a home, and for the most part, I always felt welcomed.

Now, Granny Grunt did believe in Jesus, but I don't remember ever going to church with her, other than one Easter. I dressed in that same wide-collared, light green little boy suit and "stacks." I loved looking like a grown up with my feathered hair and stacked heels.

Though Granny may not have talked about Jesus all the time, I knew that she believed Alice Cooper was going to hell—and Elvis Presley was already there. I will never forget sitting in the passenger seat of her severely old white car (even for 1977 it was ancient) when we heard over the AM station that Elvis had died. I was sad, and I will never forget her looking down at me with her teased, overly Aqua Netted, dyed-black hair almost touching the top of the car, and saying, "You know where Elvis is right now? Elvis is in *hell* because of all that hip shaking and the worldly things he's done. All that gyrating all over the stage and how he treats people." I don't remember responding or her entire tirade, because I was mad at her. I liked Elvis, his fun music, and his excellent gyrations, even though I had no idea what "gyrating" meant at the time, other than the fact that it was seemingly not an acceptable type of movement for heavenly entrance. Strangely, or not, that word "gyrations" is what captured my attention.

Later, my brother and I were staying with her for an extended visit, and one night, we were transfixed by some awards show or special. She told us not to watch it, but when she was in the other room, we slowly turned the huge knob on her black-and-white TV to the station. It would often "clunk" if you turned it, so we were trying to be as quiet as possible. When the show came on the screen, Alice Cooper was taking the stage, and thus began my first viewing of a man with teased-out hair and make-up performing a shocking number.

I was mesmerized.

Alice Cooper was an outrageous character of a magnitude I had never seen before. Maybe he, my mom's yellow charger, and Granny Grunt's large, dyed hair are why I have a heart for drag queens? I just remember us standing there, enchanted. I think my jaw was agape. I barely remember Granny coming into the living room, saying, "Boys, I told you to not watch…" She didn't finish the sentence as she too froze in her tracks and stared at the snowy, black-and-white spectacle before us.

Once Alice Cooper was finished terrorizing the youth and grannies of America, all Granny Grunt said was, "Turn that off now, and get ready for bed."

There's an urban legend that Alice Cooper bit the head off a live chicken at a concert. He accidentally killed one, but he didn't bite its head off. So, to be funny, Granny Grunt did something even grosser. She fed us pig brains.

Oh yes, pig brains. They were fried up and put in our scrambled eggs one morning.

Granny Grunt and Mom were looking at me. As Mom smiled, Granny asked, "So, how are your eggs? You like them?"

With a respect-your-elders tone in my voice, I responded, "Yes, ma'am." And I wasn't lying.

She asked, "You know what I put in with your eggs?"

I replied, "No, ma'am."

She looked at me and said very calmly, "Pig brains."

I am not sure what happened next other than being mortified that I had eaten almost all my breakfast at that point, and that I *liked* it! After that, things got blurry (literally), and my mom was lightly laughing. I think my brother thought it was awesome and wanted more. I just wanted to throw up, thinking that I had just eaten Porky Pig's brains. I was a zombie pig brain eater! I was sure I would turn into a Sasquatch Zombie Pig and go all Charles Manson on someone.

With my family, life was full of little "surprises" like that. Cruel? Not always. Funny? Not always. Dysfunctional? Seemingly, always.

Mom and I Don't Fit the Stereotype

One of my favorite memories of my mom is actually from Granny Grunt's house. At the time, a new dance called "the bump" was all over American Bandstand and pop culture. It involved standing next to each other and bumping the person next to you with your corresponding hips. My brother and I would innocently knock each other around, trying to dance. Our whole family loved music, so we had some natural rhythm, but we were silly boys looking to throw each other around the room. My mom was playful and decided to show us how to do the dance "right," but then she joyfully knocked us around into the chair and couch. I remember laughing and enjoying my mother's laughter.

That said, my relationship with my mother is challenging. It always has been, though I have always known she loves me in her way. She is beautiful, from her pin-up girl good looks of her youth to being a cute granny for my three nieces. She is brilliant and has incredible analytical skills. She isn't a church-going woman, but at a very young age, she did teach me that Jesus was the son of God, and when no one else in the world would love me, she and Jesus would. Unfortunately, that statement would be put to the test later when I was 19 and my being gay "came out" and dramatically changed that loving message.

There is a stereotype that gay men have an excessive bond with their mothers. That was not true in my case. I was terrified of my mother most of the time. I loved her, and she loved me, but I did what I could to keep my distance. However, I did have a heavy burden placed on me when I was young to be the "protector" and a good child. All the stories I've just shared of being a little bit of a troublemaker are mostly the result of acting out and not having stability as a child. When you're forced to be the stable one at a young age in an unstable environment, it can cause more harm than good. My mom did her best. I can see that now, but at the time it only made a challenging situation more difficult—and set the stage for what was to come.

But let's flashback to when we moved to Oklahoma City in December of 1971 where Ben was born. At age five, I was standing at the door of our bedroom. My little brother was asleep in the bed even though my mother and my bio dad were having an all-out war in our lovely home. I didn't understand what they were saying, but I was very fearful. I remember not crying because I wanted to know if Mom was okay. My bio dad was hardly ever around. I only have one memory of him before that point. So, when I heard her screaming, shrill and angry, I knew something terrible would happen.

Lots of yelling, stomping, thuds, and thumps, and then a *huge* crash on the other side of our bedroom door scared me into being an adult at the age of five. I recoiled backward and heard more things thrown and crashing down around the house, then the front door slammed. My bio dad got in the car and peeled out of the driveway.

That's when I heard my mom softly crying. I opened the door to the room and saw that my bio dad had thrown my favorite red stool against the door. It had the alphabet and numbers on the seat. I loved that little stool and was heartbroken to see it literally in splinters on the ground outside the damaged bedroom door. My mom's crying continued, and I walked out of the bedroom toward the sound. As I entered the living room, she was on the floor propped up on one arm, as sad as I had ever seen her before or since. I placed my five-year-old hand on her shoulder and said, "Don't worry, Mommy, I will protect you."

She took that literally, and from that point forward, I took on a role I wasn't supposed to have, and certainly not at the age of five. But instead of recognizing God's compassionate heart within me, I felt the weight of expectations from her (and myself) that should never have been placed on a young child's shoulders. What made it worse was that I failed in my promise—not that I could have ever succeeded at five— and I always felt like a failure because she hardly ever seemed happy. I never felt good enough to meet her expectations. It was probably the same way she'd felt when she was severely punished and shamed by Granny Grunt that one time she made an A-.

Frankly, all these years later, I still don't believe that I ever met her expectations or lived up to being the person she always wanted me to be. When she had a massive stroke in August of 2021, I saw the most beautiful and intelligent woman I know in a situation and state of being that was truly humbling and scary. The hospital prepared us for the worst to happen overnight. However, when I saw her the next day, though she couldn't verbally articulate her anger, she was being very cranky and moving all her limbs.

I knew she would make it. Giving the nurses hell was a good sign. Poor nurses.

Today, she has difficulty remembering things short term, and though her long-term memory is mostly there, she can't always articulate it. Throughout, my stepfather's genuine love for her has been evident. Even though she often abuses him verbally, he stays. He does so much for her, and since we have all had an opportunity to move closer to each other, our own relationships have improved. My relationship with my stepfather in particular is much better, and this may be the first time in my life that I have felt genuine admiration for him. Though my relationship with my mother is anything but typical, it's now (finally) in a place where I can feel gratitude and love.

I Still Have Nightmares About That Place

In 1976, we settled into the new townhome in Tennessee. At the time, my mother worked three jobs to keep a roof over our heads, and my brother and I became the poster children for latchkey kids. We walked home from elementary school (about a mile), and later I would go to the bus stop for the fifth and sixth grades. When we got home, we closed the door and locked it behind us. I would call Mom to tell her we were home and then watch *Gilligan's Island*, *Bewitched*, and *Good Times* reruns (and do our homework) until she got home with Wendy's or had me cook up hot dogs or some hamburger helper concoction for our dinner.

As I have more than adequately covered so far, my brother and I were very typical, awful-to-babysit, rambunctious kids. We made lots of dings on the walls, one of which I tried to hide with spitballs and white-out (used on old typewriters to hide mistakes and type over them again). We also loved jumping over the railing on the stairs, bouncing off the seats right below them to launch into a tumbling roll.

Such great fun! Seriously, think about it. You would do it too, if you could.

After my mom divorced my bio dad and started dating other men, Ben and I would test these interlopers out while she was still preparing for their date, because a lady shouldn't seem too eager. So, while she primped, we would do the dangerous jump the rail, bounce, and tumble thing as they sat on the couch. We would expertly roll up into a standing position and stare at them. The suitors who tried to get us to stop or told Mom what we did were not acceptable. My first stepdad just kept smoking, so he was all right. My second and current stepfather said, "That looks fun." So, we accepted him with cautious optimism.

My mom was remarkable in that she fought hard to keep a roof over our heads, and even if the meal was meager, we never missed a meal. However, she wasn't emotionally present or even physically present for most of our lives. It felt much more dangerous than nurturing and only got worse as I got older.

However, as time progressed, I began to hate that house, hate life, hate my life, worry, fret, and live in a constant state of fear. On one of his rare visits, I made the mistake of (offhandedly) telling my bio dad when he was stupendously high that Mom whipped us every day. She did beat us every day for some reason or another. We often had welts on our backsides and the back of our legs. She used the orange race tracks we used for matchbox cars. We were constantly sent to our room after some severe abuse done in the name of "discipline" by "whipping." In time, I preferred to just stay in my room. I was safer there. When my bio dad tried to confront her, I just got whipped again for telling him that.

⌐

The first draft of this chapter was at 17,000 words, and I realized that it could be a separate—albeit depressing—book for just my formative years. Though I have shared a lot here, the short version of all this is that, as a child, my domestic and school situation contained systematic emotional and physical abuse that set the stage for a diagnosis of posttraumatic stress disorder (PTSD) in 2005. In fact, my therapist at that time once said to me, "You know your life could be an R-rated violent movie, don't you...?"

While there was the daily barrage of emotional and verbal abuse throughout my childhood, there was also physical abuse that ranged from daily to several times a week. So much so that it was the only "normal" I knew, even though a part of me knew it wasn't normal. Even in the midst of all that, however, there were specific flashpoints that stand out.

One day I was doing something I wasn't supposed to do in the house. Because 1) Mom wouldn't let us go out without her there, and 2) I was a boy prone to rambunctiousness when she wasn't around because I knew I was going to be punished for something anyway. What was the point in behaving if you get abused either way? So, what was I doing? I was swinging my excellent green yo-yo around like a helicopter propeller over my head. *Fast!*

Looking through the window as I did it (we weren't supposed to have the drapes open either), I saw my mom getting out of the most fabulous car ever (her *Dukes of Hazzard* yellow and black charger) with Wendy's cheeseburgers in hand. She was home a couple of hours early. I panicked.

As the yo-yo's speed caused the air to whistle, two things flashed in my head at once: The drapes must close now! The yo-yo has to stop now!

And then... *Crash!*

The yo-yo went sailing through the center of my mom's favorite and, according to her, costly French crystal candy dish. It exploded into a million pieces.

I just stood there, unable to think or move.

The candy dish fragments were probably still bouncing off the wall and onto the carpet when she entered the room. All I heard was a piercing scream before I was being yanked by my arm upstairs to my room as she lost her mind with rage.

"Why do you do this to me! Why can't I ever keep nice things!"

I cried and begged her to stop, but as she went to get the orange track (she kept one in each of our rooms at all times), I knew I was in for a brand-new type of hurt.

My soul almost died.

I detached from the situation somehow by listening to my screams as if I wasn't the one screaming. I also got through it by counting the times she reared back and hit me with all her might channeled through that horrible orange track. She hit me with that thing 36 times. The only words that registered in my mind were, *I guess I am not one of her "nice things."*

When my bio dad skipped out, being a single mom in the seventies was almost impossible because the patriarchal system made her work so much harder for enough money to survive and still paid her less than her male counterparts. She only got a few hours of sleep each night during the work week. Given the immense pressure of simply trying to provide for two very energetic kids, she never had time for friends or peers who would support and encourage her. I think all of that pressure must have been overwhelming, and it regularly burst out in fits of rage. I say all of this because even as an adult I am still trying to make sense of (and possibly excuse) what happened to us.

The abuse never stopped, though it changed throughout our childhood, and went from bad to worse once she was married again. However, in those early single days after our bio dad left, whenever we were in public with Mom, we were her angels. People often commented on how cute and well-behaved we were, not knowing the truth of what went on when we were alone in our home. When we were all out together, we did our best to make her look good—which was also a hopeful play to avoid being abused later. If she wasn't around, of course, we weren't as well-behaved (remember the church story?). Either way, once we got home, we would tend to try and hide from her because, ultimately, it didn't matter how well-behaved and cute we were. The beating was coming either way.

CHAPTER 2

From Breakfast Club Allison to Rose the Brawler

Individuating From Mom

My mom told me when I was a teenager that she went to a psychic while she was pregnant with my little brother. The psychic told her that my brother would be a TV personality type and that I would be a lawyer or doctor. Growing up, Ben was the fun, relational one, and I was more intellectually focused, constantly living in my mind. I had learned that being extroverted got me into trouble, so I avoided it when I could and spent a lot of my time thinking (okay, overthinking) about my life. As such, you'd think the psychic's predictions were correct. But they weren't. In truth, we were both extroverts, but weren't necessarily supported in being who we were, though my brother got away with it more than I did. Internally, however, we were different. My brother *loves* details and strategies, which I tolerate, at best. And I love being the headline bitch on some stage in my mind. Though we both like being around other people, I am the one who truly loves networking, socializing, and making connections—a passion that would later both serve me and be part of my downfall.

While I know who I am today, growing up it was clear that I needed to be whoever my mom wanted me to be. When you combine the psychic's (mis)reading with my mom's desire to have two boys with brown hair, brown eyes, little ears, and big feet, you get exactly that. Mom prayed for us to be what she needed us to be, and she got what she ordered. At least on the surface. In truth, I think the psychic was "reading" Mom's energies and desires, not the actual truth of who my brother and I were. The end result was that our lives were boxed in long before we ever had a chance to find out for ourselves who we truly were or who we wanted to be. We were raised to be my mother's idealized version of us instead of our authentic selves.

Fast forward to my teenage years, which were horrible. I hated almost every minute of them except when I worked at the Kroger grocery store, which was both fun and a way to get away from my family on a regular basis—a break that was much needed, especially in the more trying years of adolescence. Because teenage years also meant hormones.

As my hormones kicked in, I didn't know what to do with myself and had no one to talk to. Finally, I was so anxious one day (probably having an anxiety attack) that I sat down next to my mom and said, "Mom, I think I am going crazy." She asked why, and I replied, "I just want to run and run and run and tear something up." She asked if I was angry; I told her I didn't think so, even though I felt angry with everything and everyone. Then she asked if I was doing drugs, speed specifically, and I said no. Then she gave me the reply I never expected. She told me that I shouldn't have a problem and needed to just get over it and calm down.

But how do you "get over" being a teenager and having hormones? You don't.

It's not physically possible to "get over" a pubescent testosterone rush, at least not for some years. It would have helped to have a way to channel the energy, but the clear message from my mom was that my problems annoyed and inconvenienced her. Again.

The story was the same all throughout grade school and high school. In fact, when I got beat up in grade school (presumably for being assumed to be gay—which the other kids called me, like a bad name), my mom would simply dress my wounds without talking to me. It was clear that she didn't want to "go there."

So, knowing I was gay during high school, I decided to test her. I "acted" like I was more troubled than usual and said that the kids at school were all calling me gay. I say "acted" because even though it was true and I was very upset, I had rarely let her see that before. So, my "acting" was actually more like "not hiding" things from her, because I wanted to see how she would react. She said that there was no way I could be gay because of my friendship with Serena. Serena was one of my closest friends in high school. And while Serena did give me my first kiss, I was primarily attracted to the boys my age or older. Like, *all* the other boys in my high school. (I can't wait for the next class reunion after this book comes out and they find out. Wink.)

While I don't remember my mom saying anything terrible at the time, I do remember feeling sad that she didn't offer that she would still love me even if I were gay. Instead of focusing on that possibility, she focused on how it couldn't possibly be true—which was what *she* needed. Just like I mentioned earlier, much of my youth was about being what my mom needed me to be. Unfortunately, a little bit later when I was 19, I did actually come out to her, and she had a very different and violent reaction. I'll share more about that a little later in this chapter.

As you can imagine, I spent most of my teen years avoiding my mom and my second and current stepdad, who she married when I was in sixth grade. They went to the justice of the peace and married without telling us.

As I shared in the last chapter, my stepdad was the one who could handle the staircase-banner jumping boys. I thought he was cool, as a result. And in fact, he was cool while they were dating, but he became my emotional terrorist almost immediately after they married. He often beat me horribly with his belt. The near-daily abuse would worsen and include his fists as I got older. These episodes of "discipline" never had any "teachable moments," just severe and unnecessary pain delivered with rage from an adult to a child. To this day, I don't know why he did these things. Over the years, I have assumed it was because of both my being gay and because I was unable to bond with him like my brother did. I wasn't playing the role he needed me to play in creating the ideal "family" when he married my mom. Another instance in which somebody else's projections of their needs resulted in my being punished.

The most common thing that would happen during my teenage years was that we would wake up to yelling and threats, and end the day with some form of abuse—emotional or physical (one or the other, or both). My day went like this: Get ready for school, get teased and bullied all day, come home, watch *Gilligan's Island*, *Bewitched*, *Good Times*, and *Happy Days*, and do homework. As 5:30 p.m. rolled around, the knot in my stomach would start to grow as I waited for the parents to come home in a bad mood. Which always happened. Inevitably, I knew they would punish us for something. They would make me cook, serve dinner, and clean up while they disappeared to their bedroom to watch TV. She in her nightgown and he in his tighty-whities. They did this immediately after dinner every night of my teenage years.

I wasn't allowed to say anything. My opinion was unnecessary, never considered, never an option. If I did try to speak up, I was mocked, ridiculed, and punished. So I learned not to speak up. I learned to hide, and I learned that I, as a human being, wasn't valid.

I Didn't Even Know Bo and Luke Duke Had a Cousin Named Daisy!

My only comfort was watching television and eventually masturbation. The first time I masturbated, it was by accident, and I had no idea what had happened. Having an orgasm without knowing what it was completely freaked me out. After that, I couldn't stop doing it, so I was constantly freaked out. I had *no* clue what was happening, but I loved it and was terrified of it at the same time. In truth, I thought I had cancer, so you can imagine the chaos in my mind each time I masturbated.

It first happened when I was 13. I was watching *ChiPs*, and Ponch and John were heroes of mine. When I saw them, I would get all warm inside. Of course, being gay and not knowing anything about my body, certain parts of my enthusiastic anatomy responded when they were on the TV screen. One day I wasn't even really paying attention and started touching myself. Anyone who can remember their first orgasm can imagine it in the context of having zero clues about what was happening. When things started—you know, happening—I was like, "Oh my... Oh... What... Oh, OH... What is... WOW..." and then I imagined Ponch and John in a passionate kiss, and that's when I became a man... in my hand.

I remember just looking at the aftermath—my incredibly red face and the mess that had just erupted from my body—and I freaked out. Even though that was the best feeling I had ever had, I honestly believed I had broken something. I was mortified and had nowhere to go and no one to talk to about what had just happened.

Then I learned how to use my imagination to imagine them naked in all kinds of situations. So then, of course, those situations started to include me. And well, yeah, I think it is fair to say that being gay comes naturally to me.

I soon figured out that it was fun to imagine other men on television naked. Suddenly, I developed this new and profound interest in: Sears underwear ads, men walking down the street, guys selling hot dogs at Vanderbilt Stadium, jocks at school, the produce guy at the store, and commercials with men in sportswear or tight jeans. Eventually, my erotic imagination turned to Def Leppard, Van Halen, Duran Duran, and Dead or Alive—basically any human being with a penis. My horny, gay teen brain was active all the damn time. But my sexual imagination peaked with the hit TV show *The Dukes of Hazzard*.

I even used to joke with people when I shared my "ex-gay testimony" that I was so gay that it took me until the second season to realize Bo and Luke had a cousin named Daisy. "What do you mean hot Bo and sexy Luke had a cousin named Daisy?" Of course, I knew she was a character on the show who was pretty iconic—her 'Daisy Dukes' infamy is still a part of our pop culture lexicon today—but she was so irrelevant to me at the time that I didn't realize she was their cousin. With all due respect to Catherine Bach, the beautiful actress playing Daisy, the only thing I wanted was for her to get out of the way. Move over, sis; I need to see the Dukes in their painted-on jeans sliding across the hood and jumping through the windows of the General Lee (their car). I did, however, want her fabulous yellow jeep. I liked that it was yellow, but I also liked imagining having sex with the Duke boys hanging all over it.

I was the stereotypical horny teenager of the gay variety. And yes, it was a constant source of bliss mixed with terror for a while. I will never forget when I had to tell my mom about "the eruption" for the first time.

Mom Gave Me a Brochure

Now, I knew that being gay was not acceptable to my family or friends, but I had known I was gay since I was 10. With people in my world calling me things like "Sissy" throughout my childhood, I had to have at least had an inkling—at least intellectually—that I was probably gay. The terror part was what was happening physiologically. I didn't know what to expect with my changing body. I knew it would change; I just didn't know how, why, or when. And the whole orgasm thing was a completely new, mind-blowing concept, and again, I seriously thought I broke something, kept breaking something, or had cancer. I am not lying. I was terrified but couldn't stop.

Because I was so concerned and scared, I remember sheepishly telling my mom because I couldn't tell anyone else. I hated having to say it to her. So I didn't tell her anything about my romantic feelings toward any man in tight jeans with beautiful eyes and a warm smile. I just told her, through tears and fear, that I had had an experience, and I thought I might have broken something. She kept her composure and said, "Okay, you didn't break anything, and you don't have cancer. I will do your laundry right now, but don't do that anymore."

I was so relieved that I hadn't broken anything and wasn't going to die, but I knew that I would do it as often as possible.

The next thing I knew, my mom gave me a brochure. It was small and white. It explained everything and also confirmed for me that I was gay, which helped. How? In the brochure, it briefly mentioned that "sometimes, men will find other men attractive," and that meant they were a homosexual. I don't think my mom read the brochure before giving it to me. I still wish that I didn't grow up in a time that stigmatized my sexuality. I wish that I could have talked with someone to help me understand things better and navigate a difficult time. I needed someone to explain to me that while sex is important, it wasn't everything that intimacy and love could be. During those years, I objectified sex and dreamed of romance, but I didn't know how to love or invest in another human being on any level. (Not surprising, given how my childhood was.)

Of course, as an adult, I don't beat myself up about that—I was 13! But I look back and wish there had been a safe someone to guide and help me, or at least who I could confide in.

When Harry Caused Me to See Stars

As I progressed through my teens, my relationship with Harry, my stepfather, grew increasingly hostile and violent. We hated each other, and I believe we both knew it. There was constant tension between us.

My chores were never done "right," and I was always the stupidly weak sissy in his eyes, made clear when he yelled: "WHAT'S WRONG WITH YOU, SISSY?!?" Finally, I realized he wanted to be with my mom but had no interest in me. He did show favor and attention to my younger brother, but I experienced nothing but yelling and abuse in the form of an angry, bigoted man in his underwear.

While my behavior was pretty typical of teenagers, the punishments were genuinely horrible. They involved night after night of being pushed around, called names, yelled at, threatened, and more often than not, some whipping or beating. Since I was not allowed to speak and could not hide my emotions, I got very good at glaring. My side-eye and glare game is on point! I threatened to run away a few times but had no clue where I would go or what I would do. His abuse often led to Mom joining in, yelling at me, and demanding I go to my room. My brother would often retreat before the worst of it started. When I did see him, I couldn't always understand the look on his face, which ranged from fear to repulsion, but whatever he was feeling broke my heart, and I always ended up not running away.

When my mother was not around, Harry would start slapping me across the face and putting me in headlocks to beat me. One night—I can't even remember what I had done to piss Harry off—he wouldn't stop. He got louder and louder, and angrier and angrier. As did I. My brother was in his room that night, and my mom was passively watching Harry scream and yell at me. As he got louder and louder, my heart began to panic. Harry was escalating well past the terror levels I had felt before.

He taunted, "Oh, you want to fight, boy? Do you want to fight? COME ON THEN!" He pushed me and put up his fists. At first, I did my usual and didn't physically resist him. However, that would change that night.

He came at me and punched me. As I went to turn away, he grabbed me and started wailing on my torso before moving to my head. I didn't even fight back because I knew it would usually stop soon. However, he wasn't stopping, and it was getting worse. He was pounding me on my head in the temple area. My mother, for a change, wasn't screaming at me. Instead, she was screaming at Harry to stop.

"STOP IT, HARRY! STOP IT! STOP!"

At some point, her screams hit a pitch I had never heard before, and adrenaline shot through my body with an extra-double surge. I somehow twisted out of the headlock he had me in, moved into a stance I didn't know I had, aimed, and clocked that angry asshole right between the eyes. It broke Harry's glasses, and they went flying. It also cut his forehead. The punch knocked him backward but not down. He regained his footing and threw his fists up, demanding I try that again. I shook my head, pushed past him, and went to my room. I don't remember anything else from that evening.

He would never hit me again.

I was distraught over the bruises and headaches the next day. Then, during fifth period study hall, when I usually volunteered in the guidance counselor's office, I decided that maybe I needed to share what had happened with one of the guidance counselors. They always said they would help students with "complicated" home lives. So, it took a while to get the nerve up, but I finally did, and just as I walked through the guidance counselor's door, the principal and my mom walked through the main entrance to the guidance counseling office. She told him that there was a family emergency, and she was pulling me out of school for the day and the rest of the week. We left my school, picked up my brother from his school, went home and packed everything we could into a moving van, and left. My mom was doing so because of what Harry had done to me the night before. We were leaving him. At least temporarily.

We settled into a weird-smelling apartment a few miles away from the house that night. I was scared. We were told not to tell anyone where we were and, if Harry showed up at the grocery store where I worked, to call the police. I was afraid of what he might do. For the first time in my life, I felt like my mom was looking out for my best interests, defending me in her way.

That didn't last long.

During our two-week stay at the apartment, she grew incredibly depressed. She was sleeping on a cot and watching some tiny TV in her room. It was the worst I had ever seen her.

One night she started yelling at me that it was all my fault. While I would probably finish high school at the best school in the state at that time, my brother would have to go to a terrible one because of me. We were now not living in a lovely house in Brentwood but a shithole in Davidson County because of me. My mom said that it was my fault that Harry would get so angry, and why couldn't I be a good kid and not be so selfish?

She didn't hit me that night, but she escalated her verbal attack so severely that she might as well have. I don't know what was worse, being beaten to the point of seeing stars or being scapegoated to excuse an abuser's violence. She was so angry that I thought she would have a stroke as she told me about how life had always been unfair to her. I learned things that night I didn't ever need to know. After this horrible tirade, she said that it was up to me to decide whether to go back or not.

As if I had a choice.

When I told my mom that I didn't want to go back, her verbal assault doubled, tripled, and became a maelstrom of hate and accusation. Finally, after she had gone to her room, things settled down for a while. I went to her.

I died inside as the words fell out of my mouth. "Okay, I want Ben to go to a good school. So, let's go back."

We did. I went numb for the next five years or so.

I never told the guidance counselor what had happened.

The Night I Saw The Rocky Horror Picture Show

When we arrived back "home," Harry had cleaned up the house. He was reticent as he helped to unload everything. I went to my room and stayed there for the rest of my time in that house. I never said anything to anyone, even when asked, ever again. Harry did yell at me a few times but never like before. I also lost my conscience. I stole money from work. I lied to get whatever I wanted and went wherever I wanted. I lied to sneak out of the house and got involved with drugs. That whole time was a blur because I was drunk or high almost the entire time. My grades went down, and I didn't give a shit about anything or anybody. I was a prisoner in my own home, and in my own body and mind. Eventually, when I got a car, I felt freedom for the first time. But it was short-lived.

One night, I wore my regular clothes under my Kroger uniform, and instead of going to work like I told my parents, I went out and got super high with two friends. We also convinced one of my coworkers, Jackie, to buy us a case of beer.

I was wasted when we showed up at *The Rocky Horror Picture Show*. Literally out of my mind. I barely remember trying to do the time warp and seemed to laugh through the entire movie. I don't know how we got back to the store, but I do remember Sheryl, another coworker, telling me that I couldn't pass out in the ice cream aisle where I was lying on the floor.

I don't remember getting up. I don't remember getting in my brown '81 Dodge Omni. I don't know why I was driving so fast.

I remember looking up, having had my head plastered against the steering wheel, just in time to see that I was heading straight for a rock wall. I hit it with my foot still on the accelerator and rolled the car three times.

I remember thinking that the screams—my screams—sounded like hell. They seemed disembodied. I remember it being completely black as I was thrown violently into the glass and hard surfaces. I remembered being in a state of complete pitch-black chaos all around me. I remember thinking—very clearly at the time—that I was going to die.

Everything just turned off.

I don't remember waking up, but I remember hearing the radio blaring white noise. I don't know how I got out of the car. Neither did the police. We never did find one of my shoes.

I remember looking down at my jean jacket; it was excellently trendy at the time and had 22 pockets. It's what we used to sneak beer into *The Rocky Horror Picture Show*. It didn't have any beer hidden in it anymore, and the left half looked like it had changed colors. Being soaked in blood will do that. I remember walking down the road with one bare foot, just screaming and screaming and screaming and screaming. My screams only consisted of one word.

Why?… WHY!?

I scared the ever-living shit out of the lady at the roach motel. It was about a third of a mile away from the accident. She made me stay on the porch while she called the cops. It was 3 a.m., and she didn't want me staying on her porch for long. She then said that someone had already called them because they had seen me and the wreck, and "suggested" I go back to the car. I then walked, hobbled, and stumbled, crying and screaming, back to my '81 Dodge Omni.

I don't remember the scene as I approached it except for hearing a voice say, "There he is…" followed by strong arms coming alongside to help guide me. I remember sitting on the ground next to the mangled and destroyed car and leaning against it, unable to answer the myriad of questions. All I could say was that my parents were going to kill me. I remember hearing someone drive by and fearfully screaming, "Oh my GOD, it's Randy!" I never found out who that was.

I don't remember the ambulance ride, but I remember them scrubbing the glass out of my scalp as the smart-ass EMT cleaning the wound said, "Don't give him any anesthesia, it'll kill him. Plus, look…" I felt them tugging on my head. "He can't feel shit." He was moving my head around with a flap of my scalp they had lifted to get the glass cleaned out.

When my parents showed up at the emergency room, I thought my mom would be the one to cry and Harry would be the one to cuss me out. Shockingly, it was the other way around. I barely remember it, but she was laying into me as he just sat there crying. I didn't respond in any way because I was too drunk. I remember the police officer trying to scare me straight, too. I remember only two bits of information from everything he said. The first went something like: "YOUNG MAN! YOU BLEW A 3.4 ON THE BREATHALYZER! THAT'S NOT JUST ABOVE THE LEGAL LIMIT BUT MANY TIMES OVER—YOU COULD HAVE DIED FROM ALCOHOL POISONING." The other bit of information was that he would not arrest me because my mom was a good woman or something like that.

My time in the ER passed, mostly blurry, with moments of clarity scattered throughout. However, the last thing I remember about that evening was a charming nurse who asked to speak with me privately. He shared about his past alcohol abuse and said that if I wanted help, he would connect me with some support meetings. I didn't take him up on his offer, but I have never forgotten the kindness in his eyes and the blessing his peaceful presence was for me that evening.

The days that followed were strange indeed. Harry was quiet as a mouse, whereas my mom went on a crusade against Jackie for buying us that beer. Jackie could have gone to jail. As much as I could (which wasn't much), I begged for my mom not to do that. Jackie wouldn't come anywhere near me after that. She almost lost her job because of it too.

My heart sinks every time I remember going to the junkyard to see what had happened to my car. The police strongly recommended my parents do that as a punishment and educational opportunity. My mom took me. It was the nightmare I had expected and more. There was blood everywhere, all over everything. The impact had thrown my body into the windshield before it was thrust downward, where my body violently shoved the steering wheel down toward the floorboard. Oddly, all the windows shattered except for the driver's side front door.

At school, the kids didn't know what to say. A couple of them said they were glad I was safe and didn't die. I wore some funky little hat to cover the horrible-looking gash on my head. I didn't have any broken bones, which everyone agreed was a miracle, but the wound to my head was right down to my skull.

I remember thinking I would never drink again.

I was smoking dope and drinking again less than a month later.

Creepy Chester and My First Time Going to a Gay Bar

Chester was creepy. When I was 18—before I got thrown out of the house—I was working at a fried fish counter at the mall food court.

Chester was friendly but, as I mentioned, creepy. He was in his late 30s (so he claimed), had thin, dyed blond hair, and wore mascara. He also had a whiny, high-pitched voice like Truman Capote.

No lie.

He was a hard worker, but he also worked hard at staring at my crotch. This wasn't a new experience for me. The first time I noticed my crotch being watched happened two years earlier at my first job at a different fast-food place. When I was 16, a balding, middle-aged pedophile in charge of catering liked to grab my ass or crotch and then casually walk away, winking. I never reported these guys, though I should have.

Back to Chester. Chester would help me do my side work, daily tasks that involved keeping the kitchen prep area stocked and clean, so there was that.

At some point, he and the rest of the crew were whispering and joking around after the lunch rush had died and we had caught up on all our work. Of course, I knew they were talking about me, but eventually, with all of them watching, he said in his whiny voice, "Randy, are you 'family'?"

"Am I... what?"

"Family? A friend of Dorothy?"

"I don't know a Dorothy, but I have a family."

They all just laughed and chuckled. Then the assistant manager said, "What Chester is asking is if you are gay or not. You seem to have a crush on that guy who works at the luxury coat store around the corner."

I did have a crush on the handsome guy selling gorgeous outerwear. His name is Dean (he's still a friend), and he had a super cute butt, was flamboyantly gay, and smoked Benson & Hedges Deluxe Ultra Light 100s. Are you kidding me? That's '80s gay hot right there, that is!

I felt embarrassed that I had no idea what "family" and "friend of Dorothy" meant. So I said, "Yeah, I am gay, and I have a crush on that guy."

This was immediately followed by a loud, "I KNEW IT!" from one of the female fry cooks. But otherwise, they all seemed quite happy because, as it turned out, there wasn't one single straight person that worked at that particular fried fish counter.

It really should have been a reality TV show.

Chester finally asked me, "Randy, have you ever been to a gay bar?" I said that no, I hadn't. I was too young. He said that if I wanted to go with him, he could convince the doorman, Ms. Nasty (and he lived up to his name, let me tell you), to let me in if I was Chester's date.

I was freaked out but ready to go on a new adventure to meet other "family" members. I already had a fake ID, so if Chester couldn't whisk me through the front door as his arm candy, I had a backup plan. It was decided we would go to the Warehouse 28 bar in Nashville, which was turned into an AutoZone the last time I was there. When I was visiting Nashville a few years ago, I decided to drive by, which is how I learned it had become an AutoZone. I thought that was so bizarre because the drag elite of the region performed at that club back in the day. Now you can buy car parts in the same spot where the stage once stood.

The following Thursday night, I met Chester at his apartment, and we went out. I was wearing jeans, sneakers, and a Big Dog (brand) t-shirt that was low cut in the front but hung long in the back. I had Duran-Duran-type hair (too involved with that look) and a George Michael hoop earring with a cross hanging off it. Chester kept buying me drinks—amaretto sours. Unfortunately, I was already abusing drugs that night, and eventually, the evening got blurry.

What I *do* remember is thinking that I was finally home. The men were paying attention to me, going out of their way to be excellent. We were laughing and dancing without a care in the world. The music was great, and the lights seemed in sync with my soul.

Ahhhh… (that's me breathing)

I closed my eyes to see what the lights looked like from the back of my eyelids and danced until I lost track of time. I got lost in the smiles, lights, and rhythms. I seemingly escaped the pain, fear, rejection, and horror that plagued my traumatized psyche. It was the first time I felt anything close to bliss without any inhibitions since dancing in the rain as a kid, and it was the only sign of what I thought to be true freedom at the time.

Because it was a Thursday night, it was busy but not that busy. At one point, Chester and the other guys needed a break from dancing.

I didn't stop and didn't mind dancing alone. Alone on the dance floor. No one made me feel bad about it either, especially when they learned from Chester it was my first time "out" in a bar.

I thought I had finally come to my true home and "family." And I never wanted it to end.

Of course, it did end that evening, and I went home with Chester. I did fool around with him a little because I felt like I owed it to him for taking me out, and I was pretty drunk. I felt terrible the next day and was petrified that maybe I would get AIDS even though we hadn't done anything to warrant that fear. That was when our culture, including the church, chose to further stigmatize homosexuality with hateful AIDS rhetoric rather than understanding, respecting, and humanizing us.

"Coming Out" = "Thrown Out"–The One Theological Lesson Mom Taught Me

"Honey, when everyone in the world hates you and mistreats you, you should know that God and I will always love you. You also need to know that our Heavenly Father had a Son, and His name is Jesus."

I don't remember what inspired that story, but I remember her face when Mom told it to me as we sat on the stairs at the townhouse. I was maybe 11 or 12. She was earnest and humble, and I could tell she honestly believed it. She said it so matter-of-factly; there was no question in my mind that what she was saying was true. I had always known our family was "Christian" and had been for generations. But until the age of 24, that was just another label, like "Southern" or "Blue Dog Democrats." It was an informative religious label but not a genuine relationship with God (for me) until I was 24.

What follows would put this simple lesson to a severe test. Of course, every word is exactly as I remember, but sometimes we humans can deliver the universe's beauty in one moment and then deliver the curses of culture in the next.

I was 19, and my mom discovered something that would upend our worlds. While doing laundry, she found an invitation to a gay Valentine's Day party in my pocket. There was no mistaking that it was quite the gay affair.

That is when my mother gave me my first theology lesson concerning sexuality. She informed me that God hated fags, and I would burn forever in hell. This is ironic because when I was a kid, as I mentioned before, she told me that when no one else in the world loved me, she and God would. Apparently, that wasn't wholly true.

Sidenote. Today I have a much better relationship with my mother. She's a fantastic woman, and she now knows that God does love me. But back then, a false (and indoctrinated?) application of the gospel was the *only* spiritual response she knew to the issue of homosexuality. As such, you will probably not be surprised by what I am about to share with you. It was a life-threatening moment that thousands of LGBTQ+ youth and young adults go through every day. It was one of the most horrible nights of my life that I know far too many people can directly relate to.

Mom yelled, "YOU HAVE ONE HOUR TO GET OUT OF THIS HOUSE! You can keep what you shove into your car, but you will never come back here because this is no longer your home. You are to never come by the store (they had started a short-lived clothing store), and never talk to your brother again!"

Numb and terrified, I hurriedly shoved my clothes, knick-knacks, stereo, and everything I could put my hands on into my little Aries K car. Finally, in the 59th minute of that final hour of living with my mom, I left the house and stayed away completely for over five years. I would live out of that little car for the next three weeks, but I never lived with them again.

The Divine Manifest in Drag

Then one night, my 23 year old boyfriend Todd called me at the convenience store where I worked. Todd was a relationship (a toxic relationship) that lasted about 18 months and was the main reason for the Valentine's Day party invite. He had told a drag queen friend about my plight. Her stage name was Carmella Marcella Garcia, Girl!—known to her friends as Mella. Todd had told Mella all about my situation, and Mella told him to tell me to get my ass over to her place immediately. So as soon as I could, I drove over to Mella's condo. Unfortunately, I slid on some ice and hit a tree on the way there. It only dinged my car a little, but it confirmed that my life indeed sucked, in every way imaginable."

When I showed up at Mella's door, I was as desperate as possible. I hadn't showered in a while, and my car looked like a refugee camp on wheels. I walked up to the front door, ashamed of how I looked and smelled. By that time, I felt like nobody would have me, and I was ready to give up. I can empathize with young gay teens being bullied, abused, and left homeless by religious intolerance as I know what it is like to feel desperate, alone, and confused to the point of wanting to end it all. It was the only time in my life that I genuinely considered suicide.

Mella opened the door just as he was obviously getting ready for a show. He welcomed me into his home with arched eyebrows, something on his head to pull his hair back, and what looked like a muumuu type of dress, as he said:

"I welcome you into my home, in Jesus' name."

Yes, you read that right. A drag queen invited me into his home in Jesus' name. He said he welcomed me because he knew that was what his Lord would want him to do. He also cooked me a wonderful, down-home Southern meal. He couldn't join me because he was in a hurry to get to the club for his show. I don't think I said much except "thank you." I wasn't a talker at that point in my life. Very shut down in many ways. Mella said, "God loves you, and we have to look out for each other, especially when people, even our own families, hurt and hate us." He said, "I am not going to charge you rent except to ask that someday down the road, you return the favor for another young gay person who might be homeless and helpless just for being who they are. Now go on and get some of that good food!"

As I prepared my plate, I wept. Here, decades later, as I write this, I can still smell those beans and that cornbread. I sat down at Mella's table and forgot how I smelled and the chaos in my newly dinged car. I forgot about hellfire, brimstone, and my crying, screaming mother.

For the first time, I felt unconditionally accepted. For the first time, I considered God as cool. Staying alive might be worth it. Surprisingly, when you are desperately hungry and dirty, it's not difficult to eat and weep simultaneously.

Consider this: At such a critical time in my life, the two biggest influential voices in my life presented two very different Gospels—one of cultural conditioning, fear, hatred, and abuse, and the other of Jesus' love and compassion, of Him being a Good Shepherd in our time of need. He must be a big fan of drag queens because Mella sure got it, and I am forever grateful.

Unfortunately, I was a substance abuser when I was welcomed into Mella's home. For that reason, I didn't stay long. Though Mella invited me in and gave me shelter, I didn't recognize the gift that it was until years later. I didn't know how to "adult" or what it meant to be a good room-mate. I didn't help out with bills, food, or anything else as I was almost always under the influence of a substance. Eventually, Mella (and Mella's roommates who *did* know how to be adults) grew tired and frustrated with me and asked me to leave. They were right to do so. Though, looking back, I think I was waiting for one of them—or Mella, actually—to teach me how to be an adult. This, of course, was not their job.

After I left, I moved on and was transient for the better part of the next two years. Eventually, I joined a 12-step program (still hating most Christians), and the Lord used that program to save my life again.

Mella and I were estranged for a while but reconnected in 2014. At that time, we had a wonderful conversation in which Mella said to me, "I've always felt like a mother to you, even though I am only a few years older." For that reason, I now refer to her as Momma Mella. She passed a couple of years ago to cancer and is now my Drag Guardian Angel. Love you, Momma Mella. And thank you.

I've never forgotten that icy cold day when the Lord had mercy on me and brought me out of a spiral that might have led to permanent self-destruction. I have had the honor of returning Mella's favor throughout the years, as she requested. This part of my story is why I support organizations that help homeless LGBTQ+ youth and young adults. (I've listed a few at the back of this book for anyone who needs help.)

One Hellacious Blur

For the most part, life in my late teens and early 20s was a blur. As things worsened at home before I was kicked out, I got deeper into substance abuse. After I was thrown out into the streets for being gay, my substance abuse continued—including when I lived at Mella's. As a result, the next several years are blurry. Aside from some traumatic experiences, I can't remember them very well, in general.

I had no social skills and was only slightly more weird drunk than sober. Actually, I was a weird partier when drunk, but a weird person when sober. Meaning, I was always odd and awkward. I never opened up unless I was shit-faced, and even then, you really couldn't grasp what I was trying to say or do. Not surprisingly, I couldn't either.

As I already said, I didn't know how to "adult" like everyone else around me. I had no preparation for being in the world on my own. I had no idea how to balance a checkbook (a genuine skill back in the dark ages). Any paperwork, whether it was an application for a bank account or a government form, would almost always cause a panic attack, because of my conditioned—and unconscious—fear response to doing something wrong. In my life up until that point, I had learned that even appearing to not do something perfectly would be met with swift punishment.

I got the nickname "Rose" (from the *Golden Girls*) from some of my gay friends because I was both prone to naiveté and yet could exhibit a razor-sharp wit in the next breath. I also loved to tell stories that often entertained me more than anyone else. I made most of them up, desperate for the idea that I could bring a smile to another's face. The idea of someone seeing me as a friend and enjoying my presence instead of scowling, screaming, and punishing me was like water in a desert to a dying, dehydrated man

As I got more involved in the bar and drug scenes, I got more adept at lying, partying, and stealing. I was no angel by any means. I did have sex a few times just to get drugs or have a bed to sleep in. However, I didn't sleep with every single person at every opportunity.

Between the ages of 18–21, my life was filled with the demons often associated with substance abuse. This was also the time in which I met Todd and started a relationship with him. Because I was in some sort of spiral, and because I had no understanding of what a healthy relationship meant, our relationship was truly toxic. I can admit to having a role in that, but in hindsight, the majority of it was the result of Todd's choices and toxic behaviors. I want to say it was due to his "nature," but we reconnected a few years ago, and he apologized for his behavior. He, himself, has been on a healing journey, and I am happy for him.

Todd was incredibly handsome. He looked like Tom Selleck's gay, preferred-to-be-naked-in-some-of-the-oddest-places cousin. I want to use the pseudonym of "Asshole" to refer to him for his parts of this memoir, but that wouldn't be very mature or gracious of me. Todd was energetic, always the life of the party. He said he loved me and always wanted me around, and if he didn't want me around, I stalked him until he did.

Again, we were a *terrible* combination. My behavior was just as toxic as Todd's, with one exception: I didn't quite have the sociopath thing down. Being emotionally dependent was my first go-to approach to relationships and the driver behind my toxic behavior. The main difference between us (that I could see) was that I often felt guilty about what I was doing whereas he never seemed to feel guilty for anything. On top of that, he seemed to want to have sex with everyone but me—we never did the full horizontal tango during the entire 18 months we were together. But that didn't deter my deep emotional dependence on him. It was indeed a horrible situation.

I did some truly despicable things at Todd's direction or suggestion. We stole houseplants, bar stools, clothes, food, lots of Bacardi 151, cigarettes, and just about anything and everything he determined he wanted and that I couldn't afford. He drove high or drunk all the time. He even stole my identity once to get his family brand new furniture for Christmas.

Thankfully, the Divine busted the Christmas heist.

I was standing at my kitchen sink (in our family home a few months before getting thrown out), and I somehow knew that he had stolen my identity. Neither of us were Christian, but I called him and screamed, "WHY DID YOU STEAL MY SOCIAL SECURITY NUMBER!" He was thrown off balance, something very rare for him, and freaked out, saying I was psychic and not to go all "Carrie" on him. He hadn't planned on paying it off, but then said that he would try to pay it off since I "knew" about it and was very upset.

That commitment lasted for four payments out of twenty-four.

Later, when I met his mom, I sat on the furniture my name bought. She seemed sweet, with a jet-black beehive hairdo. Not exactly cat glasses but similar. She thanked me for being good to her boy even though I was a bit of a stalker. I told her she was welcome, and he didn't run fast, so it made the stalking easier.

That is when I found out where Todd got his sociopathic tendencies.

A knock came on the door, and she whipped her hair off (a wig) and slumped over. Todd said, "Randy, don't say a word; this could be someone from the government doing their regular check-up on Mom." It turned out to be someone from the neighborhood dropping something off.

Todd's mom sat up, put her hair back on, and laughed. "Thank God I didn't have to act retarded today."

Yep. A real class act. Both of them.

She had been in a car accident years earlier and claimed to have had severe back pain and brain "issues." She was actually okay, but decided to work the system for everything from food stamps to lots of free prescription drugs. She then sold the prescription drugs to her sons (both gay) and the neighborhood addicts.

I determined that I would not hang out with him anymore after that, but of course, on the way home, those dimples flashed, and I lost my mind again.

Early on in our relationship, before I was thrown out of the house, Todd's hostile and physically abusive temper was revealed, but I ignored it because being abused was something I was conditioned to just accept (learned helplessness). For example, he once "borrowed" my car for what he said would only be a "couple of hours." Those couple of hours turned into three days over Thanksgiving. It was the only Thanksgiving where I was grateful my family had long since stopped celebrating holidays. (After Mom and Harry got married, holidays and birthdays were "just another day.")

After not hearing from Todd by the end of my shift that night, I left the convenience store/gas station where I was working. I walked a mile and a half to Todd and his gay brother's house. When his brother opened the door, he told me to fuck off. But, on my way to their house, I had spotted a literal drug den/prostitution magnet/roach motel and decided it was my only option. I stayed there for three days until Todd decided to reappear with my car.

The hotel was disgusting. I had plenty of men proposition me as I walked to and from there to work, to get something to eat, or just to get out because I couldn't stand all the bugs in the room.

Even after Todd slept with almost every man in Nashville except me, I was still convinced that he loved me. Mella had tried to warn me against him, but even though he stole my identity and my car, his actions only served to further reinforce my conditioned self-loathing and belief that I deserved to be mocked and abused. Or, more distressingly, that "love" meant abuse.

Just because you "come out" doesn't mean you come out healthy and whole. I was neither.

I can get a supernatural word of knowledge that he stole my identity but was somehow blind to the reality right in front of my face. When Todd hooked up with a genuinely lovely guy and started draining his money, time, and resources like he had done with several guys the entire time I knew him, somehow I thought I was different. I actually was different in that he was doing the exact same thing to me just without the sex, so I didn't have to be lied to as much. Anyway, Todd's new guy was nice. He sat me down privately and asked me about the deal with Todd and me. He was concerned that it wasn't healthy. He asked me if he should be worried about two things: 1) Todd and me having a secret relationship, and 2) if Todd was a trustworthy person.

I lied and did everything I could to tell this guy not to worry. I told him that Todd was a long-time friend and nothing else (even though I thought we were something more). I said that Todd was utterly trustworthy.

I updated Todd on all of this later that evening when we had dinner on the $20 Todd had stolen from the guy earlier that day. Then, Todd and I decided to take this guy's truck to Atlanta to party that weekend. He thought Todd was going to do some work or something, and he didn't know that Todd had picked me up, too.

We drank the entire four-hour drive there, throwing back Rumple Minze Peppermint Schnapps shots all the way from Nashville to Atlanta. We were pretty drunk by the time we got to our motel room on Peachtree Street, which wasn't far from some of Atlanta's biggest gay bars (at the time).

As drunk as we were, we got ready and hit the town. I was still under-age but on my third or fourth fake ID. I have to admit, we looked pretty hot. Well, as hot as '80s gay guys could get at the time. We did get a lot of attention.

We went to the first bar, and Todd was trying to put me out of the game early on. He was essentially pouring Bacardi 151 and Coke down my throat. He would do that to get me to pass out early so he could go on the prowl by himself later. This behavior often left me sleeping on strange couches, in chairs, and in cars in various places. However, that night I said, "Nope. You will not get me to pass out in the truck so you can have the hotel room alone to go fuck some trick or orchestrate some orgy." I added, "And give me the damn motel key!"

This altercation may have been the first time I was ever that hostile and demanding toward him, and Todd did *not* like it.

"Fuck you, Randy!"

"No, fuck you, Todd!"

He shoved me. I pushed him back. He went running outside to the street. I ran after him. We started yelling—remember, we were very drunk. I had no inhibitions, and everything I had been holding back came pouring out in one of the largest adrenaline rushes of my life.

He punched me. I hit him back, over and over again. Todd was furious and looked extraordinarily shocked and angry all at once.

The next thing I knew, I was being flung out into Peachtree Street. I stumbled straight into heavy traffic. There were screeching tires, blaring horns, and me running after Todd, grabbing him and punching the shit out of him in the middle of the road.

Looking back, I like to imagine a pair of old women stuck in the traffic our fight produced and one of them saying to the other, "Myrtle! I think Tom Selleck's gay cousin is in a drunken brawl with a Duran Duran groupie!" I'm sure, however, that the commotion we caused was nothing so quaint.

We fought hard. Cursing at the top of our lungs every awful name two '80s queens could make up. We punched, scratched, pulled hair, ripped clothes, and flew over the top of a bench. It was full-on gay combat, and we fought all the way back to our motel! He got the better of me and was able to break away and get to the elevator before I could get off the floor. It was a motel with external entrances to the rooms, so I ran up the stairs as our room was on the second floor. Remember, he had the only key.

By the time I got to our room, the door had an inch left to close, and I shoved that door open like a champion and screamed, "YOU GET THE FUCK OUT! I AM PAYING FOR THIS ROOM, AND YOU ARE NOT WELCOME!"

I can still see the absolute shock on his face. I had never stood up to him before, so "Rose" became a brawler that night. I started packing up his clothes, but he shoved me out of the way, and we fought some more. Eventually, he started packing. I sat in the tiny chair by the huge plate glass window near the door, looking out at the Atlanta skyline.

He cussed and fumed. People were outside looking worried and pensive. We didn't know it, but someone was calling the police. He grabbed a luggage cart and piled his stuff onto it. As he rolled it out of the room, he said, "I will leave your ass here in Atlanta, you fucking bitch." He stepped out into the hallway and, with a parting shot, said something foul followed by something about me needing to apologize when I was ready. I picked up a small bag he had forgotten, and before he could finish his last sentence, I nailed him on the forehead with the bag and said, "Goodbye, BITCH!" and slammed that door harder than I have ever slammed a door before.

And locked it.

I plopped down in the chair in front of the plate glass window and started to cry. I had no idea how I would get back to Nashville, but I felt a moment of relief.

Unfortunately, my relief was quickly shattered. I mean literally shattered.

The drapes were open on the plate glass window, and Todd could see me in the chair. (Don't forget, we were entirely drunk. Have I said that enough?) Todd tried to punch me through this huge plate glass window. Have you ever seen a sheet of plate glass shatter? It breaks into thousands of extremely sharp, jagged pieces in all kinds of sizes. Somehow I escaped the falling glass without any harm.

Todd did not. He almost lost his left arm (and he was left-handed).

I heard him scream bloody murder, as the people standing around freaked out. Without blinking or wasting even a half-second, I flew to the door and threw it open. Todd was standing there with a large portion of his forearm shredded. You could see some of his bone protruding from his arm. Blood was everywhere.

His beautiful eyes were dark, his skin ashen. He said, "Babette…" a term of endearment we had come up with some other night, "Babette, ooh… What happened?" and I told him to look at me, not at his arm. To just look at me, and he would be okay. I kept his eyes locked on mine and said to keep looking at me. "Look at me." He went quiet but not unconscious and just stared at me. I tore off my belt and made a tourniquet on his upper arm to try and stop the bleeding. He didn't ask me what I was doing or why. He just stared at me like a pale angel, crying.

As I mentioned earlier, someone had called the police while we were fighting in our room. The men in blue showed up a few minutes after I put on the makeshift tourniquet. They had an ambulance with them. The hotel owner (maybe the manager) had an absolute meltdown over the broken window. He didn't seem too worried about Todd's arm or the blood everywhere, but that plate glass window was a big deal.

The ambulance driver said that my keeping Todd calm and putting on the tourniquet had probably saved Todd's arm. As they loaded Todd up on the gurney, I remember him asking, "Where did you learn how to compose yourself, and how did you know where to put the tourniquet?"

I replied, "Mr. Davidson's ninth grade health class." He said that it must have been a good class.

The police were interestingly not that interested in pressing charges or lecturing us. They even tried to get the owner to calm down and work something out with me to pay for the window and just let it go. I have to think that was God's mercy there. My adrenaline overload was maybe hiding that I was still very drunk, but I somehow convinced the hotel owner to take our party money (minus bus fare for me). He took $300 or so and told me to get lost.

I was drunk, and my soul felt numb. It was weird to be drunk and yet have some of the most sobering moments of my life at the same time. I grabbed up all of our stuff and piled into Todd's friend's truck. It was a stick shift, and I didn't know how to drive a stick at the time, but I attempted to go to the downtown hospital anyway. It was where they had taken Todd.

I think I drove the entire way there in first gear. It took forever, and it wasn't even that far away. I don't remember parking the car or lying down in the hospital hallway. The following day, I woke up with tons of people walking around me as I had pressed my body face-first into the rubber baseboard on the hallway's wall. I was hungover, ashamed, and frightened, and I needed to wash the remainder of Todd's blood off my body.

They were able to save and do some repairs to his forearm. However, he had scars and some nerve damage, which caused him to not be able to use a couple of his fingers.

A nurse asked me if I was related to Todd as I waited for him to come out of recovery from his surgery. I said that I was his boyfriend. She said, "Okay, but if anyone else asks, you are his brother."

I was glad Todd was doing well after surgery, and I was glad he didn't lose a significant part—or all—of his forearm. But another part of me couldn't wait to get out of his life. Of course, I felt like I should stay and help (rather than catching the bus to Nashville). So, for a little over a week, I wore three different sets of clothes, took sink baths, and slept on Todd's hospital room floor. We barely talked. He blamed me. He lied to his friend (the guy whose truck he took), saying he was in a freak accident at whatever work he was supposed to be doing. Todd told his friend not to come down and that he would be fine; to not worry. Todd didn't tell him the accident's severity until we got back. A week later, we drove back to Nashville with Todd on serious pain medication. He had one arm on the wheel with the injured one propped up. I shifted the gears when he told me to.

It was a miserable drive.

Todd called his friend when we had made it to the house where I was renting a couch—not a room, a sofa—for $40 a week. My house was on the way to where they lived, but Todd needed someone to help drive the rest of the way. So, his friend came with another friend, and they drove off. As I watched them go, a switch flipped. I had no desire ever to see Todd again.

Ever.

We didn't see each other for a few months, but eventually, I saw him again out at the bars. He would flash those eyes and try to dazzle with those dimples to join him for a few drinks. He even asked to stay at my place so he didn't have to "drive back."

"No thanks, Todd; there isn't any room on the couch." The last night I ever saw Todd in person, a group of us from work went out and one of my bartender friends (a straight guy from the restaurant I worked at) was running around with us. We were hanging out at the gay bar when Todd decided to attach himself to us. My friend knew of our history and kindly informed Todd that he was my new boyfriend and didn't feel comfortable with Todd's request to sleep on the floor at my place. I was in awe of my straight friend that night.

Decades later, I looked Todd up on Facebook. Life has been very rough for him, but he is still alive and kicking. He doesn't live that far away from me now. I messaged him to say hello. It was a good conversation. He apologized for the way he treated me in the past. I still don't need to see him, but at least there is a sense of closure to what happened so long ago. The only good thing that happened while I was in a "relationship" with Todd was his connecting me with Mella.

I look back on that time in my life and can't believe I was ever that person or the extreme versions of me that were yet to come. At that time, however, I was well on my way to the bottom of substance abuse as I careened toward the rocks and further destruction. It's no mystery why it took me until my 40s to get a clue about my authentic self. I wouldn't be surprised if the Christians I briefly met in various encounters were praying for me at that time.

CHAPTER 3

Christians Suck! Except When They Don't

Before we move on beyond the epic tragedy of Rose the Brawler vs. Todd the Sociopath, here are a few more stories that happened in my formative years.

Experiencing the Spirit for the First Time

There is a picture of me in all my nerdy glory. I have a late '70s haircut and I'm wearing an odd pair of glasses. They had the Superman emblem on the stems. Next to me is my fabulous and gorgeous mother. She smiled big, and I smiled confusedly. It was the Kodak Instamatic photo the church took to commemorate my becoming a member of the church. I had gotten "saved" at some point during the six months we went to church, and this was the photo they took before I was baptized.

Funny thing, though, is that I don't remember saying the sinner's prayer or anyone explaining it to me. They might have, but obviously it did not register. However, I do remember the baptism.

I remember going into some room to take off all my clothes except my underwear and putting on a white robe. I also clearly remember that there was another very handsome man doing the same. I remember blushing as he stripped down to his undies. I was, of course, extraordinarily self-conscious, but I pretended like it was no big thing. This was an attitude I couldn't carry over to the gym locker room at school, where I regularly skirted panic attacks.

While I remember that man, I remember the soft golden light coming through the window the most. See, when asked what my favorite thing in the world is, it is always "light." I love sunlight and how it becomes the Divine Artist's catalyst to enliven all of creation. I can tell you precisely what kind of lighting was happening for every significant spiritual moment I have experienced. As I have mentioned before, sunlight is a thing with me.

That day, a soft golden light filled the room from the windows. I don't remember what Brother Paul said as he dunked me in the baptismal waters, but I know that I knew beyond a shadow of doubt that God was watching, and I had nothing to fear. My world was chaotic at home, my heart and mind tormented with shame and messages that constantly told me that I wasn't good enough. But then, God decided that He would make me feel His presence and love for some reason. I don't remember a single moment from my childhood where I felt safer and more loved than when I stepped into and out of the baptismal pool.

Later, I was told I wasn't saved because I genuinely didn't understand what I had just done to be baptized. Some people say that I am not a Christian because I am gay. Now, all I question is whether it is my understanding of the "truth" that saves me, or is it simply God's will to save everyone? I couldn't recite any Roman Catholic creed or Protestant screed at that tender age, but I knew God was there. I knew They loved me, and I would never have to face life without Them.

That beautiful and sunny afternoon, I remember going to my room and laying down on the bench built into the bay window. I watched the trees, the birds, the local pets, the other kids playing, the cars passing by on the side street, and I felt the warm sun flow in and over me. It was a divine respite in a chaotic time.

Then the Church Picked on Nikki Six

We didn't stay at that church long. One Sunday, I knew something was amiss when I saw all these teen and rock-n-roll magazines piled very high around Brother Paul's pulpit. I recognized my favorite bands at the time. Paul Stanley and his beautiful face in crazy KISS makeup, which didn't stop me from having a crush on him. It makes me wonder: Have I always had a thing for teased hair and makeup? In addition to Paul Stanley, there were Van Halen, Led Zeppelin, Boston, Mötley Crüe, and other teen heartthrobs from the time piled high on the pulpit. There were also broken vinyl records, some eight-track tapes, and some rock concert t-shirts and paraphernalia mixed into the heap with the magazines. I was hoping these would be random door prizes for single-parent kids who were there that day.

Nope.

Brother Paul had all the teens from the teen Sunday school classes bring in all their "idolatrous" items as an act of repentance to live a holy life. I certainly did not understand why someone would "worship" these amazing rock stars—a word deliberately used by Brother Paul—but I did know at that young age that there was nothing to worry about, and you could enjoy them. I knew they were just theatrical, and they were also highly talented.

Brother Paul started making fun of the men in the pictures, which prompted the considerably large congregation to laugh along with him. My brother and I didn't. Then he held up a picture of a rocker I truly loved, Nikki Six with Mötley Crüe. Brother Paul, with his big helmet hair and boring suit, held up a brightly colored image of wild, long-haired Nikki Six in *tight* leather pants. He then sardonically asked the congregation, "Do you think a 'man' that looks like this will enter the kingdom of heaven?" He started laughing, as did the entire congregation—except two little boys that found fun and even some solace in crazy, metal hair-band antics. When I heard Brother Paul and the congregation laughing, something in me hurt.

I was livid.

I turned to Ben and said, "Don't you listen to him. He is wrong. God loves Nikki, and they shouldn't be laughing at him." I was so mad. I went home and told my mother. Interestingly, she said we didn't have to go back if we didn't want to. So we didn't.

I would find out a few years later that she had gone to see some of the church leadership about divorcing my bio dad around that same time. She explained that he had abandoned us years ago, was currently living with a sex worker in Germany, and was not just physically absent but also refusing to help with finances or any support. Their response? It was her fault. She must have done something to cause him to run away and it was her responsibility to get him back. If she divorced him, that would be a sin. If she divorced him, that would be proof she wasn't genuinely saved.

Yes, they hated Nikki Six and were misogynistic assholes to my mother. We didn't go back because the church was more interested in being horrible than understanding, more "right" than gracious. The power they wielded was both abusive and unmerciful.

So I began to see that the church wasn't interested in the real world except where they could bully and make fun of it in the name of (their) truth. They were empowered by a self-righteous condescension, not compassion.

I remember seeing televangelists ranting on and on about this or that. I remember Jerry Falwell looking through the TV screen at me, a young gay teen, telling me I would burn in hell forever, that I was a pedophile. I burst into tears in front of the TV that day. Beginning that day, a hatred toward Christians burned bright and hot for many years. Even though I was a nominal Christian, I hated Christians, and now I believe that I had a lot of good reasons for that hatred. Some of them deserved it.

But one lesson I learned the hard way is that if you genuinely hate something long enough, you focus on it for so long that you ultimately become some version of it. You won't see it coming, and you will pay the price. Hatred is a sneaky bastard.

Bewitched

As mentioned in the first chapter, every day after school, my brother and I walked the mile or so home from our elementary school. Later, when we moved to a different school, we would ride the bus home. We were good latch-key children; I would unlock the door, and we would lock it behind us. Then I would quickly call Mom at work to let her know we were home. By the time I got to the phone, the afternoon reruns would be on while we tried to do homework.

JJ and his family raised us on *Good Times*. Gilligan and the crew on *Gilligan's Island* seemed like fun neighbors. There was also: *Hogan's Heroes*, *I Love Lucy*, and *The Jeffersons*. Watching TV shows where there was always a lot of fun and peaceful resolutions provided moments of calm in an otherwise chaotic life. They filled me with idealized concepts about relationships as they played out on a tiny glass window in my living room. In truth, I knew more about those ensemble casts than my own family.

The one show that caused a spiritual crisis within me, and not in the way you might think, was *Bewitched*. So, you might assume the spiritual problem was about demonic witchcraft being presented as normal and how it infused spiritual warfare into our little young minds, as many Christians do.

Silly, but no. That wasn't why.

When I watched *Bewitched*, I loved every—I mean every—single character. Of course, I loved Samantha and Darren (over time, both of the Darrens), Endora, Larry, Aunt Esmerelda, the Kravitzes, Serena, Tabitha, and all the others I don't need to name. They were all either influential personalities or simply strong characters. Yes, the show was formulaic; the Good Witch trying to be a good mortal wife finds herself having to use her "powers" to save the day, every single day! She tries desperately to please her husband and deny a significant part of herself, but she can't.

Come to think of it, that'll preach!

Plus, there was all that flourish and the flowing gowns and *smoke* when you magically entered a room. I wanted flowing robes and smoke to appear as I magically showed up anywhere I wanted to.

The spiritual crisis was that I truly believed God could give me those powers. I was young and desperately yearning for a sense of self and empowerment. I knew there was more to life than just being locked away watching television. I hated my life and felt shut down, not allowed to be happy or to have fun. I remember getting furious about the futility of my young life and, at the foot of the stairs in the condo, bitterly weeping and begging God to give me powers like Samantha. I had no idea what I was feeling or asking for at the time, but I believed in God, and I believed He willfully denied me freedom and happiness by not granting me those powers.

I was just a slightly neurotic boy, not understanding that I was going through a true spiritual/personal crisis. I know that now. I also look back at that memory of little Randy bitterly crying and begging God alone on the stairs, and it is genuinely heartbreaking until I remember how that ended. Once again, sunlight came pouring through the curtains in the main bedroom. It was just to the left at the top of the stairs. The sun's angle had the sunlight shining in slanted rays through the staircase. I remember looking into those rays and just crying, crying, crying. But the crying began to ease, and I laid down in those rays on the stairs. Then I allowed it. I allowed the Divine to minister peace to my spirit.

No, I never developed the ability to twitch my nose or pull off an Endora flourish/fireworks entrance. But in my little world that angry day, I did learn faith. I knew then that God had heard me, and while I wasn't happy that He didn't gift me with Samantha's supernatural abilities, I knew that He was with me there on the stairs. I may not have understood God, but He was there.

I may question other Christians' motivations and behaviors. I may question my own understanding of God, but I've never questioned His presence. So, when they talk about faith being a spiritual gift, I am so grateful the Spirit saw fit to wire me that way. I have never doubted that God is a truly faithful and Good Shepherd.

Party Barge and Car Surfing in Daytona Beach (1986)

A few years later, it was 1986. Somehow I ended up with a group of guys at school sanding down an old short school bus that two of them (brothers) had been given as a spring break present from their dad. We gutted the thing, painted it black, and I painted "Party Barge" on the sides. I also painted "Party Barge" on the little flip-out stop sign. It was no longer the iconic red and white flashing stop sign; it was now solid black with gold Def Leppard type lettering reading "Party Barge" on it. We thought that was so cool.

Surprisingly, my parents initially said I could go. But they got mad when the boy's father wanted them to sign a liability waiver for me to be on the Party Barge during spring break. Like all the times before when I wanted to do something, the night before, they changed their minds and said I couldn't go.

I don't remember having a fit, but I was furious. Finally, I made it clear that I was going (this was after the beating/move out in the episode mentioned in the last chapter). My parents relented at last, and the next day, the "Party Barge" crew headed to Pensacola.

Pensacola was boring. We thought MTV was there. They weren't. So we changed our plans and quickly traveled a million more miles to Daytona Beach, where the MTV Springfest was happening.

It was wild.

I will never forget pulling up on the beach with semi-naked young adults and crazy older people *everywhere*! As far as the eye could see. I was mesmerized seeing the ocean and such a large crowd for the first time.

I eventually called my parents to tell them we had left Pensacola and were now in Daytona. To describe them as "not happy" would be an under-statement, and I had a moment when I thought about what I would face when I got home. But while I was in Daytona, that thought was far away.

I think I took two showers that week, and I slept on top of the bus a few of those nights that I can remember. The guys I was with were what I would call the "nerd trust" of our high school. I loved those guys because they weren't hateful to me.

People loved *(LOVED!)* the Party Barge. Some of our friends said it showed up on MTV a couple of times in the beach scenes. I never saw it on TV, in any case. The week was a mix of glorious blurry memories, two of which included: attending a Molly Hatchet concert with a strange, topless girl on my shoulders, and participating in MTV's North vs. South best of three tugs-of-war.

Charlie, part of our nerd trust, was a gigantic fellow. He helped us by being our anchor. The series was 1-1 only because of him. But on the third tug-of-war, we (the South) tied our end of the rope to a nearby wall right behind us. We pretended to be tugging our brains out and then let go. It was great seeing the Northerners look up, shocked, and then roll their eyes. We lost that one (and the series) by forfeit, but it was worth it.

I remember falling in love with the ocean and the sun that week as I sat and stared at the waves, allowing the sun to comfort me. Swimming around in the waves was excellent, and the wind blowing my hair was delightful. I loved every minute.

In the morning, the nerd trust usually went their various ways to collect whatever interests they had that day. So, I went looking for pot. Eventually, I found a pretty, young, blonde local. I figured she would have some weed. She did. We smoked and drank Cokes (sodas, pop, whatever you want to call it). We didn't talk a lot, but eventually, I said, "Can I take a picture with you?"

She said, "No, because you'll tell all your friends you fucked me on your senior spring break trip."

I said, "You're right, I will tell them that. But you don't have to worry—I'm gay, so they won't believe me anyway." She laughed, and we crawled into the photo booth thing. By the looks of the two happy teens in the little strips of pictures, you would have thought I had a girlfriend. At least that's what I told people. The truth is that we did get high together for a day and enjoyed each other as day-long friends at the beach.

Another memory is that I was sitting on the passenger side of the Party Barge while the nerd trust was collecting shell samples or something. I was relaxed and getting high. That's when the hellfire religious zealots descended upon the beach to save our wayward souls.

My first thought was that they looked uncomfortable. Covered head to toe, boring haircuts, and scowling, scowling, scowling. They had creative protest-looking signs: "TURN OR BURN!" wrapped in hellfire flames. "FLIP OR FRY!" also enveloped in the same fiery visuals. My second thought was that I was jealous—I wished I could have painted fire like that all over the Party Barge.

One woman in a long blue jean skirt, sports socks, sneakers, long-sleeved blouse, and long, dull black hair came up to the Party Barge window where my pot smoke was escaping.

"YOU are GOING to HELL!"

I offered her a hit off my joint. You, dear reader, may or may not be shocked by this, but she refused and decided to give me a sermonette before stomping off.

I detested sweaty, uncomfortable, hell-fire-wrapped Christians with dull hair.

At another point later that week, we went to "the strip," a stretch of road where the cars rolled slowly and where there was yet another wild party-type scene. I got a little restless, so I decided to do something fun. I had scored a couple of cases of beer, so as we were driving down the strip, people would yell out, "PARTY BARGE!" and I would throw them a beer. Girls would flash us, and while I don't remember ever requesting that feature, the nerd trust LOVED it.

Of course, being buzzed, I can't remember how, but eventually we parked and went our separate ways to roam around the strip. Two of the nerd trust stayed with me because I seemed to have a magic ability to party, or at least find something to do.

Eventually, I did start doing something that I would call old-school "car surfing." Which is not to be confused with the car surfing of today. Essentially, as the traffic was crawling by; I would yell in the open windows, "HEY! Let me ride in your car for a few blocks!" The response was often, "Why?"

I would then say, "You get the pleasure of sharing your mind-altering substances with me for a few blocks! It'll be SO fun!"

You would be surprised at how many people let me do that. I am so glad I didn't die. I don't remember all the people I met, but I remember dancing through a few sunroofs. And now the 55-year-old me looks back and thinks, "What an idiot I was..." but I'd be lying if I said I wasn't smiling right now as I think about it. Substance abuse is always wrong, but the idea of my younger self—little, emotionally-traumatized and shut-down teenage Randy—having fun makes me smile.

After car surfing for a while, a group of handsome young men approached us on the sidewalk. They were winsome, friendly, and, to be honest, really good looking. Naturally, I was immediately in lust.

Then they started talking about Jesus.

Lust? GONE.

Like the Atlantic-whipped wind, my buzz was strong, but that white-hot fury with most Christians still smoldered.

"Do you know Jesus?"

"Yeah, yeah… Son of God, Moses' cousin or something, all that."

To their credit, they laughed. And then the guy with the long, curly brown locks said, "No man. Do you have a relationship with Jesus?"

I rolled my eyes and said, "Yeah, man, he's my Lord and Savior… my family has been Christian for generations."

Then his face changed; he looked almost loving, angelic even, and said, "No, do you KNOW Him, do you know Him enough to fall in love with Him?"

"Me? Fall in 'love'… with… Him?"

"Yes, Jesus is IN love with YOU… blah blah blah."

It was like a divinely clarifying moment I will never forget. I immediately felt heartsick (Spirit, I am sure) and thought, "Why would He be 'in love' with me?" I lost my breath for a second, and the guy kept talking, but it was all mumbling in my ears. I was stuck on not just loving Jesus but Him being "in love" with me.

I didn't become a born-again Christian that night, but I remember laying on top of the bus with all the revelers around us screaming and hooting. However, I wasn't distracted by them as the Divine Spirit called out my name as I stared at the stars. God typically meets me in our sun's light, but She met me with billions of stars that night. So vast is Her great Love.

Going Home

I hated leaving the beach. I was despondent. We left at sunset, and I remember vividly feeling the wind calming my soul as I looked out the Party Barge's windows. On the radio, the Pet Shop Boys were singing "West End Girls." It seemed like a perfect setting for the most fun I had experienced in my life. That night the nerd trust took turns driving us home. I couldn't sleep on top of a moving bus, so I slept in the back where we had thrown some mattresses. I woke up with one of the nerd trust members lying next to me, his hand on mine. I think it was an accident, but I let it stay there till he woke up. It was nice thinking he felt safe enough to touch me and not have it be a big deal. He said nothing about it afterward.

When I got home, I was tan tan tan. I did tell a couple of people I slept with the girl in the photo booth pictures, but no one believed me, as I had predicted. I don't remember sharing many of the other wild stories from that week. As expected, when I got home, I had to completely shut down as a coping mechanism, if I wasn't high or drunk. I would think quite often about all the shenanigans and grin because it was the most "freedom" I had experienced to that point. I didn't like taking showers in the public restrooms, but sleeping on top of the bus was excellent. And, of course, I became a Pet Shop Boys groupie.

But every once in a while, I would remember that God had sent an angelic, brown-haired young man to tell me that Jesus was in love with me, and that I could fall in love with God.

That thought would rock my heart; it still does, every time I remember it.

An Extra Seat at the Table

When I was running around with Todd, as I mentioned before, I was renting a couch (not a room or apartment, a literal sofa) for $40 a week for some time in my young adult party years. That's when an unusual situation arose.

"Randy, you *go* to that Bible study!" was the somewhat loud and earnest voice coming from the phone. It was my mom. She had called to see if Aaron had called me yet. Aaron was a guy I used to work with at the grocery store when I was 16. He was a stoic, kind of quiet guy. Built like a tank, he had a fantastic and incredibly deep laugh and would do just about anything to help anyone out. I had a crush on him for a while when we worked together. (Don't look so surprised. We all know I had a crush on just about every man that crossed my path.) My mom was calling because he had looked her up in the phone book and called her to ask about me. He had recently prayed, and told her I was "on his heart."

Aaron was very Christian—so very Baptist-y Christian—bless his big ol' handsome heart!

My mom was urging me to go to the Bible study Aaron attended, so I told her, "Sure, I'll go." She thought that was a good thing, whereas I was thinking of Aaron's good looks and only wanted to go so I could hit on him.

It's true. I was only willing to go because of Aaron's blue eyes and dimples and my straight-up lust.

Soon after speaking with my mom, Aaron called. I can even remember his voice all these years later. He invited me to a Bible study/potluck dinner he hosted regularly every Sunday and offered to pick me up since I didn't have a car because it had gotten repoed. The first few times we arranged for me to attend, I stood him up. I was still passed out from the night before or higher than a kite and couldn't manage myself, much less a conversation. He never got impatient, and I eventually went to one of his group potluck gatherings.

Nothing I did would sway him from his peaceful demeanor or get him to notice my flirtations. Oh, and I tried! He would just laugh or joke around. When I went to the first dinner, I dragged one of my nonbinary friends. "Nonbinary" wasn't a term we even knew or used back then, so nobody changed their pronouns, but that was definitely who he/they was. My friend was pretty nervous, at first, about the whole thing. I told them, "No, wear your makeup. Let's freak them out and laugh about it later." He was game, so we went.

Don't forget, this was the '80s.

After pulling up to the house, Aaron went ahead of us while we slowly walked to the door. I extra Duran Duran'd my hair. I also got a more oversized hoop earring with a cross on it, and while I didn't prance or skip, I looked as stereotypically gay as I could… on purpose. Remember, at this time in my life, anger and distrust toward Christians was starting to fully bloom into almost rage. I wanted to shock them and was only there to hit on Aaron.

I opened the door and heard clanking dishes with about 15 to 20 adults and kids milling around. I hoped the women would shriek and run to gather their children in horror as the men formed a protective barrier between their tribe and us.

Just as I presented myself as a stereotype, I was also full of stereotypical expectations of others. My Christian experiences up until that point had been my only source of data on the subject, and I fully expected it to be the same with Aaron and his friends.

What happened was nothing. My nonbinary friend put their purse and coat down at the front door with the others. The kids went screaming by, and there were the sounds of laughter as one of them tackled another, more dishes clanking and soda pop cans opening.

Then the hostess came up to us and said, "WELCOME! So glad you could make it. Randy, right? It's nice to finally meet you. Aaron told me you both worked together at one time. So come on in—we will pray before the meal."

As I sat there eating my not-that-bad spaghetti and garlic bread, I watched my genderfluid friend, the only black person in the house and the only biological male wearing bright blue eyeshadow and lip gloss, having a great time talking to everyone. I began to think that maybe I had misjudged these Christians.

Later, we circled up in the living room, where the Bible study began. They started reading a chapter from the Bible. They passed the Bible around from one person to the next. We were each to read one to three verses aloud. I thought for sure they would skip us. I am not sure why I thought this, but when the teen girl next to me handed me the Bible, I was shocked. I have no idea what I read, but I know I read three verses with extra enunciated eloquence. I then passed the Bible to the friend who came with me, who once again looked like they were thoroughly enjoying the whole thing.

After the reading and the teaching, we prayed. Well, everyone else prayed, and I watched them through my squinted eyelids. During one prayer, one of the women referred to God as "Abba." Not being raised in the church (except for my six months of trauma with Brother Paul), I went up to her later and said, "Why did you call God 'Abba'? The only Abba I know is the '70s disco group. You know, 'Dancing Queen?'" And she just laughed. Thank God she was honest and comfortable enough to laugh.

She said to me with sweet eyes full of merriment, "I call God, our Father, 'Abba' because it's a term of endearment. Abba is like saying Daddy. God loves us like a daddy."

Her eyes turned from merriment to genuine compassion and pierced through my heart with that concept. I had never had a "daddy," or at least one I would be "endeared" to. I credit this event, Mella's compassion, and the Christians in Daytona as the tipping points for my coming to Christ a few years later. I didn't know Jesus that night, but I did come to know a different side of His people than I had thought possible.

They were life-giving people, not shaming or ashamed of my "lifestyle" people. As my friend took off their makeup and we made palettes on the floor next to my rented couch that night, we talked about how unexpectedly pleasant the situation was. We had nothing to mock them over. So, we popped in a VHS tape of a Dead or Alive concert and fell asleep.

Imagine a three-story high heart made of moss-covered stone 100 feet in diameter. Howling winds and driving rain battered this stone heart. Many earthquakes have threatened to shatter this hard, invincible structure, yet it always remained unmoved. Imagine lightning hitting that hard heart as the teen girl next to me passed the Bible; a tiny crack runs down the middle and burns away the moss. Then, at eye level to the ground, a chunk falls away. If you were to walk up and look into the now-visible hole in the stone heart and squint, you would see a small light carrying the promise of the authentic creation I would become in the far distance.

…And the echo of a soul crying.

Later, as I began to process the Bible study, I prayed my first honest prayer. It consisted of one short little sentence to God, "Help me, please."

Most importantly, this group of Christians allowed God to love them so they could love me and my friend without any strings and pressure. I knew then that they trusted and loved God and cared for strangers. They were hospitable, open, and funny. I was safe to receive their fellowship without fear or hostility. It made a big difference and opened my heart to considering the issue of Christianity differently.

Regardless of where you are on the spectrum of belief concerning God's LGBTQ+ children, do you have an extra seat at your table?

Aaron did.

CHAPTER 4

Flight of the Bar Fly

There's Probably a Country Song Analogy That Would Fit Here

Shortly after my encounter with Aaron's Bible study group, I began to see my environment for what it was: awful. In hindsight, I feel those pesky Christians were PRAYING for my eyes to be opened or something!

It's not that my eyes were completely shut. In fact, from time to time, I would look around and think, "What the hell is wrong with me?" Of course, those moments only lasted as long as it took for me to get to Juanita's Bar for their 50-cent draft beer Sunday soirées. As an illegitimate coping mechanism, self-medicating with alcohol proved to be really good at numbing everything. However, I do remember the night I left Aaron's Bible study very clearly. That night I prayed a brief but honest prayer. It consisted of only three words, "Help me, please," and then I cried myself to sleep while beating myself up for not knowing what to do or what the next step would be.

Shortly after that brief prayer, my aunt showed up with a one-way bus ticket to Dallas.

Aunt J is a firecracker. Full of life and fiery Southern charm. One day, as I was lying on the $40-a-week couch, she contacted me through my mom. Aunt J said that if I wanted to move to Dallas to "start over," I could.

She and the man she would soon divorce would let me stay at their place until I could get on my feet. Like Aaron, they were Christians and felt like God told them to give me the bus ticket.

In my mind, I thought, "Great, more Christians."

I thought about it for a while, but ultimately, I took the ticket. On the day before it expired, I climbed on a Greyhound bus for a 17-hour journey from Nashville to Dallas. I think we stopped at every podunk town between the two cities. No lie. One town was called Bucksnort, Tennessee. It's the first and only time (so far) I have ever ridden a Greyhound bus.

The night before I left, all the Applebee's waitstaff (where I worked), several managers, and all the bartenders except the new guys threw a surprise farewell party at a local gay restaurant. None of them were gay, but they decided to do this for me.

Whatever spiritual or political beliefs I have held during my life, I have always sought to champion those beliefs. It is part of my personality. So with these friends, who I partied with all the time, I was gay, but I didn't force the topic or issue.

They all would share personal details too. One musician, we called him Bear, was a fantastic older guy with a red 'fro and a walrus mustache. He stated that before he met me, he thought gay guys were disgusting and always on the hunt for the next dick. However, after befriending me, he said he "got it" now and was grateful that I was approachable.

My bartender friend who had once acted like my new boyfriend to scare off Todd had a few gay impulses. One time at a party, in front of everyone, he pinned me into my chair and said, "MAN, I'm not gay, but if I were ever to try it, I'd try it with you!" And then he laid a big ol' kiss on me. I did not reciprocate. I was told I looked like a stunned cartoon character, and everyone thought it was a hoot. There was no way I would let him "try it" with me. Great guy, but that would be a hard no.

We were doing XTC at the time. Who knew that a straight guy pinning me down in a missionary position on a chair to tell me he would do me and then kissing me is something that could happen when doing XTC? Now we know.

Their honesty meant they felt comfortable with me around. I loved that crew of people, because it was the first group of friends that made me feel truly accepted, in a drug-fueled way. So that night, I was sad to leave them but ecstatic that they would throw me a going-away party at a gay establishment.

I drank 15 Cape Cods and three rum and cokes throughout the long evening into the wee hours of the morning. I remember a bit of pot going around, too. They paid for it all. We were very loud everywhere we landed. They gave me a leather conductor's hat (think S&M "masters" hat), which made me look goofy/stupid, but I loved it because it was an honest gift from friends. I had no reason, at the time, to dress up in fetish wear, but it wasn't cheap, and they bought it for me. I was thrilled. Straight people can be so cute sometimes. That night, after my 18 drinks, the brave ones of the crew and I went to the gay bars to dance and then to an after-hours bar.

Understandably, it's all a bit blurry to me, still.

The only thing I had to do the next day was catch a bus, so I slept until the very last moment. I woke up with a splitting headache, still very drunk. I grabbed my $35 and two suitcases (I am sure there's a country song about this scenario) and left my rent-a-couch. Another friend gave me a ride to the bus terminal, and I climbed aboard with my big, high-lighted '80s hair and a hoop earring with a cross on it. I was wearing some random, ugly, blue/gray/black/white, cigarette-stinking sweater (I was smoking two packs a day), jeans, pleather (plastic leather) go-go boots, and a genuine leather conductor's hat—because my friends gave it to me, and I refused to take it off.

I was a big, freaked-out, drunken, gay '80s pop culture mess boarding a bus to my future.

I got to my seat and, of course, I was sitting next to a Catholic priest.

Figures!

He was a handsome fellow in a white-collar, and said, "Hello!" with a big smile.

I grunted, "Hey," and plopped down. I went straight to sleep until we pulled into Bucksnort, Tennessee. When I woke up briefly to see the Bucksnort interstate sign and the rosary in the hands next to me, I thought that maybe God had sent an angel to knock me out for this first leg of the trip, because I was in the middle of no-fucking-where, and it was too late to turn back.

Plus, it didn't hurt that the priest was hot. I didn't try to put my head on his shoulder. However, the thought flitted across my mind right before I passed out again.

Dallas, Here I Come

When I arrived in Dallas, my Aunt J and Uncle P picked me up. I stayed in the bedroom where one of my cousins used to sleep, and they gave me a job at their screen-printing shop. I hated it. I sorely missed Nashville and realized when no cards, letters, or phone calls came that the friends I'd had were not going to be long-distance friends. There wouldn't be an Internet available to the public for a few more years, so that wasn't around to help either. I felt abandoned—a frequent theme in my life—and became super depressed. Inordinately so.

I also hated having all my money (earned at their screen-printing shop) in Aunt J's hands with 10% going to her church. Surrendering my finances was part of her condition for letting me stay with them. I hated it, but I did it anyway.

Screen printing was slightly interesting, though not nearly as interesting as Uncle P thought it was. Getting that ink to flow equally over the screen onto the t-shirt almost drove me crazy. We did it by hand, not using super-fast gizmos. Once, they let me design my screen to make a t-shirt, which was fun. It was also incredibly kind of them to recognize my artistic bent. But frankly, I was bored, paranoid, and shut down most of the time.

To put it mildly, I sucked at that job. They paid me anyway. Today, I am so grateful for Aunt J's generosity and hospitality.

I quickly decided I needed to get my own place. I got a dinky, slightly terrifying apartment about a quarter-mile from their screen-printing shop. I had no car at first, so that meant a lot of walking. The apartment's location was the sole requirement for my new place. All alone in that apartment, I was sleeping on a double mattress on the floor with no furniture. I had a little donated black-and-white TV and a radio. I didn't know anyone or have the capacity to do anything, even though there were lots of things happening all around me. I was in Grand Prairie, Texas! It is a suburb of Dallas, so it wasn't rural, but it felt like I might as well have been living on the moon.

Another problem was that I used my first month's rent (after getting my finances back under my control) to get drunk. I blew almost $300 in one night going to neighborhood bars. Not gay bars, just close by bars. After many threats by my landlord, I did pay my rent late. I would eventually settle into some routine, at least to the point of paying my rent on time and eating ramen noodles and hot dogs almost every meal.

I was miserable.

This Is What You Will Look Like When You Die

I still abused substances as much and as often as I could. On New Year's Eve in 1989, I went to the apartment complex's New Year's Eve Casino Bash. I didn't have a car, but I didn't need one for this party. We didn't play with real money, and the cover charge covered all the booze. I drank more than my share several times over.

I thought I was the life of the party. I thought I was having fun, but I was drunk out of my mind. I stumbled into my ratty little apartment at 3 or 4 a.m. where I went to the bathroom, got violently sick, and laid on the floor. I eventually got up and looked in the mirror.

I was horrified at what I saw. My face was ashen, drained of blood. I looked just like death warmed over. My eyes were sunken and vacant. My sweaty hair was all over the place. My clothes were disheveled. As I looked at what couldn't possibly be me in the mirror, I heard a very hateful voice with an evil laugh in my head say, "This is what you will look like when you die!" I still feel the echo of the terror that I felt at that moment as I typed that last sentence.

That moment terrified me to the very depths of my soul. I collapsed right there, and for the second time in my life, I cried out into the deep of night, "WHY? WHY???!!!!"

The next day, I woke up on the bathroom floor still looking like death warmed over and smelling awful. I was pretty disturbed by what I remembered from the night before. I will never forget the moment some demonic-sounding voice (probably named self-loathing) laughed at me. I also learned that I was not the life of the party as I had thought. My neighbors were laughing at me, not with me.

Demonic head voices suck almost as bad as laughing neighbors!

Being a falling-down substance abuser sucks too. I was afraid, embarrassed, and ashamed.

After that night, I knew something had to change. But I didn't know how to even begin. I was petrified of life, wounded and hurt. My therapist, who diagnosed me with PTSD in 2005, taught me about learned helplessness. I now know that I had never learned how to cope or survive, and the only thing that I thought helped me escape the pain (i.e. substance abuse) was also killing me. After that night, I started uttering more sincere prayers.

Being gay was the single thing that provided a sense of consistency in my life. As distorted and unhealthy as I was at the time, it was my identity and my community. Though we never talked about it, my aunt knew I was gay, or at least thought it was a strong possibility. I knew she loved me even though I also knew she believed being gay was sinful, and I was grateful we did not mention it. I needed to connect with my community, so I asked to borrow a car (I think it was my ex-uncle's). I can't remember the excuse or even what kind of car it was, but I do remember thinking it was old and rickety. I didn't care. I couldn't wait to go to the gay bars in Dallas.

I wanted—needed—to find some "normal." But honestly, I couldn't have recognized it even if I saw it.

These Gays Are Some Kinda Different

I will never forget the first time I showed up at JR's in Dallas. I thought to myself, "These Dallas gays aren't anything like Nashville gays." Not to diss Nashville, but there was something about there being a lot (to me) of gay bars all in one area and a lot of gay men with a lot of money hanging around these places that felt foreign. Initially, I felt out of place, but it didn't take long for me to absolutely love it.

One night, as I walked from JR's to another bar nearby (I forget the name), someone tackled me from behind. When I wheeled around to deck whoever it was, I recognized it was an old friend from the Nashville Applebee's I had worked at. Brody saw my reactive punch coming and deftly jumped backward yelling, "RANDY!!!!!"

Brody was a rich gay guy who went to Vanderbilt University. He'd made it clear that he was only waiting tables at Applebee's because his parents wanted him to experience real work before graduating from college. He hated being at Applebee's, and because of his whining about it, we all knew it all the time. He was spoiled, a little airhead in demeanor and attitude but very intelligent as well once you got past that airhead mask. He was a brat, but I couldn't help but like the guy. We both had a thing for blond highlights.

Anyway, he was in town to party with his friends for the weekend. They all told me to tag along. So I did. They wore preppy gay-lore (misspelled on purpose), unlike myself. I was wearing a green flannel and jeans. I also had a scraggly beard and a defeated look in my eyes. I looked at their excellent everything while thinking about my slightly terrifying rat-hole apartment and limited clothing options. But they were nice to me, so I tagged along with the brat frat boys all night.

That night I learned what it was like to ride in the back of a brand new, "fully-loaded" BMW with the most expensive interior I had ever seen in a car. I learned that you didn't pay for anything if you were with many handsome brat boys with lots of money. I also learned that their drugs were a hell of a lot stronger than what I was doing in Nashville.

And no, I am not taking the word "hell" out of that last sentence. Those drugs were probably manufactured there.

We went to another trendy bar having a semi-exclusive party honoring the legendary Grace Jones and her Stark Club days. One of the brat boys gave me a hit of XTC. He looked like a Superman model. Chiseled *everything*. When the X rush hit, I felt like I would fall over, so I leaned against one of the support beams holding up the second floor. I looked down into my Coke (I didn't drink alcohol when doing X). One moment it was Coke with a lot of ice. Then, in what seemed like a flash, it turned into a watery Coke. The ice had melted.

The chiseled model man appeared in front of me like an apparition. He was very concerned and was saying, "Man! Are you okay? Brody, BRODY! Get over here! Your friend—never mind. Randy?! Randy! You okay?"

I looked up at him and said with the dreamiest high X voice, "I am MORE than okay… How 'bout you, Superman?" Then I tried to caress his chiseled cheek.

He smiled, but his eyes were concerned. Finally, he said, "You were standing there staring at your drink for like 30 minutes. You didn't move."

I said, "I am GREAT! Let's dance!" So the gay Grizzly Adams guy (me) and Mr. Chiseled Superman went dancing.

Later that night, we all ended up in some wealthy guy's gorgeous condo. No, there wasn't any sex scene worthy of causing right-wing religious activist nightmares. Just a bunch of rich gay people and me, not wanting to go to sleep and laughing the night away.

Again, I felt utterly out of place, but they were nothing but kind. Brody and his friends seemed to enjoy having me around, and I loved it. Unlike the party I had experienced on New Year's Eve, these guys laughed with me, not at me.

Unfortunately, I liked those drugs too much. I was at "rock bottom," and the only comfort I could find (partying) was killing me. I knew I was out of control, but I didn't know how to stop. That strange death man in the mirror haunted me many times as I cried myself to sleep on a mattress in the middle of a small, ratty, one-bedroom apartment.

I left my aunt's little screen-printing shop a few months later. I knew I was terrible at getting that stupid ink to flow down the screen right and needed to be among other people. I was desperate, of course, as usual, and accepted a job as a telemarketer.

My Personal Earth Angel Is Named Daphne

If you don't know who Sally Jessy Raphael is, you are a poor, culturally deprived human! (Just kidding.) SJR was an icon of the '90s, especially her red-rimmed glasses, and I had gorgeous glasses that looked exactly like hers in the early '90s.

There is a picture of me with those gigantic and excellent glasses. A woman named Izzy, who I worked with, took the picture. She took it because she was in one of her other personalities (don't laugh, not kidding), and that person liked me. One of her personalities told me that another was a witch. She said, "I can trust you; you understand the fires in the mist."

Who knew I understood that? Izzy's other personality did, that's who.

I didn't know what to say except, "Thanks, Izzy! Be careful of those mist fires!" She gave me an understanding nod and walked away. A couple of weeks later, she gave me the picture. The guy next to me in the picture looked a bit freaked out, and he had every right to be scared. Izzy was known to stab people with pencils, but my glasses were hideously awesome.

Around this time, I worked at a telemarketing company, which is where I met Daphne. Daphne and I immediately connected as kindred spirits. We talked *all* the time and got in trouble more than anyone else for giggling instead of dialing. Then, on one of our shifts, she invited me to go dancing one night. I was mentally assuming that we would probably go to a gay bar or some cool "anything goes" bar, have some drinks, and dance the night away. The next day, however, that dream got dashed.

"Randy, I am looking forward to dancing with you. I think you will like my friends."

I responded, "I am looking forward to it too. It will be great to get out, meet people, and unwind."

Daphne then said, "I think there is something you should know about first…" and a little red flag popped up in my mind. She continued, "There won't be any drinking or drugs at this dance."

I was confused and said something like, "Oh… why?"

Daphne replied, "It's a 12-step program dance put on by many different 12-step groups in the Dallas area. It's an alternative for those of us who like to dance but are trying to get off drugs and alcohol."

I had never heard of such a thing. I had heard of 12-step programs, but not a bunch of former drug addicts dancing together sober. But I was desperate for friendship and human interaction, so I decided to go, even though I didn't think sobriety and social interaction was a possible mix. At least not for me. I even think I might have said this out loud to Daphne: "Well, that's fine. I will just get buzzed before going."

The dance took place in a ballroom at a nice hotel. When we walked in, I saw a sign outside the hotel bar that said, "Kamikaze shots, buy one get two!" I thought that was awesome and planned to sneak out of the dance every so often and do a few shots.

Little did I know that this night would begin my journey from trying to survive to thriving with an authentic sense of self. I had so much fun that night. I danced, danced, and danced. When the evening was over, Daphne and I were laughing with some folks from the group I would eventually join. As we left the building, I saw the "kamikaze shots" sign and realized I hadn't had a single drink the whole night.

Not a single drink, and yet I'd had more fun than I could remember having since Nashville. It occurred to me how different that night was compared to my farewell party in Nashville. For one, I could remember all of it. Secondly, I was doing the hustle between a total *Sons of Anarchy* type Harley rider who used to do heroin and Mrs. Cleaver (not her real name) who used to mix Percocet with her beer.

So, Hardcore Harley Man + Mrs. Mary Percocet Poppins + Taking the Hustle a Little Too Seriously XTC Popping Gay Guy = A Universe in Harmony. I absolutely LOVED this evening.

I did join that 12-step program (not a member today), and I credit Daphne (and our little group) for saving my life. The Universe was faithful yet again to connect me with people I could trust at my point of need. None of us talked about Jesus that much. I wore Christian t-shirts my aunt gave me, and I thought Jesus was cool. But I was still a nominal Christian at best. Regardless, I do not doubt that He used Daphne and this 12-step group to save my life.

That doesn't mean everything was peachy keen. On the contrary, I became a serious, emotionally dependent stalker without a substance to abuse. Not the criminal kind, just the creepy friend-you-can't-get-rid-of variety. I became a Class A Codependent.

I am glad they had mercy on me.

In this little group, I heard and learned about unconditional love for the first time. In this little group, I learned about proper boundaries and making amends. We would argue/debate/analyze all kinds of topics. I was shut down and petrified most of the time. Not because of them, but because I had to learn to communicate without the drugs. Growing up, I wasn't allowed to speak up, so having an opinion and sharing it sober without being afraid was something new, and I was *not* good at it.

My little recovery group seemed so wise, and I wasn't used to being treated as a peer (outside of a bar). As a result, I was constantly afraid they would throw me out or yell at me. They never did. We had a lot of laughs, and sometimes there would be tears as we shared some of our fears, struggles, or past abuse. I was a part of their crew. It was honest, gracious, and life-giving.

During that time of life, I learned how to pay my bills, balance my checkbook, and the basics of being a productive member of society. I learned more about my relational style and that I did love to talk a LOT. This 12-step program was very pro-gay, so that was never a challenge. I would also often visit a gay-centered recovery group in downtown Dallas, and at my home group in Arlington, Texas, both my sponsor and his sponsor were gay. My grand-sponsor's name was Steven. He and I dated for a while, and it ended up being a 23-year friendship that would end tragically and change my life (later in the book). We decided after a few months that we were better friends than lovers. Steven and the group taught me about unconditional love, but Steven showed that to me on an intimate level I had not experienced before.

Many people wrongly, very wrongly, assume that all gay people experience the darkness I experienced. This generalization is part of the stigmatized stereotype labeled the "gay lifestyle." That is simply not true. Many of the gay men and women I met in recovery groups and outside the bars (at work or in passing) were very loving and caring. They came from a wide variety of perspectives and backgrounds. Even some in the bars tried, in various ways, to help me. Not everyone—not even a majority of LGBTQ+ people who are gay and like to dance or have a drink—is the substance abuser I was.

Also, the gay-affirming men and women that I met in the 12-step groups that the Divine used to help clear the fog in my soul were some of the most supportive people I've ever known. God used them like He used a Christian drag queen to help rescue and preserve my life long enough to meet Jesus, eventually. Without their care and concern, I don't know that I would have lived long enough to find out what a healthy gay man looked like. All I know is that my journey includes many loving, incredibly gracious, and wonderful gay/pro-gay people—people I am incredibly grateful for and respect.

My life seemed to have finally started at this point in my story. Little did I know that I was on a path toward a transcendent Love. It would take some bizarre turns and land me in a trap for over 20 years, but I eventually got there.

Jesus, Take the Wheel of My Lime Green Mercury Marquis Land Barge

About 18 months after joining the 12-step program, I was flying high (figuratively). I was working in downtown Dallas, making more money than I ever had before. I was caught up on my bills and well on my way to making amends for the various legal problems I had left behind in Tennessee as well as the traffic citations in New York when I had briefly lived with my bio-dad on Long Island during my transient time between being thrown out and finding a couch to rent. In addition, I was making amends with loved ones and trying to do my best at this "one day at a time" thing.

There was a point where I was working on the transition from my second step to my third step.[2] I believed that a higher power could restore me to sanity (whatever that was) and I felt ready to give my will over to that higher power. This leap of faith would manifest in a way I will never forget.

I was driving down Pioneer Parkway in Grand Prairie, Texas in a land barge of a car: a lime green '71 Mercury Marquis. I had the windows down, music blaring. It was C&C Music Factory bumping and thumping through the poor, strained speakers. I wasn't thinking about God. I wasn't thinking about anything except how I should be a backup singer/dancer in the C&C Music Factory, when all of a sudden, my world would get upended by my Higher Power.

No, I didn't wreck, even though the car jerked in the lane when the Universe spoke to me. I remember looking at the big blue Texas sky and seeing one rather large cloud shredded by sunlight. The sun rays were refracting in what seemed like every angle possible. Suddenly, I just knew that God was there, that Jesus was indeed His Son, that He had a plan for my life, and that He loved me. It was like an instant Matrix download of

---

2 12step.org. (n.d.). *12 steps of narcotics anonymous.* https://12step.org/references/12-step-versions/na/

information that nearly blew a circuit in my mind (causing the car to jerk). I burst into tears, turned off the radio, and pulled over at the next convenience store. I jumped out of the car and ran to a payphone to call my grand-sponsor in the program. "Steven! Steven!!! I met my Higher Power on Pioneer Parkway!!!"

Steven said, "That's great, Randy. Come on over, and let's go get some Chinese food."

Steven looked amused and was supportive, of course. But while I knew my Higher Power was real, I didn't invest in my spirituality for a while. It was a pleasant experience to talk about, and I genuinely believe it to be authentic and life-changing. However, I must admit that my spiritual life was not a top priority at that point.

Being Weak Is a Prelude to Strength

I will never forget when my sponsor started drinking again. I was pissed and arrogant. Finally, Steven told me, "Randy, be careful. When we think we are doing well and get mad at someone who has started using again, that could be a very short slide into your own relapse."

And it was.

I remember thinking that I was now a responsible human being and that it could never again get as bad as it had been. I had even met my Higher Power, who had interrupted me during my second and third steps. As I was getting ready to relapse, I talked to my Higher Power (not prayed to my Higher Power, just spoke to Him). As I went to a very fancy bar to party with rich friends (made at my new job in downtown Dallas), I thought, "God, I am only going to have a drink or two tonight; please do not let me go back to where I was."

I only had two or so drinks that night, but just six months later, I woke up on St. Patrick's Day, March 17, 1992, very hungover. I was sliding back into the party scene faster and faster. When I woke up that morning, I knew that my Higher Power was telling me to get back to the 12-step program. It wasn't some mystical mumbo jumbo. I woke up convinced that the Big HP wanted me to go to a meeting.

And I was pissed about it!

I didn't want to go *at all*, so I had to drag myself there. It wasn't the same little group I had initially joined. That one had disbanded. Daphne and I had gotten slightly estranged, and I hadn't seen her in a while. I went to the group feeling angry at my Higher Power. I was seriously complaining out loud in the land barge on the way there. I didn't want to be there, but I knew I had to. So I walked in, and guess who was there in this new (to me) group? Daphne. She had just celebrated six years of sobriety. Afterward, we talked briefly, and she said she was happy to see me. So much had changed in her life, and we should catch up.

She said that she had become a newly devout Christian and wanted to share her journey with me. The news made my pissy mood worse... *More Christians!*

Even so, this was Daphne! I sang and danced to "Groove Is in the Heart" with her. Who doesn't love someone you can sing "Groove Is in the Heart" with? Daphne was the gal that our group went to the Depeche Mode concert with. She was with me the Halloween night I dressed in drag as Lita Ford for a 12-step Halloween party. Daphne had told the Pakistani guys at Denny's later that night that I was her favorite cousin in town for a visit, and I had laryngitis so I couldn't talk. They must have been high because they bought it and could not stop flirting with me.

Daphne wasn't just a funny chick at the center of some crazy stories. She had taught me lessons that saved my life.

And now she was a Christian wanting to talk about Jesus. Not cool!

I gave her a little bit of grief over it, but inside I was angry. I hated Christians. I hated that Christians had hijacked her opinion on morality and whatnot. But, on the other hand, I saw peace in her that I had never seen before, and I agreed to meet.

Born Again

I visited her church, and they were quite energetic, especially during worship. There was a lot of jumping around (them, not us). Several women had wreaths in their hair acting like (but not precisely like) ballerinas, and a big gold glitter Jesus banner was running by us at 900 miles per hour during worship. Some people spoke in tongues, which both amused and scared me, but not enough to wipe the smirk off my face. All in all, it was quite a show.

Even with all the spectacle and my internal giggling (and external smirking), I started crying during the old hymn "Amazing Grace."

Even with a semi-circus atmosphere, I couldn't deny these folks loved Him. I also couldn't deny that Daphne had become family to me at that point. My view of her being a "sister from a different mister" has never been an idealized projection. She is a sister to me, period.

After what I considered a tense conversation at IHOP over cigarettes, she told me that when she looked into my eyes, she saw someone that Jesus loves and a man who would love Him. In that moment, I remembered the Jesus-loving guy from Spring Break in Daytona. As he spoke to me, his face had changed. He looked almost lovingly angelic, and said, "No, do you KNOW Him, do you know Him enough to fall in love with Him?" *Me? Fall in 'love'… with… Him?*

Daphne's words hung in the air.

After visiting her church for the second time, almost 30 years ago now, I went home alone and became a Christian in my Garage Sale Chic living room. I met Jesus. His Spirit talked to me, reminding me of my path to healing and authenticity, reminding me of the angels he sent along the way to shepherd me.

I remember the young guys trying to speak to me as I was car surfing. I knew He had used Carmella Marcella Garcia, Girl! to save my life when I was made homeless for being gay. I knew He had sent Aaron to take me and my blue eye-shadowed friend to a Bible study. I knew He was the one who preserved my life through some very dangerous "party" nights, even some overdoses that I haven't written about in this book. I knew Jesus orchestrated the Greyhound bus ticket through my aunt as well as the Catholic priest sitting next to me on the journey. He had orchestrated my going to the telemarketing company, meeting Daphne, dancing with bikers and Mrs. Percocet Poppins. He, the Glorious One, had cleared the fog in my soul through the 12-step program. And now, He sent Daphne again to remind me. So, as cheesy as that roadrunner with the big gold Jesus banner was, it is etched in my brain forever.

All this and so much more tumbled through my mind as I engaged the Universe for the first time from my living room.

My Higher Power had never been passive or aloof. They had been actively chasing after me my whole life. My Spirit team, my Guardian Angel Squad, rejoiced as my spirit came alive, kneeling beside my garage sale couch in my ratty, slightly terrifying apartment.

Crying with tears of joy, for the first time in my life I knew it was transcendent love, not some weird trick of my blood pressure or drug flashback. The Universe was in the room with me. Their comfort and peace brought true life. A fresh wind cleared out my spirit as I fell in love with Him, knowing He had always been in love with me.

PART TWO

"Strong minds talk about ideas, weak minds talk about people."

–Sean Covey

"Question with boldness even the existence of God; because
if there be one, He must more approve of the homage
of reason, than that of blind-folded fear."

–Thomas Jefferson

"People expect all stories of abuse to be loud and angry but they are not.
Sometimes they are quiet and cruel and swept under the rug."

–Trista Mateer

CHAPTER 5

I'm a Crazymatic Bapticostalutherpalianite

The Gay Guy in Information Systems Just Became a Christian

At the telemarketing company where I worked with Izzy and Daphne, I used to sell crap—I mean "premium services to valued cardmembers"—over the phone. This crap was traveling programs attached to credit cards, mostly. I had moved from selling stuff on the phone to working in the branch's "Branch Administration" department. I worked their third shift collecting all the day's work and preparing it for evaluation, scrutiny, and reporting to the day shift the next day. I was the BA manager's darling until she learned that I was gay. Then she had it in for me. She started talking smack behind my back and criticizing everything she could. One coworker said that she thought our manager had it in for me since I was gay, but I never heard that directly from the manager. Her dramatic and sudden shift in attitude and subsequent mean-spiritedness gave credence to that theory, but I didn't know for sure.

Maybe to help keep me as an employee, our branch manager (who oversaw the whole call center) moved me to Systems Administration. I helped install and manage the first computer network for a branch of around 250 employees. It was fun. I moved to the second shift with that job, and it was great. The network was all DOS/Unix based and very technical compared to today's plug-and-play standards.

One night I was preparing the nightly uploads and "leads" files and accidentally deleted one of the leads files. Presumably, no big deal, right? Except, because it was worth several thousand dollars, it was not a big deal—it was a HUGE deal. I was scared out of my mind, and our shift manager and assistant branch manager were livid.

I was convinced I was going to lose my job the next day. So I spent that night worrying and creating a system of checks and balances to ensure that what I had just done could be safeguarded against and even prevented in the future. The following day, I went in as soon as the doors opened and told my branch manager, "I know that I will probably lose my job after what happened last night, but this is a plan to make sure what happened last night doesn't happen again." Then I left my future in his hands, went home, and took a nap before my shift started that afternoon.

Nobody had called before I went in to my shift, and when I got there, the branch manager called me into his office. I thought he would fire me, but instead, he congratulated me. He said that after he read my proposal to change the end-of-shift duties and file preparation, he shared my proposed changes with "corporate." Who then, in turn, made it the topic of the national conference call (all the branches, including the fulfillment branch in New York). The bigwig of them all said that what I had proposed was brilliant and an excellent example of turning a massive mistake into something that could potentially streamline the system, protect leads files, and improve the overall stability of the process. I was pleased and relieved.

Shortly after that, the corporate office called me and said I needed to apply to be a part of the IT department. My name kept coming up as a hard worker and someone they could trust. So I applied and went in for my interview. My soon-to-be boss was hilarious and offered me the job on the spot. I saw my anti-gay Branch Administration manager sitting in the lobby when I walked out. She looked at me and said, "What are YOU doing here?"

I said, "I am applying for the IT job, you?" She just stared at me, so I said, "Well, I wish you the best. See you at the branch later." I could feel the glare as I walked away smiling.

I did get the job, but the joy of getting it left pretty quickly. I learned they were going to shut down our branch in Arlington (Texas), and they wanted me to stay there until the branch was empty of people, the doors locked, and the files closed. Now that I was with "corporate," I would be there when they announced the layoffs to everyone. My job was to make sure no one sabotaged the computer systems and that Branch Administration left their office and records just as they were. I was to help the corporate team as they fired everyone by making sure no one damaged or stole anything.

That was one of the most miserable days of my life. These folks had become friends, and as the Branch Admin and Systems Admin (new computer network) departments were closing up, they said some pretty nasty comments to me. Many were quite hateful about how opportunistic it was that I had gotten the job at corporate right before everyone lost their jobs. One close friend turned vicious, saying I was a turncoat and asking how I could have betrayed them like this. Of course, I know now that they were projecting their anger, and it wasn't true. But it hurt. I cried the whole way home. I wasn't even happy to see the Branch Administration manager, whom I had beaten out for the job at corporate, hand over her keys.

After that day, I began working in the downtown Dallas office at the Crescent Office Building. The Crescent is where the first President Bush stayed one time while I was working there. It is a hoity-toity hotel and office building. My little cubicle per square foot was twice the monthly rent on my slightly terrifying and ratty apartment. When I first started there, all the "software" on my computer was DOS or DOS-driven. I remember installing one of the first versions of Windows on our computers. It was a fantastic moment in our collective technological history.

I ran weekly billing reports that equaled hundreds of thousands of dollars for just one aspect of the company. In addition, I ran daily reports for our telemarketing clients and did a lot of tech support for the corporate office. It was a fantastic job, and surprisingly, people were accepting or at least tolerant of the fact that I was "out." The executive management thought I was a fun and intelligent guy. They would invite me to their parties and out to the clubs.

But that was also the time I was in the 12-step program and friends with newly-Christian Daphne. While she "witnessed" to me in my private life, a very outgoing co-worker, Carlotta, was "witnessing" to me at the office. Carlotta told everyone about Jesus all the time. She was a fun zealot, and as such, it didn't take long to know that Carlotta loved Jesus and you needed to love Him too. I joke around, but there is some truth to it; Jesus double-teamed me with Daphne and Carlotta.

Sheesh! Jesus doesn't let up!

After sharing that I had become a Christian, Carlotta was not just excited, she was "Hallelujah!" excited. I became a Christian on May 31, 1992. Shortly after that, I was in the smoker's break room, and Carlotta came in and started coughing dramatically. She said, "Randy (cough cough), you need to put that cigarette out right now, and I mean right now, in (cough) Jesus' name!"

I said, "I know, I know, you have told me that I am the temple of the Holy Spirit now, and I need to quit choking Him. I will quit once I get through this pack."

Carlotta looked at me, wide-eyed, and coughed, "No! You *(hack-cough)* mark the date and time RIGHT NOW because that will be your last cigarette in JESUS' NAME!"

She was right. That was my last cigarette. Glad I am not choking the Holy Spirit anymore.

I had my last whole cigarette on June 8, 1992, at 10:24 a.m., and I was a bitch the next couple of months. While I have had a puff or two of a cigarette since then, they make me sick. I have had cigars and weed a few times but never smoked cigarettes.

Of course, becoming a Christian turned me into a basket case of rules and self-righteousness. I eventually quit working at the corporate office because I thought they were dishonest with their payroll (they weren't, I was paranoid). But I prayed that if the Lord wanted me to leave that place, I would have a job offer the following day. Believe it or not, I did—first thing. An executive who had worked there before called and offered me a job with her new gig. I worked with her until I started working for Tad Johnson's computer room at a ministry offering aid abroad in 1993.

About That Crazymatic Bapticostalutherpalianite Thing

My entrance into God's kingdom was through the "Charismatics go this way" door. In one particularly raucous service, a man was "speaking in tongues." For those unaware, speaking in tongues is considered a gift and a blessing as the believer is filled with the Holy Spirit and allowed to speak in a heavenly language, or a foreign language, unknown to the believer in everyday life. The Bible states that when the gift of tongues is given to a congregation, there absolutely must be someone present to be given the divine gift of interpreting those tongues. If not, the utterance was not from God and should be ignored. In this service, an elderly man was shouting in "tongues" for five minutes. I thought I knew exactly what he was saying, and it unnerved me to say the least. Eventually a woman went up front and took a microphone. She was looking right at me, and in front of about a thousand people, she said, "Well, the Blessed Lord has given the interpretation to a young believer who might be afraid to speak up... But this is what the message in tongues just given means..." And this lady, dressed in a white dress and wedding wreath in her hair, proceeded to share everything that had come to my mind while the man was delivering the spiritual message.

I don't remember the message these decades later, but I think it was about a time of trial and testing coming to that church, but whether it would survive or thrive would be dependent on their support and faith. All I know is that I was terrified that something peculiar had just happened at that moment. God had chosen me to have the interpretation and then busted me through a charismatic prophetess with flowers in her hair for not speaking up!

Over the years, and even today, I have had crazy spiritual experiences. Always have and will not apologize for them. On the contrary, they have been life-giving, live-preserving, life-improving, and make for great stories. It disgusts me when I see people parading around with business cards that have "Prophet" as a part of their title. So many are manipulating people into believing they have had a spiritual experience when they have simply been emotionally used. (By the way, I do not consider myself a prophet. Just odd—in the best of ways now, hopefully.)

Before becoming a Christian, I never understood how Christianity, which was supposed to be known for unity in the Gospel of Christ, was best known for its divisions, abuse of power, and peripheral issues. As such, when someone asked me early on, "So, do you believe that you are predestined for heaven, or do you believe that you have a choice?" I made a decision to never buy into institutionalized religion.

My answer was simply, "Yes," after which they looked unimpressed.

I explained an analogy I am sure I heard somewhere else about how you would know the complete story if you were to look at the books in the series AFTER reading them. But if you were to look at any particular page within the book, you would see a story caught in linear time. In the classic *The Lord of The Rings* trilogy, Frodo has yet to face some of the hardships and decisions he would eventually make on that specific page. YOU know what those are, but on that page, he doesn't know about them yet.

Similarly, the Divine knows our entire story, page by page, even before we are born. We live our story, creating it as we go, but the One who is not limited to our linear time—They who exist in, above, and through our time—already knows what decisions we will make. They know who all will be coming home to Him through Christ and those who will choose other paths. That doesn't mean they won't be making those decisions. Two things can be true: Free will and predestination can exist in a universe not trapped in four dimensions, and God has revealed Themself not to be limited to our four dimensions.

I should mention that astrophysicist Dr. Hugh Ross' books *The Creator and the Cosmos* and *Beyond the Cosmos* BLEW my ever-loving mind along these lines. I cried when he explained the extra-dimensionality of God in a way that made sense to me.

I have had no theological training and would rather gouge my eyes out with red-hot iron pokers than go to seminary. I find profound hypocrisy and weakness in every denomination. I find amazingly deep faith and character strengths in each one as well. I tried signing on like a Southern Baptist early on in my walk after proudly saying I was going to a Vineyard church for a while, and I realized I couldn't sign fully on to any denomination, so why try. So, eventually, I decided to call myself a Crazymatic (Charismatic) Bapticostaluberpalianite.

I have listened to conservative theologians, and they make convincing cases about everything, and then I have listened to progressive theologians, and guess what? They, too, make compelling cases about everything. So, one day, I decided that there was no way I would EVER learn Hebrew, Greek, or Aramaic. I will never have the desire to learn church history year by year, leader by leader, decision by decision—I have to take the lessons that have come to me and trust in Christ alone. I will take the experiences and my relationship with the Divine and come to my conclusions because Jesus didn't call me to learn the three original languages or take any flavor of a theologian's "word for it." He never said I would have to have a degree—or even an interest—in systemic theology to be His disciple.

So today I don't belong to any denomination. I am just a Universalist Christ-follower, and that's enough. More than enough, actually.

Charla Tan Is an Asshole

It was the summer of 1993, and Daphne called and tempted me to call in sick to work so that we could go check out the Charla Tan spectacle at Calvary Cathedral in Fort Worth. He is an "evangelist" from South Africa. The Holy Ghost was "falling" at each of his marathon meetings, "slaying people in the spirit" and causing them to be "drunk in the Spirit" with "Holy laughter."

I thought about it for half a second and immediately called my relatively new Christian bosses at Tad Johnson's televangelism ministry and lied to them about needing to take off that day (second shift). But I mean, the thought of sitting in a room full of crazy with Daphne was too good to pass up.

We were there for almost four hours. It was awful.

We sat there and listened to this huge, angry-sounding man spew random, sometimes completely incoherent statements from the stage. But what kept us engaged the whole time was the literal circus of people doing some of the weirdest shit I have ever seen at a Christian gathering. Laughing uncontrollably, falling down, barking, and plenty of manic "speaking in tongues" but no interpretation. It took about 10 minutes of this charade for me to get angry. Finally, I just sat there with a scowl on my face.

We weren't close, but we weren't very far from the stage. It felt like Charla was looking right at me and saying into his microphone, "THIS IS REAL!!!" as I crossed my arms and glared back.

I said, "NO, it is NOT!" But nobody heard it because any time he said anything worthy of exclamation points, shrieks of epiphanies of joy would mix with cackles of uncontrollable laughter.

I hated it, but I couldn't stop gawking at the spiritual train wreck happening around me. All of these people, so desperate for a touch from God, being manipulated by this person on stage. They wanted a breakthrough spiritual experience and instead were being manipulated into some kind of religious circus to feed the ego—and international clout—of Charla Tan. It breaks my heart to remember it, knowing that many people went to this event over the course of its time in Fort Worth and walked away with nothing but a memory of barking like a dog or laughing uncontrollably at nothing. All the while I am sure Charla Tan walked away with an exorbitant amount of donation money.

But that isn't all.

Toward the end, everyone who wanted prayer from Charla himself was to line up around the auditorium. Hundreds and hundreds (practically everyone there) dutifully lined up. The line was so long that it snaked in and out of the hall and through the middle of the audience. I didn't want prayer from that awful man. If you can't tell, I did NOT like him and still don't. I wasn't jumping out of my seat to take a place in line. Daphne had a different idea.

"Randy! Let's go get prayed for and NOT fall over!" I was nervous about it but thought it would be fun. So, I agreed to do it.

It took forever for Charla to get through the line to us and the plenty of people after us. EVERY person fell over. EVERY person fell over almost as soon as he touched them. Meaning it took forever because there were so many people. It wasn't like he was praying for them. All he did was bark, "FIIII-LLLLED!" It wasn't even a complete sentence, just variations of, "FIIIYYYILLLLLED!"

When he got close, Daphne looked at me and said, "Don't fall!" I reassured her I wouldn't. He got to her first, and guess what happened? She fell over like a cute little ton of bricks. Just straight down and out like the Angel Gabriel had personally KO'd her with one colossal Archangel Wing FWAP! I was like, "No, YOU did not just do that! Ugh, traitor."

However, I was determined not to fall over.

Charla and his henchmen came to me and surrounded me. They all put their hands on me, and one was laughing Dr. Frankenstein's maniacal laugh when his creation came to life. I was so creeped out. Charla put his hand on my upturned, open-eyed forehead and pray-screamed, "FFFFFIIIIIIIIIILLLLLLLLLEEEDDDDD...DDDD!"

I looked at him, crossed my arms, and said, "Nope."

Dr. Frankenstein started laughing louder, and from somewhere, more hands were touching me, and Charla said again, "FIIIYYEEL-LLLL-DDDDDDDDD!!!!!!"

I said, "NOOOOOoooPPPE."

The hands started gripping me and pressed down on me. Again, Dr. Frankenstein's laugh sounded more like Lucifer's cackle, and Charla looked angry and determined all at once. This time, when he screamed, "FILLLLLLED!!!!!" he took his hand off my forehead and pushed both hands into my stomach in a rapid motion.

I went down.

It wasn't even 30 seconds, and I sat up before Daphne did. I felt drunk, but I knew it wasn't the Spirit, and I was so angry that I couldn't even verbalize it. I didn't know what had just happened to me, but I felt violated, not refreshed; abused, and not filled with joy. A few hours later, I tried to convince myself that it was a real experience, but I couldn't get past the fact that it did nothing for me in my relationship with people or God. On the contrary, it caused me to be very suspicious and angry with that "evangelist" and that particular branch of Christianity. Of course, I know today that spending four or so hours in a chaotic environment, highly emotional and manipulated, makes you vulnerable no matter who you are. I wasn't diagnosed with PTSD at that point yet, but after counseling, I now know that the praying situation triggered all the physical abuse neural pathways in my brain. When he jabbed both hands into my stomach, my brain had a synaptic overload and shut off for a moment.

It was not a blessing from on high; it was spiritual abuse from a false prophet. Daphne and I haven't talked about it much, but I think she would agree with me, at the very least, that it was not a spiritual experience but one generated by social pressure and manipulation.

That said, Charla didn't scare me away from the church. I have always been and still am fascinated by the mystical nature of the Divine. That is why I was so angry with Charla. I know Jesus and His power are so much more beautiful and life-giving. He would never reduce people to heaps on the floor, barking like dogs, not knowing what just happened. We can experience transcendent joy without losing our senses, barking, having a break from reality and laughing uncontrollably.

Even after that experience, I knew that God does arrive and work in this world in mysterious and glorious ways, but not in a Charla Tan train wreck masquerading as a "revival" to manipulate others.

What Does One Wear to a "Promise Keepers" Soiree?

Elder Lurch is not his real name, though he looked like Lurch from the Addams Family. I don't call him that for a bad reason—I loved Elder Lurch. And for the record, I LOVED Lurch from the Addams Family! He said from the stage of the church I got saved in (but didn't stay in long), "We are renting a bus to take the men of our church to Promise Keepers in Denton on…" whatever the date of that event was.

The thought of going entered my mind. It was like Jesus was saying, "Go to this…" but I was like, "But Jesus, oh my gosh, it will be a football stadium filled with bigoted, awful, conservative Christian men! I don't even know how to speak their language, and I am sure they can't handle the gay guy on the bus for the long commute and, and, and… I can't afford it!"

I could almost swear I heard Jesus chuckle, and then Elder Lurch went on to say, "And we will be awarding a limited number of scholarships for those who need financial help to be able to go. So if you need help, stop by my office, and we will get you signed up. Scholarships and seating on the bus are limited. So drop by my office as soon as you can. Tell me, men, are you ready for a blessing?"

As the men all said in one accord, "YES" and "AMEN," I was saying in my heart, "Oh, hell no."

But the Divine wouldn't leave me alone about it.

"Randy, go."

"No, that can't be You, so… no."

"You know I want you to go."

"I am sure I am probably just hearing my self-sabotaging inner voice, and I just need to stay home."

"Randy…"

"No, seriously, let someone who wants to go get the scholarship."

"I want you to get the scholarship and go…"

I dropped by Elder Lurch's church office on the last day available to sign up for the scholarship. His secretary was there and greeted me with a mighty, delicate Texas twang. I said, "I know this is probably too late, but if you have any scholarships left to go to the PK thing, I would like to ask for one." And before she could respond, I thought of the last-ditch qualification that might stop the whole thing in its tracks. I continued, "Oh, and I also need a ride on the bus. Not sure I could make the trek in my clunker. It's probably too late for that, huh?" I was praying: *Please let it be too late, please let it be too late!* I still think Jesus was chuckling. When I get home to Heaven, I expect Him to hug me with that same light-hearted, loving chuckle.

Elder Lurch's secretary looked up, and with a smile as big and beautiful as her hair, she said, "Well, of course, hon, we will get you set right up. You are right in that the bus was full up this morning…" My heart almost exploded with relief, but she continued, "but we just had two people cancel right before you walked in! So we have plenty of room for you!"

I was smiling politely on the outside, but inwardly I was not amused with the Divine and Their mysterious ways. I like to imagine that my

Guardian Angel Squad was just hooting and hee-hawing over the look on my face at that moment.

I dreaded going. I didn't know what to wear, or how to do my hair. Should I bring my brand new, 400lb, impressive leather-bound Bible or the pocket version? How would I carry my migraine meds, which I was sure to need due to the stress? Was it okay to wear a fanny pack amongst all these heterosexist misogynists? What would happen if I was caught ogling a cutie-big-booty, or worse, what happens if I got ogled by a cutie-big-booty!? I certainly wasn't feeling compelled to be openly gay that day. I didn't give a whole lot of thought as to why Jesus wanted me to go and if I should, you know, actually pray about the whole thing.

I was terrified of Christian men. While I had met a few over the course of my life who were very kind and even sweet, most of the Christian men I had seen on TV or heard about were horribly disrespectful in many ways and also the source of a lot of pain in the name of religion in the South's history.

I remember finding my seat on the bus among many men who all knew each other, but I didn't know any of them except Elder Lurch. They were talking sports and mentioned the Dallas Cowboys at some point. So I sat there, incredibly tense, trying not to blurt out, "I LOVE the Cowboys! Such a better team since they got that new goalie Michael Jordan!"

For those reading this, that last sentence blends three different sports into a declarative statement that doesn't exist in reality. I know a little more about sports than that—not much, but a little. I did not say that out loud, but it is something I might have said by accident. I was afraid I would blurt out something like that because it had happened before.

And, of course, there was a guy on the bus that was one gorgeous man! Not just good looking—this "brother in Christ" was damn fine. Oh, my goodness! And wearing the tightest shorts and a nice polo shirt accentuated his perfect waist and chest ever so perfectly. His smile lit up the heavens, and his messy curls were perfectly messy. So why couldn't Jesus just let me suffer alongside a bunch of men 30 to 40 years my senior, men with big bellies and balding heads who didn't even notice me? But no, the devil had to get in there to tempt me to out myself by drooling, blushing, and staring. Plus, all of these chatty straight men kept interrupting my wildly and inappropriate-for-prime-time Promise Keepers thoughts.

Instead, I stayed glued to the window, watching the unexciting Texas asphalt flying underneath us. Then I just stared at the perfect reflection in the window of the perfectly laughing ideal man perfectly talking all the sporty balls talk. Then I snuck out the three Advil from my shirt pocket and took them without anything to drink. I was pretty good at popping pills without liquid from my party days.

We got to the stadium, and it was a sea of testosterone. I was a big gay neurotic mess headed into an all-day man meeting with my pocket-sized Bible, Duran Duran hair (still into it), and plain, Aunt-J-gifted Christian t-shirt, shorts, and sneakers. I hadn't even prayed yet. I didn't ask Jesus what He wanted me to get out of it. I was numb with terror. Okay, "terror" is too strong a word. I was afraid of the unknown and of experiences with large and even small groups of hetero men. My past had taught me that it wasn't always safe—in fact, it often wasn't safe. So perhaps "terror" fits.

With thousands of other men, we filed into the stadium and took our seats. I was still reticent as I watched the men from the church keep up their fun banter. The first speaker was Pastor Big Smile, and I liked him. Before the event, I had known of him because I had seen him on a taping for *Tad Johnson's Weekday Talk Show*. I loved his style and what appeared to be a genuine love for others. He was a man with a complicated past, and I just liked that he didn't seem to be hiding anything. He was the first speaker and was quite funny, full of insight, and passionate about the gospel. Then he gave an altar call for any men in the audience who hadn't received Christ. I was moved to tears and surprised that so many men there hadn't accepted Christ.

There was one problem—something wicked from the north this way comes! As Pastor Big Smile was giving the call and men were coming down from all parts of the stadium, a vast, evil storm was roiling and boiling its way in from the northwest, headed straight for our roofless event. The incredibly black clouds were rolling and billowing toward the stadium. I had been reading Frank Peretti's books since becoming a Christian (he's like the Christian version of Stephen King), and it was like something straight out of one of his novels. So I said something of that effect to the guy sitting next to me.

I pointed to the clouds and said, "They better invite Jesus into their hearts quickly because they might meet Him in a few minutes."

He said, "Oh boy, that doesn't look good."

If you have lived in Texas for more than nine months, you know exactly what kind of storm that is. That's a run to the house or some bunker as fast as you can and listen to hell unleash on Earth for a half hour to an hour, and then it's over. It took me moving to Florida to realize you could have a thunderstorm that wasn't classified as severe.

This storm came up so fast that the rain started pouring almost at once. Pastor Big Smile finished up the prayer quickly, and then all hell broke loose. Now, the sky was green behind the front edge of the storm (a sign of hail), and we (the audience of several thousand) had just begun to file out of the stadium. The storm was so furious and rolled in so fast that we all bottle-necked into the exit ramps. I went from being moved by emotion to being drenched and shoved into a crowd of men. They pressed against me on every side in one of the down ramps of the football stadium.

Then the tornado sirens went off, and where I was trapped, I wasn't getting rained on anymore but could see hail falling. It wasn't big hail, but it would still sting if you were hit with it.

Mortified, I was like, "Jesus! You made me come here, and I have been all uncomfortable, and now freaking tornadoes, hail, a bunch of drenched, armpit deodorant, smelly heteros are pressed against me in every direction! I'm soaked through to my sneakers. My hair is all fucked up, and, oh my God, now I smell like Right Guard too…" and as I was telling Jesus my list of complaints in the face of an actual potential weather tragedy, I stopped short when I heard all the thousands of men still trapped in the open stadium. I heard them, amid wailing sirens and a hellacious downpour, singing the chorus to the hymn "Amazing Grace." Thousands of men, in one voice, in the face of genuine danger, singing about God's amazing grace. I was so touched I am even choking up all these years later remembering it. I hung my head, closed my eyes, and wept over how beautiful they sounded in the midst of one helluva storm.

I do not doubt that Jesus said the following to me: "THIS is why you are here. THIS is what it means to be a man of faith, that even amid danger, trials, threats, and fear, you will see that I am Good. I do love you. My grace is sufficient to see you through. So don't be afraid of Me." And as the storm ran its course and the men sang their praises, I felt humbled and grateful. I remember tearfully saying, "Thank you, Jesus. Thank you." And as I gathered my wits about me and opened my eyes from that "moment," I noticed all these stoic Texas men I was trapped with were almost all weeping and thanking God for the men in the storm for a myriad of reasons.

At that moment, I saw them all moved with emotion and gratitude. In my judgmental head, they went from being smelly heterosexuals making me uncomfortable to being my genuine brothers in Christ. We all were drenched and smelled like wet deodorant, or worse. Nobody thought it was out of the ordinary to weep after being led into worship by unexpected beauty manifesting during a severe thunderstorm.

Many people have had legitimate and robust disagreements with Promise Keepers as an organization and movement. I will leave that analysis and review for someone else. However, my personal experience shared here was very favorable to me. Favorable in the sense that my prejudgments of these men were unfair. While we still had plenty of fundamental differences, this experience was a leveling of expectations, after which I could do away with the stereotypes of them in my brain and begin to see them as living, breathing human beings who were worthy of dignity.

After the storm, I enjoyed the rest of the day. I was relaxed, and my naturally extroverted self found his voice. It was a good experience. Later that afternoon, I threw a little nerf football around with Mr. Perfect Cutie, who was genuinely straight. Drat! We threw that and a Frisbee around with a couple of other church fellas during breaks. Riding home on the bus— hair just a fright!—our clothes had dried out, but you couldn't tell by looking at us that we were a mess. We engaged in the conversations about how the day went and that crazy Stephen-King-like storm. I smiled along with Jesus and my Guardian Angel Squad, knowing the Divine had orchestrated the day. I am still grateful.

Unexpected beauty has a way of showing up when you least, I mean very least, expect it.

A Magical Place...

The experiences I mention here are only a few of the many dramatic or outlandish experiences I had in my early days as a Christian. I also went to see charlatans like the Demon Hunter and his "deliverance" services, where he talked about demon possession and offered to do exorcisms.

That said, I was deeply ministered to by other leaders. I also grew to love and respect Tad Johnson. Even though I would imagine he and I are at odds now that I have embraced who I am as a gay man, I always loved how he preached about God's "heart" for us.

Those early years as a Christian were incredibly entertaining and either full of genuine mysticism and wonder or assholes like Charla Tan. Regardless, I wasn't drinking and partying like before, and I enjoyed going to church (mainly for the worship time).

I started learning and growing in many areas of my life. Being in an incredibly conservative culture also edged me closer and closer to becoming something I would never have thought possible. I turned into something I would have heartily laughed at if you had told me about it before becoming a Christian: an ex-gay leader in the upper echelon of a conversion therapy group, Exodus International, and a political activist for the religious right.

CHAPTER 6

The Ex-Gay Kingdom

The People Behind the Stained-Glass Closet Door

What I am about to write is mostly about my experiences with other leaders. However, any honest assessment of the movement can't be condensed to just that particular group of people. Also, most of the people that provide the momentum and get caught up in the ex-gay world are not idiots or caricatures of religious bigots. It's somewhat understandable that many people might want to put everyone in the hateful, horrible, Bible-thumping category. However, most of the individuals involved are not anything like that. Of course, some are, for sure. But that is the minority within the movement.

That being said, I believe conversion therapy and ex-gay ministry are abuse. At its core is a systemic issue wherein people are conditioned to believe that converting a sinner into a saint is their primary job on this earth. As a result, they are taught that if they don't do that, they are insulting God and not genuinely loving people. So the mandate to convert, if you will, is their primary approach to everything.

This ideology then becomes an unfortunate but obvious predecessor to believing that if someone is LGBTQ+, they have embraced sin. Therefore, the conservative evangelist believes it is their job to "save" these sinners.

They think: "You must convert to our way of thinking and behaving. You must 'change' to know true love, have healthy relationships, live a happy life, and go to heaven."

It's basic Western evangelism 101 to "convert" sinners. "Conversion" is the only approach modern conservative evangelists use to engage the world on any issue.

I have looked into thousands of pairs of eyes in the Exodus world. Almost every single participant, parent, family member, or friend involved with the ex-gay world is there because they believe it is the *only* way to truly love their LGBTQ+ loved one and be "right with God." I know they desperately want permission to love their LGBTQ+ loved one for who they are, but they are torn at a soul-deep level. They truly believe that if they affirm the LGBTQ+ person for who they indeed are, they are condemning them to hell by affirming sin.

It is their desperation and fear, when combined with the bond of community, that fuel the abuse they perpetuate. Only, they don't realize or want to believe it is abuse because they see it as their only option.

Additionally, the larger homophobic culture within the church makes it unsafe for many LGBTQ+ people within their congregation to be open about their lives. As a result, these closeted souls quietly go to ex-gay groups, thinking that it is their only oasis. And with that mindset, and in that world, it probably was.

Of course, in these groups they find friendship, a place to share something very close to their hearts, and a sense of community. Admittedly, it's an inauthentic reality, but it is probably the only sense of relief most will find in that circumstance. For desperate and vulnerable people like I was, it's very moving on a heart (trauma?) level to see a group bonded in a unique and powerful way. All of these ex-gay group participants want permission to recognize the truth deep down in their hearts that God does love His LGBTQ+ children as they are, and to know they are not abominations but intentionally-created treasures in His eyes.

I know many beautiful people still caught up in that toxic ideology. So many people are involved in that world, knowing they need to leave and wanting to leave, but they are unable to find the exit door. It is challenging to make your own way out of the religious maelstrom of presumed consequences.

Through this book, I hope to show them, especially the young ones (like I was at a critical time in my life), the way out of the stained-glass closet. Or better yet, to help them not enter ex-gay ministry in the first place.

The Most Common Question(s)

The most common series of questions I've gotten since coming out the second time in January of 2015 has been along the lines of, "How did you go from being an 'out' gay man to a Christian ex-gay poster boy to a guy who is now comfortable in saying that he is both gay and a Universalist Christian?" Yes, reader, I left that run-on sentence in for effect. It's a lot, isn't it?

For some, it seems like I made these decisions capriciously, but that's because they haven't known me over the past 55 years. Of course, nothing happened overnight, even though I have had some dramatic swings in my life. I hope that this chapter will show how despite experiencing what felt like more and more freedom, I wasn't truly free until I realized that regardless of its origin in cultural bigotry or religious stigma, a "closet" is still a "closet," and souls do not thrive in closets. LGBTQ+ people should not have to live in darkness and be subjected to the systemic oppression that wants us to figuratively kill ourselves, which can take us down a long and unfortunate path of taking that literally.

What Did He Just Say?

Even though I loved Elder Lurch, eventually the golden Jesus banner jumping, the wreath-in-the-hair-wearing female worshippers, and the Promise Keeper men became too much for me. But I didn't know where else to go, plus I loved going to church with Daphne.

Before leaving that church for another one—I will get to that in a moment—I went to a men's conference hosted by my church after Promise Keepers that was worthy of a reality show Emmy. Talk about theatrics! I was not fond of it because it was full of all the stereotypical, chest-thumping toxic masculinity I feared. But at the end of it, I went up to publicly confess that I had received Christ as my Lord. The red-faced, white-haired preacher man said that I had to show my love for Jesus. That if I did, I would receive a special spiritual blessing.

I did love Jesus, and so did another guy from across the auditorium. As I got up, I thought it would be like the Promise Keepers thing, and there would be polite clapping and a few amens. But I also knew that here at "home," it was much more raucous, which made me very nervous. We stood at the front, and the other guy and I started to share why we came up there with two other men as the speaker continued to invite people forward. We stood next to each other, and I shared, "I accepted Jesus in my living room after church a little while ago. I haven't ever declared (sounded weird to say it that way) Him publicly." The guy next to me was crying and looked very morose and strung out. He said, "I am not sure I am saved. I am... I am," and he burst into tears. Compassion immediately struck me. He continued, "I am incredibly well endowed, and I like to pleasure myself in an unholy way."

Wait, what?! Whoa! Helluva thing to pop off with, buddy!

The man praying for him put a hand on his shoulder, and the guy that was going to pray for me looked at him and said, "It's okay, son, masturbation is a sin Jesus can forgive you for."

That was news to me. Masturbation is awesome. I am a masturbation sensei: great at it. I was upset with that information, but hold on—the upset guy had more exciting stuff to share.

"But you see, sir, it's not just normal jacking off. So why would God give me such a big dick?" More genuine sobbing. "I can do things to myself that most guys can't do... Do you know what I mean? I can..."

They cut him off. We all knew what he meant.

I was SO impressed! One for such a feat and two for saying it aloud like that to the conservative Christian leader guys! I also have no doubt we were ALL jealous.

I was not turned on in the slightest but impressed, and I didn't understand why this guy was so ashamed of his unique ability. I have a better understanding now after living in that culture for as long as I did, but as a new Christian, I was shocked, amazed, and confused by what I heard in this exchange. I wanted to acknowledge Jesus as my Savior publicly. But here I was learning they thought masturbation was wrong and that a guy who could blow himself felt that that would send him to hell despite his faith in Jesus.

Life is weird sometimes.

While I wanted to give him a pat on the back and an award or something, I quickly realized my inner response was not the same as the men around us, who expressed outward concern. My heart broke seeing his obvious body shame. The men praying with us prayed for him first. They prayed he would sense God's presence, releasing him from all guilt and shame. His salvation wasn't dependent on his actions, and he would find rest in God's grace. He looked relieved and, interestingly, stayed up there while they prayed for me.

I didn't feel the need to mention anything about being gay or that I thought masturbation was great. So I just let the group of men pray for me about my new relationship with the Lord. During the prayer, they thought I had a vision. I think it might have been just the Divine using my imagination. Who knows? It doesn't matter because it was beautiful.

While they were praying, I saw myself dressed in a white robe at the end of a long procession that was leaving the earth and leading to heaven. As I took my place among the others dressed in white on our way home, I took three dice out of my pocket and threw them back toward the earth. Each of the three dice had a word on it; the three words were "Me, Myself, and I." I didn't understand it entirely, but the men explained that when I accepted Christ, I had embraced the Holy Trinity of Father, Son, and Spirit. I was casting away the unholy trinity of me, myself, and I. At the time, I only had a heavy dose of Christianese to contextualize this vision (imagination). Today I still get goosebumps remembering that moment of communion with the Divine.

Is it strange that God would bless me with a fantastic picture while standing next to a guy who could blow himself? It's not weird because God isn't afraid of context or our apparent faults. He doesn't shame us. We are the heirs She created. I do not doubt that the Divine's heart was for that other young man to know that he is loved and special.

This Heavenly Chariot Was a Creaky, Beat-Up Station Wagon

The following weekend, I walked out of the church toward my car. As I was about to step off the curb and cross the parking lot, I thought the Lord or one of the angels in the Guardian Angel Squad was saying, "STOP!" I did immediately, and as I looked up, the message in my head continued. "… That man is going to tell you about a group." This rickety—rick-et-ty—old wood-paneled station wagon jerked to a very creaky, worn-out-shock-absorbers stop. A woman in the passenger's seat rolled down the window while looking at me. Before she could get a word out, I said, "I think the Lord just told me that you would take me to a group."

She looked at her husband who was driving, and then back at me, smiling. Then, almost laughing, she said, "Get in… let's go to lunch."

When I climbed into the station wagon, I recognized that the man driving was the worship leader at the church. They were a very ordinary, plain, incredibly white couple. I mean, like, never-in-the-sun kind of white. We went to lunch, where he explained to me that he was part of an ex-gay group and that he was a "former homosexual." He had seen me go forward at the men's conference the weekend before and wondered if I was gay.

I just stand out that way.

The ex-gay group was in Arlington, Texas, and he led worship before the group started every Thursday at an artsy, charismatic church. I was so incredibly skeptical that I simply didn't believe him. He had a lovely wife and cute kids, but come on, he had to be at least bisexual.

I was much more interested in the church than whatever group he participated in. He described it in glowing terms. If he hadn't been on staff at "our" church, he would have gone there as his home church because of the worship music. I was all about worship music and knew I wanted to experience it.

The following Sunday, I visited this new church, expecting to find Christians who were just as jumpy, hokey, glittery, and conservative as the church I had been attending. I expected them to be rabid, pew-jumping, Bible-thumping, blue-haired right-wingers because they had an "ex-gay" group. What I found was not what I was expecting.

They were cool. I mean, not just cool. They were artsy cool.

The church was in a warehouse in the middle of many warehouses in Arlington, and it looked exactly like what you would expect a church in a warehouse to look like when you walked in. But the people wore trendy clothes, big, healthy smiles, and warm welcomes. They were wholly approachable and friendly. The worship music was terrific, and right off the bat, I met a ton of musicians, a poet, several writers, and plenty of people my age. I couldn't believe how (dare I say) fantastic that church was.

And they loved The Gays so much they had a "special, just for The Gays" ministry on Thursday nights at 7 p.m.

The disparity between what I was experiencing and what I expected was enormous. The man who had invited me was introducing people to me, and while he couldn't tell me if they were in the ex-gay group or not, I kept hearing about this "group for the gays" that all these incredible people kept talking about. It didn't take long before I decided to go. I mean, everyone was talking so highly of the group, so I quickly decided to visit it. What was the harm in just checking it out?

The group required an intake interview beforehand. I thought that was stupid but chose to meet with the leader, Steve. He was about to graduate from Southwestern Seminary in Fort Worth. And surprise, surprise, he was hilarious and kind, and not weird! Plus, after I started going to the group,

I would see almost all of the people I suspected were gay from Sunday service. This created a built-in feeling of safety.

Again, they weren't the rabid right-wingers with fangs and fiery torches I was expecting. Steve made me laugh a lot. Of course, I told him that I didn't want to come to his group if they would try to force me to play football or get married and have kids. He said he would never try to make me be anything; he hoped I would find encouragement to discover all that God had created and wanted me to be in the group. I still didn't trust him, and during the intake interview I gave him a few snarky retorts and pointed questions. He handled them all with grace. I remember him saying, "You know, Randy, I don't need you to agree with me. You don't have to agree with everything. If you decide to visit, all I ask is that you respect the purpose and members of the group. Take whatever is helpful; leave what isn't. If you decide not to visit our group, that's okay. I am glad we will see you on Sunday."

Where were the high-stakes manipulation and fearmongering? Nowhere. I was kind of at a loss and disarmed. Remember that no one ever signs up to be ensnared by toxic ideology. Instead, they are hoodwinked into what seems like a good idea. As mentioned earlier, I was led to believe that this was a "safe" space with no judgment to help us be able to share our burdens and joys openly, a place to discover and heal root relational problems. Basically, they hit on all of my survival instincts and deep desperation for love, attention, community, and friendship. It was all based on a lie that being gay was "broken," but no one would believe or acknowledge that this was indeed a lie. Heck, Steve even said he would never try to make me be anything. So I joined the group, which ultimately led to my living a lie for the next 21 years in the Exodus movement, plus two more years trying to deconstruct the mindfuck I went through before coming out.

In hindsight, I believe that even as relaxed and gracious as that church was on everything else, they were part of an immense system of oppression and stigmatization of LGBTQ+ people. No, of course, they were not fearmongering manipulators, but at their core they believed the same things as the fearmongering manipulators. Throughout time, they, along with millions of other culturally-driven conservative Christians worldwide, have stigmatized LGBTQ+ people. They disenfranchised us to the point that they thought they were helping (saving) us as they built a very nice, spacious, well-designed, and faux-gracious church closet to "fix" our "sexual and relational brokenness."

We were a part of the church's life but always different from everyone else. In short, if you still weren't married with children, you weren't necessarily included in some church programs and leadership positions. Oh how I wish I had heard a message of acceptance and that I was encouraged (or at least allowed) to embrace my relational state of being as a gay son of God in Christ as a gift, not a "brokenness."

But by that time in my life, I didn't have much good in my 24 years to look back on when I started with Steve's group. I went from a traumatic childhood and home life to the substance-abusing dark side of the party scene, which, at the time, I thought was freedom. That just goes to show the warped perspective chronic abuse can create in your mind. Then, on my journey to become healthy and whole, I met a God named Jesus, who kept messing up my journey and seemed to be directing me to this strange new environment.[3] Thus began my migration from gay and pro-gay support groups into the socially conservative, politically driven church world.

If I was "broken" and needed "fixing" or "saving," it wasn't for being gay; it was for being a survivor of chronic and systemic abuse. In hindsight, I think the ex-gay ministry recognizes this and uses it to justify their work. I also think that it makes survivors, like me, easy targets for the type of "saving" they offer.

I now believe it was very harmful and unfair to steer me toward denying my relational state of being and toward renouncing being gay. These folks were so fucked up but in an approachable, relatable way. But, of course, it didn't help that I was even more fucked up and thought they were probably normal.

One lady at my new home church in Arlington told me her story at a cookout I attended one Saturday. She wasn't pretentious or showboating. She just started sharing after I told her that being a new Christian was confusing. I was bewildered about many things except that I believed in Christ. She said, "Lord, honey, I understand." Then, after taking a sip of her wine, she proceeded to tell me her story. I couldn't believe some

---

3 Ultimately, I think He used me to bring an end to one of these harmful groups, even though it took some time to get there. Only He would know, of course, but it certainly feels that way from where I'm sitting.

of the things she was telling me. She was divorced, used to party like crazy, was in an abusive relationship last year, and now, while not perfect by any means, she was glad to be safe and alive and making it through life with Jesus.

She gave some details that made my eyes wide, and I just looked at her and said, "Girl, you are as fucked up as I am!"

She smiled and said, "Well, yeah. It's good that the ground at the foot of the cross is level, isn't it?"

That's the thing about this church. I learned that God is a God of grace. No one there really thought they were better than or worse than me. They didn't hate me. They knew what I was about in that regard because I kept trying to shock them with my crazy gay stories. I found out they were not shockable. But, underneath, like a dark current, was a belief that my being gay was the cause of a deep brokenness that needed healing.

My walls against Christians began to crumble, and I realized that I had no idea why I believed what I believed about God's view of who I was as a man, nor did I know what a genuinely healthy way of relating to the world around me looked like. Because of having relatively few experiences of wholeness at that point in my life (if any), I was a prime candidate to buy into the ex-gay conversion therapy world as a true believer—and I did.

Steve's Group Proved to Be a Hip Church Closet

On July 23, 1992, Sir Mix-A-Lot was singing about Baby Got Back, I LOVED John Secada's song "Just Another Day," George Bush was President, and I attended my first group meeting with Steve. Unless I was deathly sick, I spent every Thursday for the next 10 years at that group before moving to Orlando to join the Exodus International staff.

When I first got to the support group, I was nervous. There were so many more people than I had expected (about 30 to 40). Plus, it wasn't just guys. It was women and parents too. The worship leader that drove the rickety, wood-paneled station wagon was there to lead worship, and we sang about three songs. Then we moved the chairs to form a big circle for the teaching time. Steve wasn't teaching that night, a board member who was a licensed professional counselor was, and she was doing a series on emotional dependency.

That night, there was this muscle guy flexing and posing during the whole thing. No lie. We will call him Flexy. See, Flexy was blond, blue-eyed, and a scoundrel. I could tell that right off the bat because the horndog was cruising every other guy in the group. Flexy just oozed gay pheromones. I thought it was funny, not realizing how terrible it was for him to be doing that to many people feeling bad about themselves. Mr. Flexy was kicked out of the group because he was successful in more than a few sexual conquests and rumored to have passed on HIV to one of the other members. Interesting that 29 years later, Mr. Flexy is a legalistic, judgmental troll of a man whom I had to block on Facebook for his vicious attacks against me when I came out in 2015.

I realized very quickly that I was in an anomaly of a group, based on my experience up until that time. The approach at Steve's support group (back then, not now) wasn't accurate for every Exodus group that ever existed, because this group was comprised mostly of people raised in the church. Most everyone there had gone to church every Sunday for their entire lives. Only a couple of us had come to believe in Christ as adults. Very few in the group had ever identified with or participated in the gay community as I had. Many could relate to partying, but not to the extent that I had "partied." Plus, the people in this group weren't just from the same church. Some of them were driving over two and a half hours, one way, to get to the group. I kept hearing things like: "This group is a life-saver." "I come here to feel safe!" And, "I have nowhere else to go. You all are my true church family." It was fascinating to be in a room full of men, women, and a few family members who weren't afraid to share their attractions, experiences, and troubles.

Their pain and journeys deeply moved me. I was also amazed by their expressions of joy. Weren't all "ex-gays" supposed to be miserable? Especially if we were all "broken"? There wasn't a question I asked for which they didn't have what seemed to be a reasonable answer (to my naïve mind). Plus, like the Sunday church folks, they were kind of unshockable.

And believe me, I tried. I'm a stinker sometimes.

I got a little reprimand about the second or third week in. My small group leader said I should probably refrain from calling Mr. Flexy "cutie" (he was) and that not everyone was comfortable with hugging, so I should probably "ask if it was okay first."

In the 12-step program, everyone hugged me all the time. I didn't know anything else and had assumed the same in this group setting.

Aside from that, I had decided they weren't crazy or something to fear. I even started adopting some of the group's beliefs. I look back on that time and wish I would have run down the street to the largest gay church in the world at that time, the Cathedral of Hope. But I understand now why I didn't. For me, at that point in my life, this had become a non-threatening community (not the case today). They invited me to hang out at Country Kitchen after the group, no question was off-limits, and they always had answers. As I mentioned, they were seemingly unshockable and, more importantly, they were approachable. Plus, I was learning things that were helping me to improve my life. My sexuality wasn't changing, but I was finally learning healthy coping skills. Of course, I believe that all of that should have been available to me as a gay man in a different factual healing/learning context. Now I think that trying to kill my natural, God-given relational state of being shouldn't have ever been on the table, but there it was. I was experiencing a different level of freedom, something I had been desperate for my entire life. What I didn't know was that I was being affirmed, groomed, and indoctrinated to live an inauthentic reality.

It was truly the freest I had ever felt. Yet I didn't realize the shackles of cultural homophobia were only being polished to look prettier. The "closet" I found myself in had been dressed up to look like anything but, and it went from silencing me through abuse and fear to co-opting my voice to promote a culturally accepted, stigmatizing ideology. Hindsight is good, but I wish I knew then what I know now.

That last sentence has to appear in a memoir at least once, right?

Early on, the lady leading the group said they wanted to do a few weeks where people just shared their stories. I LOVE stories. I always have, and I had not ever shared mine, so I nervously said I would like to. I had the whole teaching time to share my story. When my night came, I got a migraine that day at work because of the stress. I was scared out of my mind. I shared my story, and everyone seemed to pay attention to every word. A few cried a couple of times. Everyone hugged me afterward, and none of them asked for permission first. I am glad they didn't.

Not overnight, but rather quickly, I not only adopted a conservative view of sexuality and identity, but I also became a genuine true believer. I never hid the fact that both gay people and pro-gay people had helped me along the way. However, as I have mentioned, I also experienced a LOT of bad things during my brief time in the gay community, most of which I haven't written about in this book. (I don't need to traumatize others by sharing my traumas.) The ex-gay ideology taught me that my version of "party life" resulted from sinful depravity and brokenness, as it related to being gay. To them, it wasn't "party life," it was "*gay* party life." While I was encouraged to learn and grow beyond my dysfunction, I also learned how to scapegoat the entire gay community for the dark underbelly of the drug culture and all my dysfunction. Meanwhile everyone around me was saying, with big smiles and open arms, that what I experienced was the progression of gay sin to its fullest expression. In short, I was taught that being gay was the cause or source of all the trauma and abuse in my life.

As a wounded human being, it was easy to shift the blame for my drug and relational abuse to the ethereal "result of sin" argument that abdicated me from taking full responsibility. It also gave me an excuse to project these very dark parts of my journey onto an entire community that is so much more and so much healthier than that one aspect of the "party" scene I experienced. One can find the substance-abusing and dark aspects of life in any bar, gay bar, or Star Wars cantina scene in the Universe. But, of course, I was encouraged in my projections, as it served the underlying narrative the group needed me to embrace.

Unfortunately, instead of digging deep, maturing, and taking personal responsibility as a gay man, I minimized, objectified, and scapegoated the gay community. I will spend the remainder of my days correcting that mistake.

By adopting the worldview and bias of those around me, I received the approval and affirmation I had never gotten before and so desperately craved. The voids of my childhood were slowly being filled, or so I thought at the time. Again, since I was so desperate for connection and approval, I quickly started helping the leadership of the group with various activities, such as setting up the circle for teaching time, putting the handouts on the table, and putting the chairs back in place after the meeting. I even volunteered to help Steve write to gay prisoners looking for help to "overcome" while they were in prison.

Not surprisingly, the more I was embraced, the more connection I felt, and the more I volunteered. I easily moved from helping to becoming an advocate. I started leading a small group, and the ministry's leadership LOVED how I handled groups. They said I was a "natural." For the first time in forever, I thought I had found a place in the world—*my* place in the world. However, the director was moving across the country after he graduated from seminary, and the board was thinking of shutting it down.

I begged them not to. The other small group leaders and I said we would run things until the board found a new director. Oh, how I wish I had just let the fucker shut down! They, of course, did hire a new director, and I eventually became the assistant director, then co-director, and then the executive director from 1999 to 2002. I wish things had been different and I had kept my mouth shut.

In time, I was invited by other ex-gay or church leaders to travel the country and speak at different conferences and workshops. When I started sharing my ex-gay story, I would often say, "I came out of the closet only to find out I was in the wrong house!" In front of these audiences, that almost always got a hearty laugh. Today I now say, "I came out of the closet, found out I was in the wrong house, moved down the street to a hip church, and eventually moved into their much bigger and better-organized 'closet' with the sign 'Support Group' on the door and 'Freedom From Homosexuality' on the trapdoor." These "support" groups had more space, great music, and LOTS of other gay people trying to make sense of it all.

The problem is this entire world was built on shame, condemnation, and the systemic stigmatization of LGBTQ+ people born of the cultural homophobia that has seeped in and tainted the church. It is so systemic and widespread for generations across the globe that in today's world, it is still (wrongly) considered an act of compassion and love to steer people like I was toward one of these conversion/ministry groups. This malicious assault against our personhood and relational state of being is so conniving that it convinces good-hearted, well-intentioned people like those at the church I attended that somehow this is a proper and healthy response to the fake homosexual "crisis" in our country. My walls of distrust and cynicism weren't crumbling because I was finally learning to trust, they were crumbling under the weight of systemic bigotry delivered with wine and smiles.

Moving into this strange new world, I felt like Alice falling down the rabbit hole, and I was all in for the ride.

I know now that the quest for approval and acceptance lies at the bottom of an endless well when we seek it outside ourselves. At the time, I think I would have done anything to try and keep the group going in order to prevent myself from having to experience the loss of connection. Anything. And I do believe that God uses us despite us.

I hold on to the suicide interventions that we did and the various good things that happened over the years. But in general, I mourn the loss of two decades of my life to the ex-gay movement. I hate the what-if game that can often breed unhealthy despair. Still, a part of me wonders… What if I had been treated as an equal and given the same access to resources and opportunities in the church as a gay man? Where would I be today? Would I be in a vastly different and more prosperous place? Would I have not felt like a complete idiot in the dating world at the age of 47 (when I went on an actual first date, not a party hook-up with a man) because I had never actually dated before? Regardless, while I think a person my age having questions is healthy (who doesn't make mistakes, big mistakes sometimes?), living in guilt, shame, or condemnation isn't healthy. I'm not and never have been omniscient (thank God, literally). I find comfort in believing in God's sovereignty.

Today I hope to take these experiences and help LGBTQ+ people take their place in the church and not settle for some para-church group advertising itself as a safe haven. Ex-gay groups are not safe, nor are they a place of refuge. Full stop. We deserve to take our place as who we are in the Body of Christ or be affirmed for any spiritual or non-spiritual path we take. The church doesn't belong to a creed or culturally-conditioned statement of faith. The church consists of people of faith, including the LGBTQ+ ones.

Walking the Waterline

In 1995, I wanted, so badly, to know what my "calling" was. I chased down Pastor Square Jaw, a stoic former military man who gave seriously stern sermons. We met over lunch, as I explained to him that I wanted to know my calling, but I didn't know how to go about figuring it out. At the time, I didn't know if I was supposed to go into ex-gay ministry or do something else. I was looking for an easy answer, but instead of telling me what he thought, he said that when the Lord revealed my "calling" to me, I would know it beyond any doubt. Before leaving, he and a couple of elders who worked out of the church building lay hands on my shoulders and prayed for the Lord to show me my calling.

I left the church after their prayers and went on with my day. I didn't think about it again until later that night. As I slept, I had one of the most vivid dreams I have ever had in my life. It was like I was in another dimension that was more real than this one. In the dream, I was walking down the waterline of a beach. The waves were coming in and repeatedly flowing over and away from my feet as I walked northward. The beach was to my left, and the waves were to my right. As I walked, I heard what sounded like a church congregation out in the ocean screaming obscenities at a group of gay and lesbian people walking onto the beach. (I don't know how I knew it was a church congregation; It was just one of those things that happens in dreams when you know you know something.) They were screaming, "FAG! Look at those dykes!!!" And then laughing at the group.

As these homophobic people in my dream continued to curse and bully, I went to turn to the hecklers and rebuke them, but before I got a word out, the LGBTQ+ group of people on the beach behind me started yelling at me, "See what you are a part of!" They were genuinely upset with the church and confused about my being of the same faith. I suppose this scene and interaction is partially what made me know it was church people out in the ocean.

I remember feeling overwhelmed with sorrow about the church group and turning to the LGBTQ+ group, filled with love toward them, and quoting Romans 3:10, saying, "There are none righteous, no, not one," followed by Romans 3:23, "For all have fallen short of the glory of God." I then shared that Jesus came to atone for and save us. In that moment, I felt the veil of separation rupture, so that we could go to Him without fear. And the next bit is tough to describe, but it was so vivid. I lifted my hands in the dream, and the Holy Spirit rushed from heaven onto the LGBTQ+ group, and they rejoiced in experiencing the Divine. I woke up crying with joy.

When I told Pastor Square Jaw about my dream, we both believed that the Lord had answered my prayer and I had received my "calling." Of course, a simple "calling" wasn't enough, and we had to impose the conservative ex-gay narrative onto it. For Pastor Square Jaw, the dream meant that my calling was to be an evangelist for the gay community to invite them into our world and save them from themselves. It would take 20 years before I realized that my actual calling was to take my place as a peer in the gay community as a gay man of faith, and not become a scapegoat for the religious to curse the gay community.

Today, I am more of a Universalist Christian, and I still believe that the dream showed me my calling because it is as vivid today as it was then. My heart and love are with my community that I was never supposed to leave. Somehow, God knew I needed to swim around for a while, aloof and estranged, and disconnected from the truth of who I am. Thinking I could adapt to and uphold an institutionalized religion was simply wrong. God knew I was in a mainstream cult, and I would eventually find my way home. He loved me through it, which eventually allowed me to be in the right place at the right time to help shut down Exodus.

I now know that my calling is to humbly walk through life and do my best to love, serve, and be in community. It's God's part to love others, including those of us who wander a bit. My job is to keep walking and be available to His love. The Divine guides my feet and, like the waves, washes them as I go forward, experiencing life as a man of faith.

The church does deserve rebuke for her condescending judgment and insults hurled at the gay community as a whole. She is unapproachable and distant. The LGBTQ+ community has a right to know that Christ is in no way a part of the cultural stigmatization of the gay community that has come out of the church. He is living, dynamic, and willing to relate to us, not curse us. The Universe transcends our humanly-contrived religious machinations.

Blessings in the Closet

One point that I hope comes across about the ex-gay ministry is that people involved in ex-gay ministries are not idiots. I mean, well, some of them are, and it's really clear who they are. I believe the other 98% of the folks think like I did: That this is the only possible Christian response to the issue of "same-sex attractions."

Part of the reason this belief can be so compelling is due to the tremendous amount of affirmation that comes through a broad and profound system of belief and an international network of adherents. But, again, no one signs up to be in a toxic belief system. They are duped with what seems like positive, life-changing ideas. Plus, when it comes to the peripheral issues (because sexuality doesn't change and shouldn't have to), they are often handled well (in some cases) in the ex-gay world. What are "peripheral issues"? They're the things that we deal with as humans, regardless of our sexuality. These are things like mental and emotional health. As I mentioned earlier, I learned how to deal with emotional/codependency and learned healthy boundaries and interdependence in ex-gay groups. I discovered my voice, talents, and gifts in the church and ex-gay support groups. At the 1995 Point Loma conference, I also learned from The Celebrity Ex-Gay (beloved by ex-gays and Hillsong church out of Australia who sent him all over the world) and Roger (the future leader of Exodus and my future boss) that it was okay to be yourself in many other ways that had nothing to do with my sexuality. These people were funny, bright, and a joy to be around. I laughed so hard many times during that week.

Communal Showers, Unexpected Grace, and Lesbian Avengers–
My First Exodus Conference

I had never flown into San Diego before. It was 1995, and I flew in via Southwest Airlines in Dallas through El Paso and Las Vegas. And it was a long, nerve-wracked day. But finally, we got to the Point Loma Nazarene College campus, and I discovered that while it was beautiful and calm, there were communal showers and no air conditioning.

Did I mention there were communal showers? When I realized this, I was like, how is a conference full of people trying not to be attracted to the same sex going to pile into communal showers? Plus, the folks walking around campus didn't look like they would want to avoid this "temptation." I struggled, big time, with body shame issues, so I got a migraine just thinking of having to deal with ANYONE in the shower. Plus, it wasn't like it was a typical public situation. This conference was full of "not-gay-but-gay-looking" guys primping or playing the false masculine jock-boy theme. That's a lot of high-maintenance bathroom behavior to force into a communal shower situation.

I wasn't thrilled. Since this was my first time attending the conference, I went to the "first-timers" orientation. After the meeting finished, Carrie, an Exodus ministry leader from Denver, Colorado, introduced herself to me. She was so approachable and seemingly full of grace. She helped instill a sense of peace in me.

From that point forward, I met all kinds of ex-gay legends and pretty much every ex-gay leader who was or would rise to prominence in the late '90s up until Exodus closed in 2013. It still amazes me the far-reaching, global, negative impact the folks at that conference made. It is remarkable and unfortunate for many ex-gay survivors and those still trapped in that ideology around the world.

I also met the "Lesbian Avengers." To be clear, I didn't "meet" them, but they crashed a special worship concert that was open to the public one evening. A host of angry lesbians with specially decorated shirts came running and screaming down the aisle with a *SPIN* magazine reporter and photographer in tow. They took over the stage, took the microphone away from the singer, and did their own modified version of "Amazing Grace." It was crude and lewd.

Interestingly, at one point when the lesbians started singing, literally everyone in the crowd stood up, raised their hands, and started singing the original Amazing Grace. I was one of them, weeping as I held up my hands, and our crowd drowned out the anger on the stage. Even as the lesbians were being escorted out, a few of them screaming shame at people as they passed by, we sang my favorite hymn, and I was appalled that the angry women would change the words the way they did.

The *SPIN* reporter had been at the conference as an attendee. They duped some of the attendees into interviews without disclosing who they were talking to or what was happening. The Exodus board, including Carrie, and the director graciously defended themselves and confronted the reporter and *SPIN* and talked with the Lesbian Avengers.

I mention all this because I don't feel that what the Lesbian Avengers did was successful or practical. If their end goal was to cause disruption and/or prompt thought or disagreement, they failed. I fully understand and relate to their anger today. However, what they did only ended up falling on deaf ears because it reinforced existing beliefs about the LGBTQ+ community. Their lewdness and mockery, and the bullying of the singer, only solidified the attendees' beliefs through a communally shared experience. It was like a negative affirmation that what we were doing and what we were there for was a loving and proper way to view and live our lives, in contrast to the way the Lesbian Avengers behaved. In fact, the members of Exodus leadership, at least the ones I knew, appeared strong, kind, and wise as a result. Of all the things that happened that week to solidify the ex-gay worldview and us as a movement, the Lesbian Avengers significantly contributed to nailing the door shut on our church closet.

In the end, the Lesbian Avengers were correct in their anger. But protests like that don't work in the conversion therapy/ex-gay world. Instead of changing hearts and minds, it had the opposite effect, and, in my opinion, it only fuels more ex-gay talking points that serve to diminish and stigmatize.

An Unexpected Repentance

It was also during that week that all the chips on my shoulders against the church fell away. One evening, the keynote speaker invited a pastor to come up to the stage. The pastor started listing the sins of the church against gay people. After each point, he would offer an apology.

I paraphrase because I don't have the transcript, but the pastor essentially said, "For our sin of indifference, I apologize. For the sin of bearing false witness against you and the gay community, I apologize. For the sin of ignoring your struggle and making fun of you, I apologize."

I sat in the seat with my arms crossed. While everyone around me was crying, I sat there thinking, "Yeah, you better fucking apologize, you fucking asshole." I was filled with rage. The church had stigmatized, ignored, and torn families apart. The church was horrible—at that point, I liked my church and these people, but I still hated "the church" and couldn't stand Christians for the most part. The pastor seemed to be genuinely atoning and could get as emotional and teary-eyed as he wanted. I felt that he meant it and it was a nice gesture and all, but in my mind, I still said, "Fuck you."

Then the keynote speaker got up and said, "Now it is our turn." I uncrossed my arms and thought, "Our turn to do what?" As if reading my mind, the speaker said, "It is our turn to apologize to the church." My instant reaction was, "OH, HELL NO!" I scowled, crossed my arms and legs, and thought this skinny runner man (he ran every morning) was batshit crazy.

Unfortunately, I became his fan that night. That all ended, of course, when he mocked me publicly after shutting down Exodus. Today, however, I don't know that I would modify his crazy with "batshit," because the truth is that he isn't crazy—he is actually the wolf he warns others of. I believe he is a self-righteous, manipulative serpent.

But the night he called on us to repent for our sins against the church. I don't remember anything else he said. I was not a happy person, but when he gave "the call" for us to come forward for prayer (and as an act of repentance), I believed God said I had to forgive the church and release my toxic anger toward her. That realization made me angry, but 10 minutes later, I was at the front of the auditorium, crying my eyes out in prayer.

As I prayed, I imagined the Lord on the cross looking at His Bride, the church (past, present, future). He was there because of her. She was literally and figuratively the reason He was crucified. Yet instead of hating her, He asked the Father to forgive her because she knew not what she was doing. If Christ could look on the church with love and forgiveness, it was in my best interest to do the same. It was not ignoring her sin. It was not justifying her contributions to oppression, pain, hurt, and evil behavior. Instead, it was recognizing that it's not in the church that we find atonement; in

Christ alone, we find our hope and home. If Christ was sacrificed for my sin and could forgive her, I could at least try to forgive the institutionalized church, too.

My heart completely changed. The church went from being a cultural institution of ignorance and oppression to a spiritual being that the Divine calls Their Bride. The cultural institution needs to be overthrown, but the Bride exists regardless of our faith or lack of faith. We are all on our own journeys, which should be celebrated, protected, and, most of all, respected.

It was in that moment that I unwittingly gave the institutionalized, culturally-derived church carte-blanche to infuse a stigmatized view of homosexuality into my life, not realizing that ex-gay ideology was a manifestation of deep cultural bias, not Spirit-led compassion.

Climbing the Ex-Gay Ladder

Even though I was as gay as I ever was, I flourished in finding my voice and natural assertiveness. It turns out that the supposedly brainy introvert that I was raised to be wasn't the real me. I loved talking with people and facilitating small groups. As I mentioned earlier, before being a small group leader, I wrote prisoners in response to their letters for help. In writing—literally handwriting (this was before email and beneficial home computers)—I learned how to compellingly articulate my feelings and beliefs into words. Of course, initially, Steve would read over the letters before I sent them to make sure what I was sending out was helpful and in line with what the ministry believed. It didn't take long, though, before he said he didn't have to do that anymore, and soon thereafter I began to lead small groups. Again, I flourished in leading small groups. Eventually, I would start teaching during the significant group teaching times, as well.

Then when Steve left to move back to the East Coast and I pleaded for the board to let us keep the ministry going, the small group leaders would take turns teaching. A short time later, I became the associate director when the teacher from my first ex-gay meeting was the interim director, co-director with the next director, and then executive director from 1999 to 2002. When I was in leadership, Steve's group (which was now led by us after his departure) started having an actual budget.

Honestly, at the time, I had no clue how to run a non-profit organization. However, I learned very quickly, usually through trial and (many) errors. I felt I had the "ministry" side of things down, but dealing with a board (that eventually was full of personal agendas and dual interests) was challenging.

Along with the infusion of reparative/conversion therapy into all the materials and resources produced in the broader ex-gay movement, I was unaware that the grace I had found at Steve's group was slowly disappearing, though it was still there (to a degree) when I left to join the staff at Exodus. However, once I moved to Florida in 2002, I would hear horror stories of what the board had done to the ministry after my departure. I am sure some of what I heard was biased, but I know that when I went back to Texas a year or so later, several board members made it very clear they didn't want me to visit the regular group because it might be "confusing." I, in turn, made it very clear that I was going to visit the group I had helped establish whether it was "confusing" or not in no uncertain terms.

It made for an awkward evening.

From 1995 to 2002, though, I built the first (or at least one of the first) ex-gay ministry websites and the first online ex-gay forum (bulletin board). It would eventually grow to tens of thousands of participants (mostly young people). Again, after my departure, I was told it was "confusing" for me to take part, so I realized some on the board, through the mask of compassion, had a plan to rid the group of any of my influence. In their eyes, even though I was now a card-carrying religious rights advocate, I was too liberal. One board member even went so far as to tell Roger Tompkins (of Exodus) before he officially hired me that he shouldn't hire me because I wasn't ready. The board member told Roger that I would cry a lot when I was upset (hello, I was healing decades of trauma!) and that I brought technology into the groups as a personal crutch for my own well-being. What made the situation worse is that this specific board member was my mentor, and he was supposed to keep the things we discussed confidential. He was supposed to be a safe person to share my pain with. In reality, though, he used our conversations against me as he tried to ruin my reputation and opportunities in national ministry.

When I finally left, they gave me a Mont Blanc pen as a thank you for my service (charming). But after I left, I never received a single phone call, email, or letter. They avoided me at the national conferences, and I heard from others that they were telling people negative things about me instead of talking directly to me. I grieved their manipulation and betrayal, but I got very good at helping other non-profit boards avoid the same mistakes. I learned a lot about how functional and healthy boards worked and was able to counsel other ministries through various trials and development opportunities. I wouldn't say I am an expert, but I learned valuable lessons about leadership, board management, and team development due to my experiences after taking the helm of Steve's group. Those lessons would be incredibly important as they were put to a pointed and consequential test years later as Exodus started to implode.

The Motherland, the Fatherland, the On Your Own Land

I will never forget June 3, 2002. It was the day I started as the new Exodus membership director. I was scared, totally excited, and wearing a pair of Walmart shoes I got for, I think, nine dollars. Roger was very kind, but during that first week, he looked at my shoes and said, "Where did you get those?"

I said, "I got them for a great price at Walmart."

He said, "Very nice. But you will never wear Walmart shoes again."

And while I never was genetically predisposed for fashion or cared about shoes, I never wore Walmart shoes again.

Adjusting to Florida was not easy. It felt like a different universe. I grew up in Texas and Tennessee, then moved back to Texas, then Florida—all Southern yet very different. I call Tennessee the motherland, Texas the fatherland, and Florida the "you're on your own land."

People here are simply different and not nearly as open and ready to feed you as they are in Tennessee and Texas. My mom decided to move down here from Tennessee shortly after I moved here, so she came down to look for a place to live. I told her, "Now, Momma, it's different down here. The people aren't as nice as they are in Tennessee and Texas."

She said, "Oh honey, I am sure they are just fine. Florida is the South, too."

I said, "Well, there are pockets of the 'South' here, but the true 'South' stops somewhere around Gainesville/Ocala and turns into an odd, New-York-flavored international melting pot the further south you go on the peninsula."

She listened, but I don't think she believed me until after the first day of driving around. That evening, she said, "Randy, you were right."

I replied, "Right about what?"

She said, "The only people who were nice to me today were the people at the toll booths… and that's probably because I was giving them money."

I laughed and said, "Well, the people here are nice. They're just a different kind of nice."

And it is true. It's a different kind of nice. It feels much more aloof than anywhere else I have lived. That said, I have found Floridians to be just like everybody else in their desire to build relationships and create connections. I have also found that the people here love every single reason to party. Maybe it is because this is a worldwide tourist destination, but the folks around here really know how to enjoy a bottle of wine, the beaches, lavish dinners, and the nightlife. It took a while, but I have grown to love and call Florida my home. Even though our three seasons are:

1. Hot.
2. Hot as Hell, Hot.
3. Hotter Than a Steam Bath in the Hottest Part of Hell, Hot.

I do love it here. But don't ask me the "do you love Florida?" question in late July, August, or September.

In June of 2002, though, while I loved the wide variety of nature and the incredibly diverse population, being on the Exodus staff became my sole focus, and it consumed me.

I thought June 3rd was the beginning of a long lifetime of fulfilling ministry to help people find "freedom from homosexuality" and "become who God created them to be." Little did I know that God had a different plan to liberate me from an abusive childhood and culturally imposed homophobia into a healthy, whole, mostly sane gay man. I now believe the Divine guided me through all the various events in my ex-gay life to meet the people I met, to eventually join Exodus, and to be an integral part of helping to shut it down (which we did, eventually). However, I had to get through a turbulent, life-threatening ride first.

CHAPTER 7

The Ex-Gay Kingdom Part 2

Richard: A True Ex-Gay Superstar!

When Richard called the office and was on hold waiting to talk to me, I may have made him wait a little longer than necessary. To be honest—I did not want to talk to him at all!

I mean, not at all.

Richard was an ass. Not just an ass, but a high maintenance, let's-throw-down-in-front-of-the-whole-world kind of an ass. Richard had been thrown out of our Exodus conference several years before for yelling at and interrupting workshop teachers. He was an ass to just about every person he met.

And now, after a few years and a turnover in leadership, he was on the phone wanting to talk to Roger Tompkins, the new president of Exodus, but ended up talking to me.

I cannot remember the exact prayer I said before I picked up the line, but it went something like this: "Dear Jesus, please help me not see Richard as an ass and have the grace to not treat him like one either. Amen."

After taking a deep breath, I picked up the phone and said, "Richard! How are you?"

Richard talks fast, and he doesn't need you to verbalize words to feel like he is having a conversation with you. So not only did he want permission to come back to our conference that summer, but he also proceeded to tell me we "needed" him to do a keynote address.

I was stunned. Richard was a man who insulted and threatened almost all of his peers. He had burned every bridge imaginable and was now expecting us to make him a keynote speaker at our biggest yearly event.

I resisted the temptation to call him on the carpet for all the awful unresolved situations he had created over the years and told him a truth that I hoped would get me off the phone faster. I said, "Richard, there are some issues we would have to resolve before that could ever be a possibility. Regardless, we have already confirmed all of our guest speakers."

He replied for about 10 minutes in as many different ways as possible to say that we needed to make room for him to be a speaker and utilize him more often. I told him, "Again, we have some serious unresolved issues with you and how you treated many of our leaders. If you would like to work through all of that to reconcile our differences, we can. But having you as a speaker of any kind at the conference is not something we can do."

Richard got mad. He said I had offended God by not inviting him to speak. I doubt that very much.

He then recited his ex-gay resume as an ex-gay leader to me, going on and on about all the amazing things he had done to counter the evil gay agenda. I took a deep, inaudible breath as he kind of went berserk and almost shouted, "Randy, I have been an EXPERT in this field for years! I was one of the top ten ex-gays globally for over a decade."

I laughed out loud. You could hear my belly laugh reverberating around the office. Controlling my laughter was not even an option. It was hilarious to think of a "top ten ex-gay list." Then my mind started coming up with all the criteria one had to have to make that list, and I cracked myself up even further.

My guffawing response did not improve Richard's disposition in the slightest.

Over my eventually stifled chuckling as I tried to stop laughing, Richard asked angrily, "WHAT are you laughing about?"

I replied, "Top ten ex-gays? That has got to be one of the stupidest things I've ever heard. If you were to be in the top ten of anything, why would you pick THAT list?"

He went off, and I apologized for laughing. When the conversation finally calmed down somewhat, I stuck to my boundaries of needing to resolve past conflicts before entertaining ideas of working with him again. I even convinced him to set up another phone call with me to try and do that.

The truth is that being "ex-gay" is such a rare novelty that even as an operationally defunct, dysfunctional, 50-ish-year-old movement (at the time of this writing), we never really figured out what "ex-gay" actually meant. Plus, being "ex-gay" was cultish at worst, plain bizarre at best. Who would want to be in the top 10 of that?

To go from 1976 when the founders of Exodus were first trying to find their way to Richard somehow thinking he was an ex-gay superstar was an incredible leap not based in reality—it was a product of what Exodus had become. At the time, Exodus International was a niche ministry with cultural oppression and stigmatization of sexuality buried in its foundation. For all our smiles and hugs, Exodus was not a pure, grace-based approach to understanding the gospel for LGBTQ+ people.

As the culture shifted toward blessing the LGBTQ+ community as the morally acceptable and beautiful expression of love it is, the voice of those with a stigmatized religious view of LGBTQ+ people would prop up the Christian ex-gay worldview as the testimony du jour on Sunday or public policy battles. In short, ex-gay/conversion ministry testimonies provided cover for ongoing systemic hatred within an organized Western evangelicalism.

The church is waking up to the fact that it is not and never was acceptable to shun those of us who are gay. While there may be nuances and a few unique issues that arise from being gay, the truth is that LGBTQ+ people can come to Christ, walk out our spiritual journeys in loving relationships, and receive His atonement and the Divine's blessing.

Being gay and understanding how that plays out and what it means in my life does not make me forever unique. The gay community, for all its bravado and flair, isn't that different from any community at large. Humanity is humanity, frailty is frailty, strength is strength, dignity is dignity, faith is faith, and love is love.

Remembering Richard while writing this has brought some sadness. He passed away suddenly a few years ago, dying way too young. I hate that my interactions with him were so contentious. But he chose to stigmatize the LGBTQ+ community and thought that was a noble cause. I hate that he was in a place where he thought he was doing good by hurting himself and us. I hate that he was rewarded by the activist fringe religious right in the church and validated for living an inauthentic life. It grieves me that he might have gone to the grave never having known peace with his Creator concerning the truth that he was a gay man.

I hate that the Exodus "product" was to produce false experts who could tell good stories that wrought so much hurt and devastation. It became about us, our projected idealizations and self-loathing being declared as facts, and our carefully crafted (and curated/managed) message then became more important than God's unconditional love and grace to LGBTQ+ people.

My Learning a Lesson Richard Never Seemed to Grasp

Let's take a step back for a moment. In 1992, I started working for Tad Johnson who had his own Christian weekday talk show based in Texas. I worked in the computer room and had just begun my ex-gay journey. In 1993, I began praying for an opportunity for Tad to produce four shows about the issue of homosexuality on his weekday talk show. I had them all planned out. But the deal, the "fleece before the Lord" (spiritual test), was that I wouldn't initiate the idea of creating the shows. Then, in late 1994 or early 1995, one of the producers who knew about my journey came to me with the idea of doing four shows. Three of which were exactly what I had envisioned.

I was elated.

They brought in some of my Exodus heroes at the time (Hank and Gladys Smooten and Dante Harrigan) and had me as a guest on one of the shows. It was my first time on TV for an interview, and I was scared into anonymity. The digitized effects made me a blurry, effeminate Arnold Schwarzenegger. It was hilarious. After the taping, I went to IHOP with Dante, and we spent a good long while talking about Tad, Jesus, and modern-day Levites. That night seemed to be an affirmation that yes, Randy, you have been through a lot, and we want to know how God saved you and is now walking with you on this journey. Constant attention and affirmation were something I was desperate for without realizing it.

From Being in Front of Millions to Where the Fuck Am I?

A few months after my digitized television debut, I left Tad Johnson's ministry and moved to Shelbyville, Tennessee. The plan was to live in my

Granny Grunt's house, even though that furnace in the floor still freaked me out. She had passed away, and my mom and two aunts were trying to sell the house but thought maybe I could live there and finish up college first. So, I thought that perhaps God was providing this rent-free option to get my degree. However, things didn't quite work out as planned.

The doors closed at the university because they would not give me the in-state tuition break (I had been in Texas until I reapplied for college in Tennessee), and I couldn't afford the out-of-state tuition rates. In addition, I couldn't get financial help because I had made too much money the year before. So, I enrolled at the local community college in Tullahoma, Tennessee.

Shelbyville, pronounced Shebvull by the locals, is a horrible version of a Stephen King town. Actually, it was even worse than a demon-possessed Stephen King town. Yes, I said it. There were only 15,000 people there at the time. One time, as I watched a Cowboys game on TV, I realized that you could fit about four or five Shebvulls into that one stadium.

I started to get panicked and felt like I was trapped.

Then I met this cool guy in one of my classes. He was intelligent, witty, and just intellectually intriguing. I met him at Pizza Hut, where I had just gotten a job delivering pizzas. I was the youngest driver, and it was the best-paying job in town unless you wanted to work at the Tyson Chicken plant. (You DON'T want to work at the Tyson Chicken plant. There is a reason they get paid somewhat decently—for rural Tennessee.)

So this friend is cool, his girlfriend is fantastic, and I am thinking, at least I can relate to someone here.

Until I didn't hear from him for a week, and finally found out why—he was in jail for selling cocaine.

Who knew? Everyone in town but me.

I am an unabashed extrovert and genuinely love people. However, I didn't fit into Shelbyville at all, and not for lack of trying. I won't say anything negative about the residents of Shelbyville. However, I will share a single incident that made it clear to me that I was an outsider. On one of my pizza deliveries, I witnessed the worst case of racism I had ever seen in my life. I was from the South, and racism was nothing new to me. In this instance, though, I was shocked. Shocked. Not only was I shocked by what was being said, but there seemed to be an expectation that I would agree with what was being said because of the color of my skin. I must have looked like a deer in the headlights, because I couldn't believe what was happening. At that moment, I realized that being ex-gay wouldn't matter to these people. If they discovered or knew about my past as an openly gay man (part of a marginalized community this type of homophobia helped produce) that meant I truly wasn't safe (again) where I lived. To top it off, I was the only man in town that used hair products, so I also knew the glares I got from people meant potential danger.

I had severe culture shock in Shebvull, and I felt increasingly isolated. I couldn't connect with anyone even though I did visit all five or so churches near the house. Unfortunately, even there I was afraid.

I asked my parents for help to get out of there, but no dice.

One night I was desperate and quite upset. In Texas, I'd had a good job, friends, and a church family. I had come to Tennessee thinking that God was leading me there to get my degree, and here I was relationally starved, isolated, and failing college algebra.

I had NEVER failed a test before.

How had I gone from being on national television six months earlier to delivering pizzas to some racists who wanted me to warn Pizza Hut to never send non-white drivers to their keg parties? People at church had "prophesied" that I would be lifted up before the rulers of this age, kings and leaders, to share my story with them. How did I go from that to my only friend being a lying (to me) drug dealer?

I cried as I lay in the middle of Granny Grunt's living room floor. I thought about driving up to Nashville and going to the gay bars. I wrestled with that temptation for quite a while, but eventually, I stood resolute, believing (then) that I couldn't go back to that life.

I truly believed that I had met God and thought He had called me to a greater love than I could ever find with a male partner. Like I have said before in this book, I was a true believer at this point. As I declared this in prayer, I thought Jesus would manifest some comforting thoughts or give me some encouraging words.

Instead, I got rebuked by the Spirit—no warm fuzzies at all!

She (I now believe the Spirit is a feminine energy) had a lesson for me. Without even thinking along these lines, the Spirit interrupted me and reminded me of the four TV shows with Tad. She revealed I was proud of what the Lord had done 'through me,' but I wasn't necessarily proud of those shows.

A spiritual "fleece" had not been answered. My passive aggressive manipulations in the name of religious conviction led to the shows.

So instead of being coddled, the Lord disciplined me.

At that moment, I believed the Divine said They don't need "me" to get Their message out. They could make the "stones cry out" with praise if They wanted to. But I felt convinced that I was to treat the poor, the average, and the rich the same way and that I was to never again compare myself to them or worry about being "lifted up" in front of high-profile individuals or lots of people around the world.

My only response was, "I just want some encouragement, and now I feel worse."

I believe the Divine led me to go into the wilderness of Shebvull to teach me an important lesson that I would maybe have never received amidst all my "normal" life in Texas. Humiliated and humbled, I begged God to let me go back to Texas. BEGGED. In two phone calls that took less than a half hour the following day, I had my job back at Tad Johnson's ministry and a place to live down the street from it.

From that point forward, I had unique opportunities that would put these lessons to the test. I shared my testimony around the world and on Capitol Hill. As a result, I have met most of the current national and international Christian leaders, including some of those who would eventually help to get Trump elected as President.

Yes, it was exhilarating to have lunch with senators, House reps, White House staffers, and leaders in DC. But looking back now, all I can do is mourn the thought that the toxic ideology of conversion therapy and religious stigma is so systemic that these leaders welcomed me with big smiles and open arms.

As a result, when coupled with the praise I got from my leaders and peers in ministry, there was a time in the early days when I thought about myself in the same way Richard did: as an ex-gay superstar. My bottomless void of self-worth and addiction to people-pleasing seemed to only point to public affirmation as the answer to what I needed. And I got it. Unfortunately, the ex-gay/conversion therapy world rewards self-loathing narcissists in order to get them to continually recommit to the cause. The only acceptable LGBTQ+ people in Western evangelicalism are the self-loathing ones. LGBTQ+ people who are too willing to be put in front of mics on a stage only go home to inner torment afterward. They are eager to walk in the halls of power to tell a story they would like to have as reality, but to do so, they are killing themselves from the inside out and providing proverbial ammunition to the far right to continue the systemic oppression of LGBTQ+ people and their fundamental human rights.

The "Ex-Gay" Movement Outside of Exodus

Part of my experience with Exodus was liaising with other ex-gay conversion groups that weren't a part of Exodus. While Exodus was the largest network of these groups in the world, there were probably just as many organizations lone-wolfing it out there or trying to develop networks themselves.

Many times, there was a lot of friction between outside groups and Exodus. It might be surprising to the outside world, but the differences between these groups was vast. Those differences ran along many lines, including: theological, political, ego, jealousy, competitiveness, and all sorts of slander and backbiting.

I went to many meetings attempting to rally the various groups together to accomplish like-minded goals, but none of it seemed to go anywhere. One time I went to one including Mormon groups, Jewish organizations, secular counselors, and independent ministries, and we spent a whole day trying to come up with a name and purpose statement that led to nothing. We may have met one or two more times, but it only ended up being a ridiculous waste of time and money.

Once, a well-known conversion therapist (in that world) came to me after we ended the day and said, "Wow, that was stressful. I can't wait to get to my room, get naked, and stretch all this tension out." Then he stared at me like a creeper at a bar wanting to know my zodiac sign and restated, "Nothing like the freedom to relax au naturel."

So I said, "Yeah, you have fun with that. Nice to see you again." And I hurried out as quickly as I could.

Mr. Naked-Yoga-But-Somehow-Ex-Gay-Man was not fun to be around. Like Richard, he loved being the center of attention and was best known for screaming "prophetic" laments as prayers in a van full of ex-gay leaders when we protested at the APA in Chicago.

Camp of the Scary Woods

Speaking of Chicago, I once visited an ex-gay ministry in the deep woods of the rural Midwest. I was going to see a specific person who had "checked in" there. He used to be a very popular speaker, that is until he was busted for being HIV+ and having unprotected sex in a state that made it illegal to not inform partners of your status before having sex.

This man had unsafe orgies or hookups in the gay community on Saturday nights before heading to church on Sunday mornings and speaking about how God had made him straight.

When he was reported to the police by a man who had contracted HIV from him, he fled the state and ended up at this camp in the woods. He had been there for a while when I went to see him and confront him over some of his lies to us as well as his unscrupulous behavior putting other people's health in danger. When I arrived, I was welcomed and given a tour of the compound and asked to stay for dinner and the evening service.

It was everything you would expect in a cult. The leadership planned every moment of every day for the participants. Sleeping quarters were like makeshift dorms with way too many people in them. Everyone had chores and meetings scheduled throughout their day for the entire time they were there. They were intentionally separated from the rest of their lives, isolated out in the woods. The power dynamics and mantras gave me the chills. I knew then that if they ever tried to join Exodus (they never wanted to), I couldn't in good conscience recommend them—even in our rabidly conservative network.

I did confront the man, and he admitted his hypocrisy and sense of invincibility. He told me he would make amends, somehow, to the people he had infected and whose lives he put in danger. He also told me that he knew what he had done was only for the show (entertainment) and money. As a final blow, he said that he had finally gotten truly "saved."

In response, I said, "Please forgive me, but you took a lot of other ministries' money saying the same shit. How can I trust that you are 'truly saved' now, given your track record?" He said I couldn't, and that his actions going forward would show his true repentance and change of heart. I never saw or heard from him again. I guess he decided to keep hiding deep in the woods with people who thought they were helping him.

There were plenty of ex-gay camp type of events but one that was long lasting and still running at the time of this book seemingly had a successful weekend retreat. It was popular with some male leadership and group participants within the Exodus network. The retreat was run by men who were licensed counselors, but of a different faith, so they were not a part of Exodus by their own choice because they couldn't agree with some theological and cultural issues. However, that didn't stop them from wanting Exodus to promote their retreats. We couldn't do that because of the tactics they would use to desensitize male sexualization, such as having the participants sit on or against each other in very personal ways. They would also facilitate recreating trauma through roleplay between group participants or rage therapy (my words for intentionally inciting rage).

They gave a scholarship to us to have one of our staff people go to "experience the truth." The staff member willing to give it a shot didn't last past the first day and left. He felt incredibly uncomfortable and didn't like what was happening to the participants. After that, we made it clear we would not recommend their retreat and advised member agencies not to recommend them. Still, some of the Exodus member agencies bought into it and did recommend people to that program. We received consistent pressure over the years to recommend them, but we would not.

What is it with some conversion therapists doing bizarre things in the woods?

The Hated Big Dog

When talking about Exodus, I think it is also important to show that while Exodus was the biggest conversion therapy organization to ever exist in the world (to date), there were many ex-gay groups that had no affiliation with Exodus. Some of which I have no doubt had big grins and a wagging finger saying, *I told you so, they've sold out to money and the devil!* when Exodus closed. It's important to note a few examples of these groups because many of them grew larger and even more were created after Exodus closed. This evil ideology—ex-gay/conversion therapy—can be found in mainstream theological views of almost all conservative religious groups of any faith.

In other words, Exodus didn't create the toxic theology it was based on and promoted. That existed before Exodus and clearly has carried on since its closure. That theology was and is so much bigger than Exodus ever was because it is taught as the default theological view in every conservative church, mosque, and synagogue across the world, to name a few. At the same time, while the same beliefs on sexuality and gender are present across the board, the groups themselves are very different. This is also important to know if you want to understand how this pernicious dark strain flows in various ways to continue to ensnare and hold hostage more and more people—both the LGBTQ+ community *and* the well-intentioned and good-hearted believers who think they are helping.

Now, About Those Groups… Exodus + Outside Ex-Gay Groups = Non-Starters in Most Cases

In many situations with outside groups, it was a futile exercise to try and work with them. I went into every meeting with good faith that something would work out. It usually didn't.

And there are many other stories with different groups outside of Exodus whose idea of "working together" was about promoting their resources within our networks. However, a vast majority of the time, significant differences prevented a working relationship. For example, Exodus was too liberal, too conservative, too political, too controlling, too hands-off, too arrogant and personality-driven, or too much of whatever this and that was.

Now that I have been out of that world for over a decade and have gotten a glimpse into the gay advocacy side of things, I know that competitive and self-promotional aspect exists probably within any advocacy or ideology-based movement.

However, again, the underlying toxic beliefs of the ex-gay world are focused on drawing in vulnerable people who are hurting and seeking relief only to continue the damaging abuse. In the end, the entire movement, while full of many different manifestations of conversion therapy, will never be able to solidify its efforts. I believe that because the efforts themselves are built on shifting sand and "leaders" (including me at that time) passing themselves off as experts on the issues within their bubble despite having no qualifications, experience, or credentials. Once they get beyond the edges of their bubble, frail egos usually stifle any real forward momentum as a true movement.

And today, I am very grateful for that.

Unfortunately, it must be said that the corrosive effects of ex-gay ideology and the Gospel According to Conversion Therapy continue to exist in smaller bubbles, and there may be more of them than ever before. It seems all the suds in the bath don't disappear when the biggest bubble pops.

So far I have shared mostly a macro level of the movement. Now I want to share with you some individual stories from when I was out on the road and some specific instances of what the day-to-day looked like.

Of New Age Shaman Priestesses and Gender Complementarity

I was on a plane taking off out of Salt Lake City. It was the size of a pencil, and we were all crammed in like sardines. I was in a mood, and not a good one. So as people got on the plane after me, I buried my head into my drawing and tried to ignore everyone. That's not my usual. I am not the guy to force a conversation on a plane, but I am the guy that kind of person likes because I usually don't mind talking. But not this time. I was in "leave-me-alone" mode.

As we were taking off, I couldn't draw. (A plane moving hundreds of mils per hour + wind resistance makes for a difficult drawing climate inside a pencil-sized aircraft.) As we ascended, the lady next to me, who I found out later described herself as a New Age Shaman High Priestess, threw up her hands and very loudly and enthusiastically sang the chorus of The Beatles' classic *Let It Be*:[4]

There will be an answer; let it be
Let it be, let it be
Let it be, let it be
Yeah, there will be an answer; let it be
Let it be, let it be
Let it be, let it be
Whisper words of wisdom; let it be.

Along with every passenger on that plane, I stared at her in disbelief. She sang this song at the top of her lungs as we climbed for thousands of feet until the plane leveled off its ascent. In hindsight, I think she was nervous about the takeoff. She didn't notice our bemusement or seem to care about the many faces staring at her. I prayed, "Jesus... You are going to make me talk to her, aren't you?" and I don't know for a fact, but I think I heard Him doing the Jesus chuckle, again, in response.

So when the plane leveled off, and I could pull my art supplies back out, I started drawing. Shaman lady started quietly—"quietly" to herself—practicing the speech she would be giving at a convention she was about to attend. It concerned the metaphysical symbolism and mystical beauty of horses. Horses were a topic that was very important to her.

I just kept drawing. If Jesus was going to make me talk to someone, He would have to make them speak to me first.

"Excuse me, excuse me, sir?" Shaman Lady asked." I LOOOOOVE your drawing; the energy behind it is so amazing!"

I thought I heard more chuckling coming out of heaven.

---

4 The Beatles. (1970). Let it be [song]. On Let It Be. Apple Records No copyright infringement intended.

And that began a conversation that eventually turned to her asking me if I was an artist for a living. I said no. She followed up with, "Well, what do you do?" So, I told her I worked for Exodus International and gave a brief description of what we were about concerning homosexuality. She scrunched up her High Priestess face and said, "You do know... Don't you? That gender is nothing but a social construct?"

I went from being slightly annoyed to Insta-Super-Ex-Gay, and a genuine excitement came over me for the topic in a heartbeat. Then it was my turn to "witness" the beauty of God-created gender complementarity. I was well-practiced with my talking points, so I was very passionate about the whole thing.

Then I noticed that everyone on the pencil-sized plane around us was now looking at me. The in-flight entertainment for the day was a lousy karaoke version of a Beatles song and a bigoted, too-loud-for-any-public-space sermon on gender. The now-chatty Randy and his new Shaman High Priestess friend talked the rest of the flight, which I am sure no one appreciated but us. I gave her the drawing I was working on at the end of the flight and wrote on the back, "Read the Gospel of John Chapter 1." She said my drawing would make a fine addition to her home altar.

I am still not sure what that means.

Of course, all these years later, I know that all feminine and masculine attributes can be seen in all genders and are not limited to heteronormative/binary couples. Our patriarchal, gendered cultural constructs do not define these fantastic attributes worshiped in ex-gay/conversion ministry circles. These traits are a transcendent part of who we are as humans. These transcendent traits are not only for earthly purposes but to point to a beautiful, mysterious, and glorious God who created us individually and in relationship with one another to reflect the Divine to the world and beyond.

It's beautiful enough to make a New Age Shaman High Priestess and a recovering former ex-gay leader cry. While the rest of the plane rolled their eyes.

Don't Drop the F* Bomb in a Church Van

Back in the fall of 2009, I spoke at an Exodus Latino America Conference. It was a very well-attended conference, and I met many fun people. The only tension was when we were going over the border into Mexicali. The border patrol stopped the man driving me and decided to call me awful names in Spanish. My driver said, "Did you understand that?"

I said, "Enough to know that he didn't have a high opinion of me."

And the driver shook his head and said, "No, he didn't. I think he was trying to relate to me by insulting you."

A US Border Patrol agent insults a US citizen to score points with Mexicali locals? Okay…

Other than that weird encounter, the people in Mexicali and all my friends from Latin America were warm and welcoming.

The interesting thing, though, is that Mexicali is in the desert. It felt like a furnace blast the whole week. Driving into Mexico was not tricky, but driving out, crossing the border back into the States, was a two-hour snail's pace in hell type of an adventure.

Let me explain.

Street vendors were *everywhere*, selling just about everything from concrete gargoyles to temporary tattoos. One lady was walking up and down the line of cars with old issues of *Playboy* and *Hustler* lined up on one arm, and, I am not kidding, about a thousand plastic rosaries were hanging off the other arm.

She was a one-stop-shop for sin AND confession. Now that, my friends, is clever marketing!

Anyway, vendors kept knocking on all the van's windows and getting our attention. Some were quite persistent. Our host told us not to make eye contact and ignore them. However, a vendor started pounding on the driver's window at one point. We tried to ignore him, but the guy was getting louder and saying that we were in danger.

Finally, the driver listened through the glass, then rolled down the window and looked back at the ground. His eyes got big. Then, he thanked the man, looked back at us, and said, "I have some bad news and some worse news."

Did I mention yet that we had been smelling gas fumes for a while? Finally, the driver said, "The gas cap is cracked and leaking, and we have left a trail of gas."

I said, "Ohhhhh…." as I imagined the van blowing up while all the passengers looked back and saw the little river of perpetually flowing gas evaporating in the 110ish degree weather.

Then the driver said, "And the worse news is we have to turn off the air conditioner to put less stress on the gas and see if we can stop it from overflowing."

I had visions running through my mind of being blown up in a tan van with a Holy Spirit dove on the side amid 110 degrees of desert heat, so I said the same thing Ralphie from *A Christmas Story* said: "FUUUUUUUUUUDDDDDDDDDDGGGGGEEEEEEE!"

Except it wasn't the actual word "fudge." You know I said "fuucccck!" right? Just to be clear.

One younger guy in the van smiled broadly after hearing my dramatic and drawn-out F* bomb. However, another, more pious co-passenger was not amused. She said, looking straight at me, "Sometimes, after a fantastic conference where the Lord is glorified, Satan tries to steal our joy!"

Of course, I didn't respond except with a little voice in my head: "Yeah, pious lady, well, you are right because it is about to get hotter than hell in here. And if anyone behind us decides to drop a cigarette, we are about to find out what it's like to burn in the fiery lake next to the porn and rosaries lady!"

I am not proud of dropping the F* bomb in a church van. It's not something I intend to keep doing. But oddly, it just seems like the exact right word to manifest during visions of explosions or being trapped in a mobile inferno for two hours.

With the air conditioning off, the gas stopped bubbling over, but I was afraid we would have heat stroke. I thought about walking the rest of the way, but we were told not to get out of the van. (You know, cartels were upping the game on kidnappings at the time.)

The heat was awful.

Of course, we survived. No explosions or exorcisms were needed. We even ended up laughing a lot (gas fumes?), and the pious lady, surprisingly, turned out to be a lot of fun. We drank a LOT of bottled water and Diet Coke. Eventually, we got over the border fine and drove directly to a Pep Boys a few blocks away to get a temporary fix. Ultimately, we made it back to San Diego without much bother.

When Was the Last Time You Passed Out on Top of a Bus?

They were Fresno Grannies. I am sure they have probably been friends since grade school. They had that vibe. One dressed in earth tones with salt and pepper hair pulled up into a loose bun. Her friend looked like

Mrs. Claus (you know, Santa's wife) but in all blue and white. Her mini-malist color scheme matched her eyes and hair, respectively. She was very prim and put together. She also had her hair up in a tight bun. Earth-Tone Grandma was talkative while Mrs. Claus had left the North Pole perma-frost and instead adopted a perma-grin. She never stopped smiling the same smile. Mrs. Claus was cute, and though a perma-grin can tend to be unnerving, Mrs. Claus' wasn't.

We were at a Love Won Out conference put together by Exodus International and Focus on the Family. Yet another controversial con-ference presenting stigmatized views concerning homosexuality and Christianity from an ex-gay/conversion ministry perspective that we honestly thought was "loving." I was there as an employee. I went to over 30 of these events over the years, and all kinds of folks attended them. As such, to see a pair of older women walk through the doors was not uncommon. It was also not unusual for people to ask me questions; my name tag let them know I worked with the conference.

When this pair walked up to me, Earth-Tone Grandma looked up with squinted eyes, a shaky, elderly voice, and a pointy, arthritic finger. "Are you *that* Randy?"

I answered, "Yes, ma'am," while wondering why she emphasized the word "that."

Her eyes opened a little further; the pointy finger became a soft-ened hand resting on her opposite shoulder. "The Randy who wrote a few chapters in Roger Tompkins' book about God's grace and the homosexuals?"

Not exactly sure where this was going, I answered again, "Yes, ma'am."

Her bright brown eyes were Earth-Tone Grandma's most fantastic attribute. They were wide now, not squinty, and she said with a bit of excitement in her shaky voice, "You're the Randy who went to Daytona Beach on your senior vacation, got high, and passed out on top of a bus?"

As she spoke, her friend (Mrs. Perma-Grin Claus) didn't bat an eye, and her grin never faltered. As her eyes locked on me, I nearly peed my pants. I've never been asked a question like that before at 7:45 in the morning by a grandmother.

I did write about that wild Daytona experience for Roger's first book (which was ripped off the shelves by his publisher when we closed Exo-dus), but that was the last thing I expected to come out of Earth-Tone Grandma's mouth. After catching my breath, I looked from one to the other and said, "Uh… Yes, um… yeah. That was me."

Earth-Tone Grandma's eyes lit up with joy. She threw both arms out wide and with the biggest, most heartwarming smile, cried, "Oh my goodness!! WE ARE KINDRED SPIRITS!" And while she was hugging the life out of me, as all good grandmothers know how to do, I looked at Mrs. Perma-Grin Claus standing to the side, and her perma-grin was a full-on delighted smile.

Earth-Tone Grandma smelled like toast. I didn't have a choice but to notice the toasty aroma of her embrace. I enjoyed Earth-Tone Grandma's exuberant, happiness-filled hugs and exclamations of "I am so happy to meet you!"

I was amused and said, "Well, I am glad to know that we are kindred spirits, and thanks for the encouragement!" At the same time, I was dying to ask the question of my newly declared kindred spirit, "Soooo... When was the last time you got high and passed out on top of a bus?"

I didn't ask, but I should have.

I'm the Bad Cop and Fire-Putter-Outer and Poster Boy

I used to half-way joke (because it was true, in my opinion) that regardless of whatever my title was, my job description was to do whatever Roger didn't want to do. Which was pretty much everything negative regarding member agencies, especially the peer-based ministries. Don't get me wrong, he dealt with a lot of the issues head-on, but I was the primary point person for oh-so-many bullshit arguments and situations.

One of the reasons Roger hired me was that we both agreed that Exodus was full of really weird ministries and leaders. We wanted to either bring them along and help them become better ministries or move them along and out of the networks. Of course, some readers may think that *all* Exodus ministries were weird and should have been shut down long ago (which I agree with). I understand that perspective and also know that the reality is that there were many Exodus ministries. Some tried to stay trendy and appear knowledgeable in order to continue selling stigmatized lies and spiritual abuse against LGBTQ+ people as God's truth. Then there were the other Exodus ministries, who were even more ridiculous and promised to "cure" people of homosexuality with hypnosis in three hours. Or there were the whacked-out "ministries" that hosted weekend retreats where the icebreaker was to give your dick a name and take a communal shower with three hot jocks (the leader's description), an ex-gay leader, and two other ex-gays.

Yes, that sounds like the script for a porn movie. It sounded like one back then, and it sounds like one now.

That communal shower was a literal programmatic element in the weekend retreat to help participants with their body shame and desensitize them to the sexualization of males. It would be laughable if it didn't con so many men into setting themselves up for even more sexual incongruence in the name of "change."

When talking with the group leader, I asked about the "naming the penis" thing, and he said every guy does it in high school, and it was a way to disempower the sexualized nature of how the ex-gay men saw penises. Even then, I didn't believe him for a second. Matt's dick will sexually turn on the "ex-gay" dudes whether you name Matt's dick Mr. Floppy Schlongmeister or not. I then asked about the showers, and he said no one was forced to do it. I said, but if they don't, they are missing out on not just a shower but a programmatic element they paid for. Plus, you are making it sound like it is an essential part of them reclaiming their masculinity and healing their homosexuality. That's a LOT of pressure for something that seems contrived and ridiculous to impose as a "programmatic element." He disagreed, and after hearing him talk about how healing it is for him to be a guy among other "hot" guys... I asked, "So... What are you getting out of this?" He was a little surprised by the question. I repeated, "You describe the straight guys who help you with the retreat as 'hot.' Are you using the showers to fulfill some desire within yourself?" Not surprisingly, he got mad.

Are you noticing a pattern of accountability making Exodus leaders "mad?" Even from within their ranks? Yes, that is evidence of a very cultish ideology. From 1976 to 2003, you could count on two hands how many times Exodus held the member agencies accountable for outrageous behavior and claims. That just didn't happen before I joined the staff there. I wasn't very popular with other Exodus leaders for a while because I made it very clear that I wouldn't be a true membership director if I referred people to ridiculous or abusive (even to us) groups.

After I moved to Florida, I learned some hard truths about the dysfunction of the movement as a whole. I had previously only experienced, in person, the group I had been a part of in Texas. While still a product of anti-LGBTQ+ Christianity, there weren't genuinely horrible people involved. After moving to Florida, I learned quickly that the overall movement had all kinds of nasty stuff going on.

While in public, I was doing speaking engagements, working conferences, appearing on billboards, sharing my testimony in the Senate building on Capitol Hill, and lending my image for a full-page ad in *The Los Angeles Times*. But it was a much different story behind the curtain.

- Behind the scenes, I was trying to convince an Exodus ministry leader that yes, indeed, it was against IRS regulations for non-profits to use the ministry newsletter to raise money for her cat's stomach operation.
- Behind the scenes, I called state licensing boards (in three states) to report sexual misconduct allegations against licensed professional counselors.
- Behind the scenes, I was consulting member ministry boards on how to survive press attacks (uncovering truth), board splits, sexually "fallen" leaders, and why using the word "sodomites" in their literature was a bad idea.

In my job, I found myself doing all sorts of things I never anticipated. There was one thing I expected in the job description: flying around the country with the sole purpose of visiting with leaders and trying to convince them to work with Roger and his new staff (us) in making Exodus stronger and healthier.

Even though that was part of my job description, I soon learned that these leaders were only interested in us promoting them and their resources and resented that we would "pry" into their day-to-day operations or programs. They were autonomous organizations, but we had the power to refer to them or not. We were the international beacon that directed people to local efforts. And, as I said, I was not comfortable referring anyone to member agencies when I had no idea what they were doing. The outside leaders may have considered it "prying," but we considered it due diligence. The people who called us for help and support were in pain. Unfortunately, when I did "pry," I was often horrified by what we found.

I wish I'd had the power, knowledge, and will to help shut down Exodus much sooner than we did because, in truth, none of the ministries (including the one I went to) were good or healthy. They were all abusive. I am trying to reveal here that there has always been a vast spectrum of "Exodus member agencies." They were not cookie-cutter in their abuse, and some of them were nightmares to me even when I was a "true believer."

Additionally, the old guard of Exodus would get mad at us for over-reaching our "authority" by imposing accountability. But unfortunately, Exodus leadership, as a whole, was too myopic to consider that the movement was full of incredibly narcissistic hypocrites who called themselves leaders and pastoral counselors without any real merit to their claims. The misguided, well-intentioned leaders who knew nothing about the legalities of running a non-profit also had no real professional credentials or credibility to draw upon either. Yet they could tell a good story and kept getting the proverbial megaphone to perpetuate the wildest forms of denial and confirmation bias.

It was a constant battle of egos, will, and manipulations. Finally, within a couple of years, three to be exact, I presented a summary report to the board of over 70 "fires" (serious to severe) that Roger and I had had to put out. I created that report to make a case for developing standards and guidelines for member ministries to abide by to be a part of our referral network.

Because of all the stress, the horrible revelations of abuse, and the incredible dysfunction—plus all the public scorn and condemnation I felt from the "world" (Christianese for the general public)—my undiagnosed PTSD was triggered 24/7, and I felt shut down and miserable again. I started having regular migraines and episodic bulimia. I was tempted to self-harm by cutting myself (something I briefly did as a teen). So I went to counseling and deliberately picked a secular, non-Christian therapist. I wanted to freely cuss in our sessions and not worry about it bleeding over into work. Dr. Buddha (I eventually found out he was a Buddhist) diagnosed me with PTSD.

You Will Learn to Soar

"God just showed you that?" My therapist asked this with a perfect, incredulous look on his face.

"Yep." Tears were pouring down my face, and I was finding it hard to catch my breath.

"Well, in that case... I was going to wait for a few sessions before going over this with you, but it seems you are ready. Let's talk about 'learned helplessness'..."

More on that in a minute.

What the Divine had shown me in this session was simply stunning and a life-moment. My therapist was helping me deal with my trauma through a technique called EMDR.

> From Wikipedia:[5]
> "The goal of EMDR is to reduce the long-lasting effects of distressing memories by engaging the brain's natural adaptive information processing mechanisms, thereby relieving present symptoms. The therapy uses an eight-phase approach that includes having the patient recall distressing images while receiving several types of bilateral sensory input, such as side-to-side eye movements. EMDR was originally developed to treat adults with PTSD; however, it is also used to treat trauma and PTSD in children and adolescents."

At the time, I initially thought it was secular therapist voodoo, but I was in so much pain I eventually submitted to it with the caveat that I could pray first. Of course, my therapist said that was okay.

After I said a silent prayer for protection and for the Spirit to guide my thoughts, we began the EMDR treatment. I believe my therapist asked me to focus on a specific episode of abuse, lean into it and let it manifest the deep pain it produced. I very quickly got lost in a vision.

I saw myself as a mourning dove (an actual dove species) on the ground in the woods with a horrible shackle around me. It looked like the kind you see in pictures of human slaves. Jesus was standing in front of me, trying to reveal that the restraint wasn't binding me. It was just around me and wasn't designed to constrain me. I falsely believed I was enslaved because I hadn't known life any other way. Plus, through systemic physical and emotional abuse, I wasn't given a choice to see it any differently. I, as this falsely enslaved mourning dove, was filled with absolute fear through every part of my being and soul. It immobilized me.

In the vision, I saw the Divine, in His human incarnation as Jesus, looking at me with compassion, and then He did something amazing. He

---

5 Eye movement desensitization and reprocessing. (2024, April 7). In *Wikipedia*. https://en.wikipedia.org/wiki/Eye_movement_desensitization_and_reprocessing

transformed into a mourning dove Himself and started cooing and poking me to scoot out of the shackle.

In our session, I was on the brink of losing touch with reality. I sobbed and sobbed and sobbed. It's hard to explain, but at this point, I was full of terror and felt like I didn't have a choice but to stay in this "vision." Without prompting from me, my therapist said, "Randy, stay with this, but don't lose the sound of my voice."

As the Jesus dove was prodding me to scoot myself out of the slave shackle, I eventually did. Again, still as the dove, I stood up on shaky dove legs that had never been used. The Jesus dove got a little more animated and spread His wings, encouraging me to do the same. I did. He started walking around, and I followed Him. He started hopping and flapping his wings; I did too. Then He jumped/flew from bush to bush. I was more reluctant to leave the ground but eventually did the same. After doing practice jump flights from several bushes on the last one, He launched out like a dove but transformed into a beautiful majestic eagle. I followed suit and transformed into a beautiful, glorious, FREE eagle.

Then I believe the Divine said, "Now, it is time for you to soar!"

I don't know that I have ever cried that hard.

"Randy… Randy… Randy, come back to the office. Randy, I need you to take a deep breath and acknowledge that you are hearing me. What are you feeling, Randy? What did you experience? Randy…? Randy…"

I told him what had happened, and he genuinely looked astonished. That's when he said what he said at the beginning of this section about "learned helplessness."

That night I just cried the whole night with relief and the feeling of liberation, yet at the same time, in the deep grief of acknowledging that the abuse and hurt had robbed me of my power and taught me learned helplessness, I couldn't have any different options because I wasn't deserving. I grieved that I wasn't fulfilling my God-given purpose and ability because the hurt and abuse had convinced me I was powerless to escape the pain when in fact I could. I embraced the truth that slave shackles can't enslave a dove; others' curses, hurt, and abuse can't enslave me unless I don't know that their lies are not my reality. This learned helplessness was ingrained in me from the very beginning, from my first breath. I was never good enough, smart enough, or handsome enough. I wasn't lovable or even likable.

Others made every decision for me. I adopted their ideas of what was best for me because I didn't know or have the skills to decide for myself.

All lies. From 1968 to 2005, I lived in the false enslavement of learned helplessness. It would take quite a while longer to learn how to stretch my wings and fly independently. It would take till 2013 to see how being "ex-gay" was also a part of that false enslavement and learned helplessness. Even as I write this, I am mindful of how pervasive learned helplessness can be.

However, in 2005, I immediately began to assert myself more as a person and leader. I was no longer comfortable grinning and putting up with bullshit for too long. Maybe I was a bit too aggressive at some points, but I started to recognize and reject patterns of abuse and dysfunction within Exodus that triggered my PTSD. I began to see how the PTSD dynamic was rife throughout the movement.

The earth started shaking under my feet. I was freer than ever, but not truly free.

My journey with PTSD and everything I learned about myself in therapy mirrored my experience in the ex-gay/conversion therapy world. Both addressed the "peripheral issues" often associated with mental health (such as codependency and substance abuse) within a larger construct or system. PTSD has its own method of approach that encapsulates everything a human can experience. The toxic ideology of the ex-gay ministry does exactly the same thing. Both seek to empower the individual to find healing, only one is based on lies and perpetuating systemic abuse, whereas the other is seeking to heal the results of systemic abuse. Guess which is which.

Great healing occurred during my time in the ex-gay world, because I sought therapy *outside* of that world. However, while I was feeling more freedom than ever before, I still had no idea of what true freedom and self-confidence looked like. I forced my healing into the ex-gay mythology of becoming more "not gay." Instead of seeing this healing for the miracle it was, I tried to see it as proof that ex-gay ideology works. For the first time in my life, I started seriously dating a woman. She was gorgeous, fun, intelligent, and a GREAT kisser.

I didn't consciously manipulate the situation, but a part of me loved being able to say I had experienced a degree of change and had this beautiful blonde woman on my arm. Not only that, I was genuinely attracted to and in love with her.

She treated me with respect. We loved laughing and visiting with friends. We never had sex, but we came very close a few times. We both wanted to (honestly) but didn't because we believed you couldn't have sex outside of marriage. So we had some major make-out sessions that were very hot. Very.

I was still gay as a gay goose and had a crush on my gym trainer at the time, but for the first time in my life, I was genuinely bi-curious and not afraid to explore that curiosity. To this day, I know that a small part of me is attracted to confident women. But while I could have a romantic relationship with a woman, it would never be the same as or to the level of having a relationship with a man.

And currently, that man is my now-husband, Dan!

Also, at that point in my life, I traveled, spoke, wrote, did interviews, led staff and volunteers, and flew first class hither and yon to give my testimony. I did keynotes and workshops in everything from small churches in rural communities to Senators and members of Congress on Capitol Hill in DC (in the actual Senate building). My recovery from past abuse and other dysfunctions was progressing and transformative, and I thought that I had arrived at the pinnacle of my "calling." I felt I was going to be in this role for the rest of my life.

As I typed that last paragraph, I realized that was now over 10 years ago, and today, as an out gay man with no one inviting me to Washington, DC anymore, I am freer than I have ever been. I may have felt free then, but I was not truly free. The slave shackle had become ornate because my environment had become much more distracting with the trappings of success and purpose. But it was a false success with an inauthentic meaning, created at the expense of the LGBTQ+ community. Even though I felt more freedom and hope than I had ever felt before in my life, the foundations of what I believed began to crack during my sessions with my therapist.

What started as world-shifting tremors unbalancing me would quickly turn into upending earthquakes that destroyed the Exodus movement and permanently changed what it means to be an LGBTQ+ person of faith. Thankfully.

CHAPTER 8

Scandals You May Know, and a Few You Don't

These episodes in my history at Exodus still give me nightmares, so much so that my hands are shaking as I type this!

Honestly, even though I'm writing this memoir, I don't actually like owning embarrassing stories and terrible mistakes I've made. Nor do I want to expose others (hence changing all names). In fact, during my time at Exodus, I was conditioned to believe that it was my job to protect and "deal with" any scandals as much as possible, keeping them outside public scrutiny.

I now understand that the "core mission" of the organization was the actual bomb-throwing firestarter in and of itself. As a result, we continually dealt with an endless stream of scandals and controversy because the core mission—the literal mission statement of Exodus—was destructive, and we were too blind to see it. The only good thing to say about that is that we did eventually see clearly and shut Exodus down. It also means that I am trained to reflexively deal with scandals by burying them—this is something I work on changing to this day, especially as it relates to exposing truth.

Many people don't understand the level of denial—that cult-like ideology—that being willfully blind requires, and by the end of this chapter, you will probably have even more reason to think there is NO way we couldn't see everything before we actually did. All I can say is that blinders forged and framed by denial are precisely that: blinding. Furthermore, what little you might notice is darkened to the point of not being recognizable—like walking around in a dimly-lit and foggy room without your glasses—making everything appear utterly different from reality.

I share the stories to come in order to clarify and educate, not to throw shade at people, even if they deserve it. I am sure some may feel that I have it in for them. I do not. I share this because people are often shocked at my passion for telling the truth. Conversion therapy undermines church and local communities in its ex-gay form. It is destructive to families, and it can be deadly to individuals. Perhaps more importantly, I have a unique perspective that few have or have access to. I saw it all. Not just the issues that affected the one ministry I led before joining the Exodus staff, but ALL of the issues—both public and private—that all the member agencies underwent. It still breaks my heart to realize all the evidence that Exodus was destructive was everywhere you turned, even in the leadership. Yet we held on to our firm grip of denial and doubled down on confirmation bias instead of allowing for a dose of reality or truth to enter into our sphere. Our grip was further fueled by the tenacious determination of a malignant narcissism unwilling to let go of its projected self. Unwilling, because it felt like we would die if we let go of our false reality, not just physically but eternally. Fear can be a great motivator for denial, in all the ways it shows up.

Another reason I am sharing this is that I know that all of this is probably still happening in the networks and standalone ministries that continued after Exodus shut down. Leaders are still making these same, or similar, shit piles and not being held accountable by their referral hubs or local leadership in any meaningful way.

Three Scandals You Probably Know About

1. All Those Ex-Gays Who "Went Back" or "Fell" to Sin

It seemed that the unspoken process for dealing with defectors was first to figure out if they were repentant or going off to gleefully dive into the deep end. I am talking about John Paulk, John Smid, Yvette Cantu Schneider, and myriads of local ministry leaders and group participants who would "go back" to being gay or "fall" to sin.[6]

Though the process wasn't official, or officially written down anywhere, for those of us who remained, if the "fallen defector" was repentant, we would work out a plan of accountability and restoration with their ministry board or church oversight committee. If they were running half-naked through a pride parade, we would shake our self-righteous, tone-deaf heads and lament for about five minutes before we collectively—without actually discussing it—decided to "ghost" them forever, because "light cannot mingle with darkness."

What was never spoken publicly, or even privately, was that we had scriptures teach us that someone who returns to sin is vile. Cherry-picked scriptures added that we should not associate ourselves with that person. And since these folks were challenging every fiber in our self-loathing beings, we were quick to say a word or two of sadness, maybe make a statement about how our door was always open, and then wave goodbye quickly before conveniently severing all ties. They were explained away by saying:

- *"They didn't run the race to completion."* (Hebrews 12:1)
- *"They never really did work out all of their issues."* (Book of second opinions, chapter fuck:verse you)
- *"They must have been leading a double life or always were double-minded."* (James 1:8)
- *"They have always been on a 'slippery slope' with the way they acted."* (Galatians 5:7–8)

Now I know that most of those who "went back" to their true selves did so because they actually dealt with their issues. In truth, they didn't "go back." In fact, they actually grew in their spiritual maturity and healing to transcend the homophobia and false paradigms of ex-gay ministry that had trapped them. Of course, those of us who were still trapped didn't understand and couldn't think of their escape as transcendence. We didn't think being a healthy and whole LGBTQ+ person was possible. We were so incredibly wrong.

I was so incredibly wrong.

---

6 While I state that all names in the book have been changed, these were public individuals whose names and stories are easily and readily available, and therefore are left as is.

Gratefully, I am now living that truth and know that being your true self while also being a man of faith is 100% possible.

What's even worse was the countless number of leaders who would tell me they "fell" to masturbation while watching gay porn or had some random hookup or had fallen in lust with a group member but not acted on it. Then, a week later, the same person would ghost someone else for their decision to leave the shackles of the world of ex-gay conversion and embrace who they indeed were. The truth is, in both scenarios, the individual in question was still gay. The difference is one was healthy enough to locate the ex-gay exit door to find their way out of self-loathing and live a healthy LGBTQ+ life, while the other gay person was acting on their God-given relational impulses in shame and darkness while admonishing the one who chose to live in truth.

2. Uganda, Jamaica, and the Truth of What Happened Overseas

Uganda: One weekend, I learned that an Exodus board member named Eric Proctor was speaking at a conference in Uganda. While there, the news broke that this "conference" was organized by Ugandans who wanted to criminalize homosexuality and had some horrible guest speakers like antisemite Mr. Fascist. To make matters worse, some of the penalties proposed by the conference would include death.

We were immediately called to respond and explain why we would send a board member to such a hateful event. People had a hard time believing we didn't know he was over there. The truth is, we did not know he went there and did not pay for his expenses. In other words, he wasn't there as an official representative of Exodus. In fact, board members were never required to tell us where they were going when it involved conferences or situations that might implicate Exodus. Nor were the member agencies required to inform us of their speaking engagements or activities. These people weren't attending various events as representatives of Exodus, yet they fully expected us to hold the shit bag when it was on fire.

So when Uganda happened, we at the Exodus office were utterly clueless until after the controversy started.

To make matters worse, we couldn't get in touch with Eric for the longest time during and after the Ugandan conference. Once we did, he refused to say anything in-depth publicly. We were practically begging him to state that he hadn't vetted the conference organizers, that he went there on his own accord, and to roundly condemn efforts to criminalize LGBTQ+ people.

Unfortunately, he seemed perfectly willing to allow us to be thrown under the gay blogger bus, stating that he didn't want to "add fuel to the fire." He didn't want to risk his employers, the Johansens (incredibly wealthy couple), and their Johansen Foundation being dragged into the controversy. His attitude made me so mad. Add on the snarky pressure from activists, blogs, and media outlets, and it all became too much for me, personally. As a result, I advised Roger not to respond because I felt like the activists weren't interested in the truth, and it was Eric who needed to make an apology and explain himself (even if he didn't want to), not Exodus.

At the time, I made some bizarre public statements on which I look back and think, *Man, that does NOT make sense.* It only made matters worse. We eventually drafted an open letter to Ugandan President Yoweri Museveni on November 16, 2009. Then, *finally*, we presented him with an open statement signed by 51 various Exodus leaders and board members (including Eric) in 2010. In a nutshell we called on President Museveni to not sign into law the criminalization of homosexuality in Uganda. Eric never went to bat for himself or us in that situation on his own and eventually, reluctantly, gave in when we called on the leaders to sign the statements. Unfortunately, our statements came after the anti-homosexuality bill passed. Our response was too little too late. Ultimately, the statements we eventually made about Uganda appeared self-serving, because they were. From our perspective, we still condemned homosexuality as a sin, but felt that gay Ugandans needed help from organizations like ours, not prison.

Looking back, I am not sure how much of a better option help from Exodus-like efforts would have been, as both are a form of punishment.

I deeply regret the public statements I made at the time. We didn't meet the expectations we set (like going to visit the Ugandan leaders) and did not meet the basic expectations we should have met (quick, decisive response condemning the conference and the efforts to criminalize gay people). I apologize for advising that we shouldn't respond simply because I wanted Eric to. I naively thought he would want to protect Exodus and take ownership of his colossal mistake. He didn't. It didn't help that my anger with certain gay activists and bloggers over the whole thing made me dig my heels in even deeper. I should never have done that. Again, that is one of the many regrets I have of my time in that world.

We were our own worst enemies, yet again, and didn't want to admit it.

Jamaica: Not long after Uganda, a different board member and, at the time, board vice-chair, Dante Harrigan, went to Jamaica (which we understood to be a very homophobic nation) where he made what we considered to be several awful comments. He condemned President Obama for threatening sanctions against Jamaica because of their laws criminalizing homosexuality. He also publicly supported the developmental view of homosexuality, saying "if fathers did their job," it would prevent their offspring from developing same-sex attraction.

Once again, it wasn't anything he ran by us before going. However, having learned our lesson from the Uganda incident, we responded very quickly this time. Harrigan felt his words were misconstrued to support criminalizing homosexuality but admitted it was an error to say what he said. The worst part was that his words could be used, just like in Uganda with Eric, as an argument promoting and supporting the criminalization of homosexuality. However, what was different this time was that Dante was willing to talk with and work with us when the shit hit the fan. We quickly drew up an official policy against the criminalization of homosexuality and published it with a press release. We also accepted Dante's resignation from the board. In my opinion, though we could have responded even quicker about Jamaica, it was lightyears faster than the Ugandan situation.

Where some of our most ardent critics got it wrong was in willfully believing this was an organized effort from our office to evangelize the world with ex-gay ideology whenever and wherever the opportunities presented themselves. It was not. Instead, it was evidence of the poor communication and accountability between our office, board members, and ministry leaders, as well as proof of the destructive policies occurring around the world against the gay community.

What many people may not realize is that there were many different "Exodus" organizations around the world. Exodus International (our office, which I refer to throughout this book as simply "Exodus") was known for most of its life as Exodus International North America. The previous Exodus director, Bob Davies, led the effort to create the Exodus Global Alliance (EGA), which was based out of Toronto and is still a Canadian non-profit. After EGA was formed, they did their own thing by communicating with other regions around the world that also called themselves Exodus, such as: Exodus Asia, Exodus South America, etc. The Exodus Global Alliance became the hub for most of the world's "Exodus" regions.

However, we barely had any relationship with any of them, and our office rarely shared what we thought the other regions should do or say, as we believed them to be autonomous. Interestingly, the Exodus Global Alliance tried, at one time, to claim they had spiritual and structural authority over our office. That did not go over well, as they had neither. To say our relationship with EGA was strained is an understatement.

The bottom line is that I don't think we were as monolithic or organized as people thought.

3. The "Pray Away the Gay" iOS App

As part of our plan for outreach, and back when Apple's platform was going full steam ahead with their app store, we decided to develop an app. We paid too much money for it (several thousand dollars), and it was wonky and ugly. I think its only function was to pull in content from the Exodus blog and the monthly newsletter, and we were going to use it for announcements.

One staff member said, "You know they are just going to yank it from the app store eventually."

I responded, "Well if they do, it will get us some media coverage, so it's a win-win!" But, of course, I was only (kind of) teasing.

When the activists and the media caught wind of it, they said, "Want to Pray Away the Gay? There's an app for that!" It caught fire. All around the world, the news outlets mocked the app, and it didn't take long for Apple to pull the app from their store. While the activists were crowing, I smiled at ALL the support flooding in. I wouldn't say we planned on creating the app for that reason, as we wanted it to be a resource for people to stay in the loop with announcements and what we were writing about. But Apple pulling the plug on that ugly, wonky thing didn't bother me because it provided a rallying point for our supporters and ministry leaders.

The world was having a field day scoffing at the app and didn't realize that once again, they weren't undermining the movement but strengthening its resolve. They laughed at us, but our base knew that what they were saying was not the real intent of the app. The news outlets were using this situation as an opportunity for clickbait and to entertain the ones who were already angry. If they had gotten past the sloganeering and sought an accurate analysis of its content, they could have been much more effective at undermining Exodus' toxic ideology. Instead, they did little more than mock us while our supporters sent a flood of encouragement.

And as all good "Christian" religious activists know, being able to claim persecution is a great rallying cry. It wasn't persecution, of course, and I am pleased Apple pulled the app quickly, but this is another situation where I believe gay activists declared a victory but didn't actually accomplish much. Because it was perceived as persecution, it did nothing to dampen the momentum within the ex-gay movement.

Four Scandals You Don't Know About

1. Conference Shenanigans

The annual Exodus International conference used to bring in around 800 to 1000 people. Each year, it was my responsibility to help escort people off campus who broke the "don't fuck your dorm roommate" clause in the behavioral expectations sheet we made everyone sign. (There were quite a few of those over the years.) It was also my responsibility to deal with any conflicts that came up. I was there when gay protestors threatened to break into the conference through the rear of the property. When one conference attendee was physically threatening our assistant, I was there. When a known gay activist snuck into the conference on the sly, I drove him off campus in a golf cart. If there was controversy during the conferences, I was usually in charge of handling it.

That didn't sound right. Eh, whatever.

I was basically the ExoPolice for conferences, except for my first conference as a staff member in 2002. That first conference was where I learned that the fellow staff member I was sharing a room with had confessed to our boss that he had been with his boyfriend the week before. When I heard that, I remembered the guy who had dropped him off at the airport—it was his boyfriend. Needless to say, he didn't come back to work at Exodus, and the last I heard, he is in a gay throuple.

I also heard rumors (though I was clueless at the time) that quite a few of the young men on campus organized a game of naked musical chairs. I can't say that happened for a fact, but the rumor has been around a long time and, quite frankly, it wouldn't surprise me.

2. Why Is Sam in His Underwear, Passed Out in a Dorm Hallway, Laying in His Own Vomit?

Sam was an Exodus regional rep until we found him passed out from drinking one and a half bottles of gin mixed with prescription pills. We know this because the half-drunk second bottle of gin was still in his hand as he was laying semi-naked on the floor about twenty feet from his dorm room. The door to his room was open, and he had completely wrecked it.

As it dawned on me that it was Sam on the floor, I ran to the group of leaders, shocked and angry that they were just standing around guffawing. Zack was the only one trying to help Sam off the floor. I yelled to the others, "Go get a blanket or something to cover him up!" Zack checked to make sure Sam was breathing and not in danger of choking.

We had been on campus all day. We found him not long after the afternoon meetings had concluded. When other leaders found the prescription pills, I told someone to call 911. There was a slight pushback from one leader, and I said, "We can't take the chance. We don't know how many of those pills he took with the gin." They immediately agreed and called 911. As the ambulance drove off, I remember thinking what an asshole Sam had been at the meetings earlier and wondering if that was a cry for help. As he was carried away by the ambulance, I stayed behind, but a couple of leaders followed to check on him at the hospital.

Thankfully, Sam was alright. But I never heard from him again—no explanation, nothing. I tried contacting him a couple of weeks after the event to give him time to regroup, but he wouldn't return my calls or emails. I had to write a letter to his board about his removal as a regional rep and to see if they wanted to continue as a referral agency. They were friendly, but with Sam going through whatever he was going through, we agreed that the ministry he ran would also need to be dropped from the Exodus roster.

Unfortunately, Sam was not an anomaly at many of these conferences. I often saw leaders drink to excess in a way that seemed unhealthy and, in fact, harmful. Keep in mind that this was Christian-based ministry work, and that kind of behavior was incredibly frowned upon by most and delivered consequences to some.

That specific leadership conference was very contentious. It occurred before our regular annual conference in 2004, and coincided with my appearance in a full-page ad in the *Los Angeles Times* that same week. I always disliked the leadership conferences because of how often they developed into confrontational events. But that specific conference was especially contentious because we were discussing the crafting of "member ministry guidelines" for the first time in Exodus' history. These guidelines were intended to help with accountability and communication. We naively believed they would strengthen both the ministries and Exodus itself. We wanted to do the guidelines because on our team, we had determined that the networks weren't cohesive or consistent, and we thought the guidelines would give a baseline summary of what each ministry was agreeing to if they wanted to be a part of the Exodus referral network. That idea was shot down in flames, which resulted in my presenting a summary of "fires" to our board after the conference was over. I included dozens upon dozens of examples like the one with Sam, and the board saw fit to approve drafting the guidelines immediately after I shared with them. The silver lining of this situation was that it triggered my PTSD so badly that it prompted me to get professional counseling, which ultimately led to my healing and ability to change my life's path to one of truth.

3. "Inappropriate Touch"—What Exactly Does That Mean?

Over the years, many leaders in the Exodus networks would tell me, or announce in their newsletters, that they had to take a sabbatical or step down altogether from their roles because they "fell" with group partici-pants, other leaders, and/or someone anonymous, etc. The sexual "fall" was usually explained as an "inappropriate touch."

That always aggravated the snot out of me. What the actual fuck did that mean? I thought we were being "transparent," yet this language made it sound like they had accidentally poked someone in the eye with their pinkie. Of course, the confession was always accompanied by tears and stories of being lonely and vulnerable. But the transparency was obviously, and purposefully, blurred. The apology always came across as acceptable, but not real or meaningful—one where the leader would face the consequences of their actions. Where group participants were always held feet to the fire when it came to accountability, leaders somehow got a pass on being "transparent" about their sins. Even the ones calling for complete transparency, to this day, didn't apply the same rules to themselves.

It made me angry. No, hon, you weren't "lonely and vulnerable." You are gay and horny. And someone flipped your trigger, so you abused your power (if you slept with a client or group member) and were (are?) a hypocrite.

In most cases, this translated to full-on oral or full-body bumping uglies in all the usual ways of, you know, the gay kind. However, the description was often toned down to not "embarrass" or "shame" the leader who "fell" or to tempt those of us they were confessing to with impure thoughts. By whitewashing or glossing over the truth of what happened, it was easier for them/us to deny what their "fall" represented: the fact that no one has changed or ever will change sexualities. Gay conversion therapy did not—does not—work. The leaders' "fall" was proof that you cannot escape your natural state of relational being by bottling it up with highly consequential behavioral modification without it leading to excessive and risky behavior once the dam bursts.

In another case, remember the board member who was teaching at my ex-gay group the first night I was there? Much later, she confessed to having sex, (I mean, "inappropriate touch") with a female small group leader and needed a break from the ministry.

Finally, just as I was coming on board at Exodus, another director in the Pacific Northwest also stepped down for, you guessed it, "inappropriate touch." There were so many situations like this, but the following was the most egregious, in my opinion, which is something only a handful of us know.

4. The Time Yvette Was Right About Mrs. Kilt, and We Didn't Believe Her

When Peter Donovan was photographed running away from a gay bar in Washington, DC a couple of years later, he left the wildly (in those circles) successful conference he created that traveled all around the country spreading the Gospel According to Conversion therapy, which left the organization in a position to have to juggle a few of the staff positions. His second-in-command was promoted to his job, and then he hired an incredibly popular female speaker to replace him as the new second-in-command.

She was a hit on the speaking circuit. People laughed and cried, riveted by her story of "change" and "freedom." She always drew a great amount of engagement and applause, especially when she shared her story about the time she met a red-headed man in a kilt and how that got her flustered (touted as evidence of "change"). She would usually say at the end of that story that she is still waiting on that redhead in a kilt to propose marriage. Which always got a laugh and sometimes applause.

But one time, my soul-sistah, Yvette Cantu Schneider (name used with permission), told me while we were watching the future Mrs. Kilt speak, "Watch, she'll cry on cue... and there she goes." And right then, this dazzling speaker cried on cue. At first, I thought Yvette was just being snippy and unfair, but now I know she had good reason to be suspicious. After that, I could no longer not see how perfect the timing of her crying was when she spoke the same message over and over. Plus, if anyone is going to pick up on a pattern, it's Yvette. I love that about her.

Later, when Yvette was the women's ministry leader, she contacted me and said the future Mrs. Kilt was sleeping with a member of the group she, Mrs. Kilt, used to lead. Yvette learned that it had started before she joined as a speaker at this conference and continued over the years, all while she was on stage, dazzling crowds with her story of "change."

Roger and I didn't believe Yvette at first. We were even a bit rude to her in our protestations and defense of Mrs. Kilt. Yvette had copies of the emails from Mrs. Kilt's former group member and she had permission to share them with us, but we couldn't accept them when she forwarded them to us. However, eventually, out of deference to Yvette, we decided that we would have a meeting with Mrs. Kilt about the allegations.

Instead of being defensive or in denial, Mrs. Kilt confessed that "it only happened a few times." But it was enough to show that it was an affair over a long period. As a result, she stepped down from her volunteer role at Exodus, stopped speaking on behalf of and at these conferences the next day. Instead, she told everyone she would take her ministry in a new direction solo. We never said anything publicly or within the Exodus networks. Some of the watchdog blogs speculated, but it quickly died out.

This one shook me to my core.

Why this one? After everything I had been through, why did Mrs. Kilt's betrayal actually rock me at a heart level?

Well, for starters, I thought she was beautiful, and she was one of the first friends I had made when I started working at Exodus. We even went on a few dates. I thought I knew her. I trusted her. I had put her on a pedestal as one of the most godly people I knew, and—in some ways, I think—I revered her for the life she had created and was living. She was the shining beacon on the hill, and I thought that she was everything I wanted to be in order to live this life.

Therefore, it was the most shocking because it was the deepest betrayal. It *felt* like the deepest betrayal anyway. I had no idea anyone could live that deep of a double life without someone knowing, without someone figuring it out. But nobody had. I hadn't. I had no idea. And that hurt. It hurt when I found out, and it still hurts a bit today. I'm sad for the loss of friendship, but I think I'm mostly sad for the loss of the piece of myself that I had invested in her—when she was a walking lie. I grieve the person I thought she was, and now I grieve the harm she did and the damage she caused to others as a narcissist wrapped in a beautiful bow.

I was also angry about the abuse of power she displayed, in an almost sociopathic way. She showed no remorse for what she had done to others— the woman who came forward was also a friend of mine, and my heart broke for her. I knew what it was to be abused, I knew what it was to be taken advantage of and to be trapped in an imbalanced situation with someone in power. I knew these things, and now I knew that my friend, a woman I admired and trusted, was a perpetrator of this abuse.

Mrs. Kilt and I had had so many laughs and fun times together as we traveled the country, but after she finally confessed, I remember going to the back parking lot of the Exodus office and weeping. I wept for her, I wept for the group member she took advantage of (and the others I could only guess she may have taken advantage of), and I wept for the loss I felt in that moment. I never saw her again and have no idea what has become of her or what direction her ministry went in. I can only hope that her victims have found healing in some way.

Speaking of Conferences… That Greenroom, Whoa

I loved hanging out in the greenrooms at conferences. There were a lot of fun and inappropriate (for us at the time) jokes. They usually had good food, too. There, I learned the father of reparative therapy (now known as conversion therapy), Joseph Nicolosi, cussed like a sailor and was a bit high maintenance, if "bit" equals extremely and especially when he was upset about something.

We were friends until he started harassing me about dealing with my apparent "unresolved issues" that "manifested" in effeminate mannerisms. Finally, he offered to pay for me to go to the secular "Warrior Weekend." I was offended enough to say no, but instead I said, "I doubt running around naked in the woods, yelling like we think warriors would yell and trying to prove our masculinity will help me project a deeper voice and slow down my talkative hands." Plus, my version of "camping in the woods" is going to a Hilton Garden Inn. So there was no way in hell I was going to ever do Warrior Weekend.

Usually, the greenroom was full of all of us catching up and giving updates on our lives. This is where I met Anne Heche's mother, Nancy

Heche. Nancy had become a regular speaker on the ex-gay circuit and was very popular with the parents, at her own daughter's expense (in my opinion). At the time, I liked her, but now it disappoints me that she is still a favorite speaker at ex-gay conferences. I never got the whole truth from her about her relationship with Anne, and I am sad we gave Nancy a platform she was still using to bolster ex-gay ministries up until at least a year before Anne's passing.

Another time when we were in the greenroom, I brought the whole room to a screeching halt as it filled with silence. Dr. Z and a few others were somehow on the topic of anal sex. They couldn't wrap their heads around how it can be, and is, pleasurable. They understood the "top" part but not the "bottom" part. One person was inappropriate and made fun of it, but Dr. Z seriously didn't get it as he was an "ever-straight" (never gay, always straight). He wasn't an actual medical doctor, but you would think as a male he could have figured gay sex out. Plus, he was one of the smartest people I have ever known.

Being the helpful person I always tried to be, I asked if they wanted to know why it was pleasurable. The jokester warily nodded his head, and Dr. Z was genuinely curious. That's when I explained that stimulating the prostate can help create a full-body orgasm and is possibly the only way for males to have multiple orgasms.

What followed was the most silent silence I have ever not heard. Everyone was speechless. Eventually, one of the leaders said, "Well, thanks for the education, Randy," as he rolled his eyes and walked out.

We all know that Mr. RollyEyes knew, from personal experience, what I was talking about.

Today, I find it interesting that the Creator would purposefully design that as one way a man can receive pleasure. It's almost as if it was—(gasp)—natural! And, admittedly, I get a good chuckle and smile inside when I remember that story today.

A Rundown of Various "Situations"

I could go on and on about all the scandals that happened, but we would need another entire book just to write them all down. So instead, here's a summary of other things I ran across in my position with Exodus regarding ex-gay leaders:

The Sick Cat Lady: Ms. Meow had a 501(c)(3) and chose to leave the Exodus network, convinced I hated cats. She thought this because I told

Ms. Meow she couldn't use her ministry newsletter to raise money for her cat's surgery. I was trying to tell her that the IRS could fine her or even remove her 501(c)(3) status. Then when I found out she was depositing donations into her personal bank account, I asked her about it and she said there was nothing wrong with that. So before I could remove her from the network, she left.

That Smarmy Bastard: I submitted an affidavit in the case against Chris Austin in Texas. This smarmy bastard and I never got along. He was never a part, or a fan, of Exodus. He always thought I was soft and made fun of the charismatic church I attended. I met him when I led the group in Texas. He started conversion therapy with what he referred to as a "cognitive-behavioral" approach, but was actually aversion therapy. In my opinion, it was akin to a sadist getting off on his power over the group attendees. The abuse included having people "shoot" ammonia sticks up their noses whenever they were "tempted" to imagine gay sex or masturbate (his group was only for men). He was also a big fan of having attendees wear a rubber band around the wrist and pop it any time they had a "temptation." He also did other unethical things, like having the men form a circle in their underwear (I heard reports that some would get completely naked) while he taught and facilitated "group activities."

I never referred people to him. I never wanted anything to do with him, and then I started hearing reports that he was sexually assaulting his clients during their one-on-one sessions. A young man who was one of his clients reached out to me and another leader about the allegations. When the state of Texas brought charges against Chris Austin, I was asked to submit an affidavit explaining my role in the young man's experience. I had already reported him to the state licensing board with other accusations before he was caught, so I gladly submitted the affidavit. Austin was found guilty and had his license to counsel revoked, and I think they put him on probation for a long time. Thankfully, he no longer leads a conversion therapy group that I know of.

Speaking of predatory counselors: During my time at Exodus, I also reported several other Exodus referral counselors to their state boards in Texas, Louisiana, and one in Tennessee, who thought naked massage was a form of talk therapy. Even I knew that being a "doctor" of psychology did not equate to being a professional naked oil massage therapist.

There was also a report of a licensed professional counselor in Louisiana, who we will call Fannie, "dating" one of her clients. Her excuse was that she was mentoring the former client for a more personal and valuable experience. Well, Fannie initiated changing their dynamic from professional counselor and client to mentor and protégé because she felt it would free her to help this "client" more broadly and personally. When I talked with Fannie about this, she said it was going great! *"Why, just the other night (the protégé) came over, we went and had a nice dinner, attended an Indigo Girls concert, came back to the house, and (the protégé) let me 'hold' her in my lap, in my recliner, until 2 a.m."* My brain said, "WHAT?" but my mouth was speechless.

"It was a cathartic moment," Fannie added. "It was all perfectly healthy," she implored.

"You do know that was a date, right?" I asked. I also said it was not above reproach for a professional counselor to instigate that kind of power shift with a client. So we also removed Fannie from the Exodus network.

A house divided: Over the years, many member ministries expressed their hatred for one another. There was one such ministry from Oklahoma City that called and demanded I not allow a different ministry from Tulsa to become an Exodus referral. In his demand, he said they were backbiters, liars, and manipulators, and they had caused all kinds of trouble with his ministry, therefore we shouldn't let them into the network. As it turns out, the Tulsa ministry felt the same way about him. The situation was irreconcilable.

That wasn't the only example. There were also ministries from Fort Lauderdale and Miami that hated each other. They couldn't even be in the same room without it turning into a shouting or insult contest.

The "hatred" wasn't limited to ministries, however. There was one time when a board in Tennessee had a falling out and split. Half of the board joined a staff person in accusing the director of using ministry money personally. We flew in and joined the regional rep in taking a look at their accounting, but we couldn't find evidence of the misappropriation of money. That didn't matter, though, as the damage was already done.

Then there was the example of another board in Houston where a long-term ministry leader and volunteer tried to lead a hostile takeover of the ministry and have the director fired. We flew in on that one as well, and it was awful. I later determined it was a waste of time because it was an in-house dispute on which we couldn't weigh in. The volunteer eventually left, started her own thing, and never applied to be an Exodus referral.

Infighting within Exodus was always around. Many Exodus referrals would not refer to other Exodus referrals because of everything from something akin to a blood feud to: "I dunno, he's just weird thinking he can hypnotize the gay out of people in three hours or less." True story.

Conflicts of interest: Exodus regional reps were not supposed to use their position for personal gain while volunteering in their role for Exodus. During my time there, I noticed that one particular regional rep's area never grew. In fact, it lost member agencies. I contacted a large megachurch in that area directly and asked them what happened to their application because they had dropped off the face of the earth. I learned that the rep told them that for them to even apply, they had to hire him to come out and do a weekend conference. This went directly against the agreement to be a rep, and was a bold-faced lie. I assured the megachurch that they could apply at any time. However, because they didn't like the rep, they chose not to apply. I don't blame them, and the rep and I had a very heated discussion as a result.

Another example of conflict of interest was the 501(c)(3) organization's board members, including ours before Roger overhauled the board. These organization boards were all "rubber stamp boards" where the trustees were often family or people who volunteered to do other things within that particular ministry. Some of them behaved like you would expect a board meeting to behave, but most were boards in name only and lucky to have even one meeting a year.

Then, there was the strange and perilous saga of the Exodus Board of Directors. If you were to listen to the old guard of Exodus, they would say, "The Exodus Board was fully elected by member ministries and populated with member ministry leaders. It was supposed to be that way for the serving and equipping of Exodus to its member agencies." That mantra is a bunch of idealized horseshit.

In truth, the board was once fully elected by member ministries. But it was always the same group of people rotating in and out of the board. When there, they benefited, but no one else did. When I was the director at the group I led in Texas, I didn't get a single benefit from the Exodus board except being asked to do some interviews. I never saw board meetings or had any board decisions sent to me that would impact our local group. I wasn't looking for anything other than referrals, so I wasn't disappointed, but it was clear that the original parameters of the Exodus board only reinforced its self-serving nature. The idea that this small group of people was in it for anyone other than themselves, along with the power trip of micromanaging the Exodus staff (literally giving directives straight to the team, not through the director) was absurd. The only thing I consistently saw come out of the board meetings were the group photos of the current board lined up "to serve" us.

Pffft...

I also learned that back then, if you were the loudest voice in the room, you usually got what you wanted, which is not a healthy dynamic for any organization. Before Roger came along, the "membership-driven" board got at least two free vacations annually for one to two weeks each to attend a board meeting. All expenses were paid every time. One would be at a lovely retreat center for the winter meeting, and all costs were covered to have them at the annual conference in the summer. Not surprisingly, they would often come in for the conference much earlier than necessary.

One final thing about the "membership-driven" board: They were clueless about running a "national" organization. They may, or may not, have had local board experience, but it was clear that none of them had experience with having to think through a myriad of issues on a national level with hundreds of member ministries, thousands of leaders in those local ministries, and tens of thousands of group participants around the country.

Their experience leading a group of seven people after church on Sunday was not sufficient in preparing them for being able to speak in an informed way to guide Exodus on a national scene. There was no way they could adequately examine all the issues, and though the board meetings were profitable for some, they were never actually helping Exodus establish credibility or have a national vision for the movement. Moving the Exodus board to directors being appointed took a long time, and they were much shorter meetings with much more effective board oversight and objective accountability and analysis. I believe that is one of the major reasons that helped the board see clearly that Exodus needed to close when it did.

June 19, 2013, the day Exodus closed, was one of the hardest and best days of my life, and it was only made possible by all the hard work we did up to that point.

The Real Reasons Exodus Shut Down

One of the reasons I decided to dust off the rough draft of this memoir and see about getting it published was what manifested after the film *Pray Away* was released on Netflix. It seems like many people were riding the energy of the documentary and started repeating and spinning stories about the demise of Exodus and their roles within Exodus.

Interestingly, some think they were the "key" person to take down Exodus in various ways. For example, someone I love dearly printed on their new book jacket that they "led" the takedown of Exodus. Another was a gay activist who honestly believes the one meeting they set up was the lynchpin that took down Exodus.

Then there are the former colleagues who believe splitting off from Exodus to form the Restored Hope Network irreparably gutted Exodus as an organization. Little do they know we added one to two church memberships for every member ministry defection. So, the number of "member agencies" in Exodus grew when the old guard marched out the door. In fact, we had more than a few churches say they didn't like or didn't trust the peer-based ex-gay groups.

The old guard's departure hurt us, but it wasn't the sole reason Exodus closed—unlike in the '80s and '90s when a large number of ministries defecting would have been sufficient to shutter its doors. But in 2013, the dynamics had changed so much that these groups' departures were not the death-knell for Exodus.

In fact, Exodus could still be around today because the tide was turning toward the church moving more to the forefront of the "pastoral form" of conversion therapy, and Exodus was actually positioned to expand our church network. The parachurch groups (peer-based ministries) were and are disappearing in favor of support groups within local churches. Churches started developing their own groups instead of referring people out. So for every peer-based ministry that left, we added at least one or two more churches to our network. While one may be tempted to rejoice over the decrease in peer-based ministries, consider this: Toxic ex-gay ideology has become the mainstream evangelical response. I would argue that it is more widespread than even Exodus could have dreamed of because the church has become the mask that hides the conversion therapy that has created and uses a false gospel to survive.

Unlike 501(c)(3) groups, church-based conversion therapy is hidden behind freedom of religion, making it less vulnerable to civil suits and government accountability. In-house church programs are replacing parachurch groups, and as they did in the last days of Exodus, they keep growing and growing. The ex-gay movement didn't die with the end of Exodus; it has been hidden under the wings of homophobic churches, denominations, and individual supporters.

Ideally, survivors' stories would be the most compelling reason for shutting down Exodus, but like everything I've already mentioned, they alone weren't enough. However, it was after years of hearing them and then finally seeing them aired on a national TV program, *Our America* with Lisa Ling on the OWN Network, that the weight of the situation became unavoidable. It impacted our hearts in a way that made it impossible to ignore. It became the tipping point and the catalyst for what was to come.

The survivor stories were vital to making us (me) self-examine our "truth" and voice. It took longer than it should have, but eventually, I began to relate more to the survivors than to the old guard I used to idolize. I found myself relating to them on a genuine level. My mind was still at war with itself, but in my heart I knew what the survivors were saying was true. Unfortunately, it took Steven's suicide to bring it all home in a horrible, undeniable moment of reality. The survivors tried to warn me, but I didn't hear them, or didn't want to hear them, until I could no longer deny them.

I am genuinely sorry to the survivors I offended and hurt in those years. Thank you for your courage and for telling us the truth anyway.

The absence of common ground: From 2008 to 2012, the Exodus office withdrew from political activism and eventually reparative therapy.[7] As is mentioned in other parts of this book, Exodus ministries covered a vast spectrum of theological beliefs and cultural approaches. However, political activism and reparative therapy (now known as conversion therapy) were great solidifiers for our base supporters and participants. Who had time to worry about theological differences when we could distract and refocus by fighting the mythological "gay agenda"? The more we got involved with the religious right and culturally-driven Christians, the more support, money, and cohesion we had within the three Exodus networks that existed at the time. In addition, the more we integrated reparative therapy, the more credibility we had (among our own and the religious right).

---

7 Gritz, J. R. (2012, June 20). *Sexual Healing: Evangelicals Update Their Message to Gays.* The Atlantic. https://www.theatlantic.com/national/archive/2012/06/sexual-healing-evangelicals-update-their-message-to-gays/258713/

Therefore, as long as we could keep feeding the machine with these very polarizing topics, we could distract our member ministries from the shifts taking place that were steadily building pressure and keep them from attacking us since we were at the forefront of the culture wars. This approach allowed us to continue to increase our resources, build, and grow. The dark side of this strategy meant that we had to continually conform to the messaging of the super-secret (but not-that-secret) groups in DC that genuinely did not care about our goals and voice. That realization eventually led us to stop pimping out our voices to the religious right.

Then we realized all of these psychologists were the most significant source of open scandals, hidden scandals, and client abuse. They were treating clients like guinea pigs (and sometimes playthings), and they were an absolute mess themselves, so we distanced ourselves from reparative therapy. When we started removing professional counselors who openly professed to be reparative therapists or listed "reparative therapy" as a service they provided, you should have heard all the squealing and hollering coming from the old guard and the ex-gay ministries. (It was *loud*.)

In both situations, we did the right thing. Unfortunately, however, those two arenas were significant, and their absence caused a huge void for many unhappy members of a self-loathing movement. Without a "them" to focus on (distract themselves with?), the leaders in the networks started concentrating on criticizing each other… and the Exodus office staff.

It all blew up when Roger and I (who went to the same church at the time) shifted our theological view of God's grace and its availability to LGBTQ+ people. This theological evolution strengthened us to not return to our crutches of political activism and reparative therapy. It also gave us the space to reconsider our messaging and finally have "ears to hear" what survivors and critics were saying all along.

We were anything but flaming liberals, but you wouldn't know that if you listened to what the old guard was saying at the time. The resulting bullying, public shaming, donor poaching, and intimidation that came from that world was eye-opening, to say the least. It was also one of the ugliest moments I've ever experienced in my Christian life.

No vision or mission: For a couple of years leading up to Exodus' closing, we had considered rebranding, from rewriting the vision and mission statements to even changing the name. As I said, we weren't flaming liberals, but we weren't pawns of the religious right anymore either. We were still trying to implement our new insights, so rallying a movement based on principles and beliefs we weren't sure we agreed with anymore was impossible. However, trying to rebrand and create a new, compelling vision and messaging was beyond our grasp.

Even the donors who still loved us were reluctant to donate because they no longer knew our mission and purpose. It makes sense that if you give to an organization, you would need to be fully on board with what the organization was doing and where it was headed.

The old guard did poach a few large and a lot of regular donors. But it wasn't the loss of donors that closed Exodus' doors, it was the disconnect from our donors and supporters that ultimately caused the organization's demise. The internal struggles and lack of vision manifested in decreased funding and emotional support, which meant the organization began to fail structurally. Having to lay off people (eventually, including me) hurt like hell.

The watchdog blogs: Today, I am grateful for the bloggers' efforts to change the hearts and minds of those considering going to one of our member agencies, confront our wishful thinking and confusing speech with facts, and be a resource to fact-check our messaging and actions. I talked with a few of them about their intent, motivations, and goals for what they were doing, and none said "we" (the Exodus leadership) were their target audience. At the time, it felt like it, but we were not. One even told me they had no hope for us to ever change. This would explain why none of them took any credit for Exodus closing.

One admitted to being overly harsh toward us at the end of Exodus. This admission is why I mention these blogs here. Looking back, I still think they were sometimes indulgently harsh toward us. However, now, it makes more sense. I don't blame them for doing what they did, but it hardened my heart to many legitimate points they made because their anger and snark clouded my ability to truly listen to what they were saying.

I have only had a couple of people over the years say that they knew those blogs would take us down. Of course, they didn't, but they did influence us, even if it was unintended on their part.

It all turned into one massive pile of "shut it down... now." No one person or group can claim to be the only entity who shut down Exodus. Even though I wrote the report that helped Roger make the case for closing down Exodus to the board and was with him in that meeting, I wouldn't even say that I "led" the takedown, though I was in the room for all the years leading up to it.

In my opinion, the only person who can probably say they "led" the takedown would be Roger Tompkins, the President of Exodus when it closed. He tasked me with writing the report, he edited it some and approved it, and he brought it to the board meeting, prompting them to vote unanimously to close Exodus. Roger didn't have to do any of that. Though he had the authority to make, or not make, the case to close it down, he did decide to argue for closing it down, and the board unanimously agreed... and the world is a better place for their courage to do so.

Now I Need a Drink

It is not an exaggeration to say I could write multiple books about all the scandals and unhealthy dynamics that produced them. We were all a product of institutional self-loathing and religious bigotry created by modern evangelical culture vultures. This firmly instilled a mindset that essentially had us believing that the only "right" way to love God and respond to our relational state of being was to turn away from our truth— who we truly were. To buck the system meant turning your back on God and being cursed to live a tortured life of sin that would extend into a tortured eternity. It wasn't as simple as saying that we didn't want to get found out or that we were knowingly living a lie or living a double-life. It was that we had a genuine existential fear of living any other way.

CHAPTER 9

The Earthquakes Came, the Walls Fell, We Are All Bitches Now

That last chapter sucks. It's heavy, and chock full of things over which some might experience upset, anger, or even rage. That's the chapter I have had the worst time trying to write about in a way that conveys the truth of my experiences as *I* remember them. It's also the chapter that tempts the ghost of my self-loathing to say, "There were so many times you were given reasons to leave and you were too stupid to realize you had blinders on." Self-loathing is an asshole, and I am not going to let anyone's hate for me, especially my own, determine my course in life. Moving from self-loathing to true self-awareness and care is what helped me exit Exodus and ex-gay ideology altogether and move into the truth of what it means to be me. I left the lie with a commitment to unflinching honesty, which was the precursor for developing a thriving life.

At this point in my life, this chapter is the hardest to write, reflect on, and think about. Everything I've shared up until now has been processed, thought through, and reclaimed in one way or another. Subsequently, this chapter represents the worst time in my life as an adult and a Christian. Everything I had invested into my life at that point fell apart in a disastrous implosion. While many things had happened before Steven died, his death ripped my blinders off with a fury that still stings sharply all these years later.

Steven, sweet Steven, how you are missed.

I want to start with Steven, even though his death was the final piece of the puzzle that made everything fall apart. He deserves to be honored in that way. There were many things leading up to that day that ensured that my perspective would come tumbling down, but ultimately, Steven's death was like the keystone in a Roman arch—as soon as it was removed, nothing else made sense.

I Love You, Steven, Always

Before brushing my teeth, I checked my email and read some of the worst news a person can receive. Stunned, I wandered out of my room, still in my nightclothes, into the living room and stood there shaking with grief as my eyes filled with tears.

Steven is gone. Our beautiful Steven… gone.

Gone by his own hand.

The punch to my gut lasted all day. The tears came strong, and quickly. The 23 years of memories flooded in, and all I could do was pray and remember.

As mentioned earlier in the book, Steven was my sponsor's sponsor in the 12-step program I had joined to overcome substance abuse. At some point, we became romantically involved, but we quickly determined we were much better as friends than partners. This proved to be true as we had remained friends all those years.

I first learned about unconditional love in our little recovery group, in which Steven was affectionately dubbed "Group Guru." Another person I love dearly, Daphne (who I grieved with on the phone that day), and who I consider my sister, mentioned the unconditional love principle one night in our meeting, and they all showed sincere compassion when I sat there, confused. Unconditional love felt like a brand-new concept for me, and at the time, I doubted it existed.

Steven wiped my tears away later as I received the truth that unconditional love might exist. It was Steven who became the first man with whom I felt safe, even when he looked me straight in the eyes, holding my attention. It was Steven who I called after having my third-step epiphany. Steven and our group tried to speak into my life in those early days and beyond, often saying that I did not have to live in shame or remain shut down.

It was Steven who was the first friend to ever send me flowers. A dozen yellow roses. I love flowers. I love yellow roses.

Of course, 23 years means we had plenty of disagreements, laughter, lots of coffee, more laughter, late-night Denny's, his wedding, singing in worship, praying, debating, laughing, and encouraging. I always believed that if I ever needed him, he would come quickly in whatever way necessary.

I wish I had known what he was going through, because I would have run to him without hesitation.

One night I remember being with him and a few others as we talked about spiritual stuff. He said, "You know, many people think we only exist in the space right behind our eyes and don't inhabit the whole of our being. Furthermore, they believe they are human beings having a spiritual experience, but I believe we are spiritual beings having a human experience."

That always stuck with me, and I believe the Divine used that simple truth to bring me home to Him eventually.

And now our beautiful Steven has gone home to Him, face to face. Our Heavenly Father is now lovingly holding Steven's gaze, wiping his tears away without fear or condemnation.

I love you, Steven, always.

What I Learned About the Why of Steven's Death

I wrote the above numb with pain and in shock. At the time, I remember being afraid to ask Daphne if she thought that Steven's suicide had anything to do with his struggle with faith and sexuality. But I eventually did, and she said that, in all honesty, she believed that many things contributed to his decision but that they included his struggle to "pray away the gay."

After hearing her say that, it would take months for me to feel my heart again. Even today, it feels like there is a black scar where the knife killing my delusion plunged. Steven's suicide drove home the fact that the fruit of stigmatizing religion and ex-gay/conversion ministry is not the life-giving "Fruit of the Spirit." Instead, the fruit of religion that teaches LGBTQ+ people to hate and deny themselves often results in bitterness, destruction of personal self-worth, destruction of relationships, and sometimes even death. It is the poisoned apple.

Steven's death was the final blow to my falsely constructed world. From that point forward, there was no foundation left to fortify. The earthquakes in my soul wouldn't allow that false foundation ever to be rebuilt again.

However, leading up to this, there were quite a few WTF epiphanies that chipped away at my inauthentic reality. Thankfully.

The Love Won Out That Shall Not Be Named

"Oh my God, get him off the counter!" We were in Detroit, and one of the main speakers at the Love Won Out (LWO) conference in that city was drunk as a skunk, saying hilariously crass things, leaning back, and flinging his legs up in the air.

We were in a fancy hotel, by the reception counter, and a person on the Love Won Out team was drunk prank-calling guests on the lobby phone. It was so late that I didn't see any hotel staff around trying to quell the mayhem.

I was a little buzzed, but I still couldn't believe the shenanigans I was seeing. A new friend found his way to sit down beside me. "Randy, does dry humping other guys make you gay?" This is what this new friend and Focus on the Family staff member (who was also new to our crew) asked me after he'd had more than a few drinks.

"Wait, are you telling me that you—YOU?—dry humped another guy?"

"Yes, it was a group thing my unit (military) did with recruits after getting us drunk."

"Was it consensual?"

"Yes."

"Did you like it?"

"It was funny."

"Did you orgasm? Is this something you want to repeat or explore more?"

Silence.

I said to him, "Man, I am not hitting on you, but if this is something you have continued and would pursue, you probably struggle with same-sex attractions (ex-gay speak for gay)."

"Randy, I am just telling you this because I am drunk. Don't tell anyone about this part from my past. I honestly have no desire to do that again, but I don't want to be a hypocrite in helping out this conference with unconfessed sin."

I told him not to worry about it. It sounded like some stupid hazing thing, and as long as it was consensual, and he didn't have the desire to want to repeat it or pursue a romantic relationship with another man, then I chalked it up to drunken curiosity.

This type of thing happens to me all the time. For some reason, straight or closeted men feel comfortable sharing their bi-curious escapades with me, which even occurred with some religious leaders and staff of religious leaders.

At this particular LWO conference, however, I learned much more than I expected. Several of the key speakers got trashed. I mean really trashed. It didn't happen at the other 30+ LWO meetings, but that night I saw two of my idols turn into crass "mean gays." For some reason, one of them couldn't keep his hands to himself at dinner. Though everyone else said that his hands weren't down someone else's pants, I was across the table and saw what I saw—and I saw one man shoving his hands into another protesting man's pants. At the time, I was so afraid of what I saw that I explained it away by telling myself that this was just two men taunting each other like they always do, and it got out of hand. (The old "boys will be boys" mentality—which attempts to excuse a lot of truly awful behavior in the world.) With tears in my eyes, I told one of them the following week that I had never envisioned him as a mean bar queen before, and now I couldn't forget seeing him act like that. At the time, seeing this "humble man of God" that I had admired acting like a fool was devastating.

Today, however, I am more likely to laugh (if it's consensual). While I don't recommend abusing substances or repressing yourself so severely that you go crazy when given a chance, I now look back on that night and wish the authentic people who lived behind those friendly Christian smiles on stage had true freedom to be themselves in all their gay glory. I wish their genuine and honest selves would smile with peace and contentment and not push down and hide anymore, and that they could be themselves as the belly-laughing, tears streaming down their faces, drunk and smiling guys they were.

That night in Detroit was unforgettable because I saw a side of several of my ex-gay heroes I had never seen before. But, I knew there were measures of truth in the revelation. Most of the other leaders got away as soon as possible and never mentioned it again. But I stayed for the whole show. I knew I was seeing them unfiltered, and I loved them more for it. Something in me knew they weren't "acting out." In spite of the wildly inappropriate behavior, what I saw were their true selves trying to come up for air now that alcohol had removed their inhibitions. I saw parts of their authentic selves that surprised and scared me at the same time. I also saw the pain of what living in the stained-glass closet cost us, all of us. At that point, though, I had no idea what to do with these revelations, so I simply noted them in my mind.

All Shits and Giggles Until You Don't Toe the Line

In 2011, I got a call from a ministry leader asking me when I would come out publicly to either align with Roger Tompkins' heresy or denounce him. The caller and other network ministry leaders were distraught, with Roger having publicly said several times that 99% of people in ex-gay ministries had not "changed" at all. He also said that gay people could be saved and go to heaven.

I didn't make the ministry leader on the other end of the phone happy when I said that I was still working through what I believed, and regardless of whether I agreed with Roger, I would never publicly attack him, since I considered him to be a long-time friend. Even if I profoundly disagreed with him (and we do profoundly disagree on many things now), that would never happen. Friends don't do that to friends. At least, I don't.

From that moment forward, I was never friends with that leader again, which is a good thing.

For a few years up to that point, those who were Exodus spokespeople and representatives chose to be more honest with our messaging and personal stories. We wanted to be truthful about what people could expect when going to an Exodus referral ministry and what we believed theologically regarding "once saved, always saved" when it comes to God's grace and "the homosexual."

The old guard of Exodus would not have it. Roger got hammered by their constant griping, whining, and backstabbing. It happened to me as well but not to the degree it occurred to him. They were doing it daily, every day, for several years. It was excruciating being screamed at by people we had loved, served, protected, promoted, and worked with in various ways for two decades. It was like they instantly turned from being trusted friends and confidants to manipulative, vengeful, and malicious enemies.

Finally, when they couldn't bully Roger and the Exodus Board of Directors into firing Roger and hiring one of their approved leaders, they started the Restored Hope Network with the blessing of the "founding fathers and mothers" of Exodus who were still a part of the movement.

I wasn't the only one getting calls from leaders demanding we publicly separate from Roger and Exodus. Some took it upon themselves to call through the Exodus networks (member ministry, the church, and professional counselors), demanding that these member agencies leave Exodus and publicly denounce Roger Tompkins. They also started calling large donors to Exodus and saying all kinds of lies to scare them into thinking we were heretical and leading people off a cliff and straight into hell.

Some of them said I was throwing ministries out of the network left and right for not believing what I thought they should. Not true. They willfully left because they had determined they couldn't align with our statements, vision, and beliefs or be held accountable for how they implemented those beliefs. I kicked some ministries out when I first got to Exodus, but not during its implosion. I didn't have to, and I was glad to see them go.

So This Is What the Underside of a Bus Looks Like…

Day after day, phone call after phone call, email after email, there was a constant flow of bitching and backbiting. Our former friends went on a crusade to "expose" us to everyone they could and convince them to join and support their new efforts. Mind you, we were still very conservative! We believed in a politically conservative view of identity and sexuality. I was still living as a "lifelong celibate who'd experienced a degree of change." But these folks would tell others that we were secretly promoting and living in sin, and encouraging divorce. In their words, we were: false prophets, apostates, possessed by evil, selfish, narcissistic, and spiritually rebellious.

Transference, much?

They would assume the absolute worst, make conclusions based on those false assumptions, spread those erroneous and horrible conclusions as fact, and scare the snot out of other ministries and supporters, who would then repeat these false accusations and condemnations repeatedly. It was heartbreaking and numbing.

I tell people it was like they threw us under the bus, ran over us, put the bus in reverse, ran over us again, invited a caravan of buses to form an extended circle, and kept looping around to run us into the ground over and over and over and over again.

Today, I look back upon these former friends and their curses and can't believe I ever thought they had something I wanted. Friends who had once told me their hopes, dreams, and fears. Friends who had confided in me about some deeply personal issues. Friends I had shared deeply personal matters with now looked at me with malice and hatred; they treated us with nothing but condescension and condemnation.

All in the name of love and concern.

What the fuck, indeed.

Not Isolated Incidents—A Pattern

While what was happening to us was horrible, on every scale imaginable, it was the typical experience of countless individuals who have come to see that ex-gay/conversion efforts are not healthy, effective, or trustworthy. Even though I was now on the receiving end of the attacks, I realized how awful I had been in some of the same ways. I was terrible to those who had begun the process of being more honest about their experiences and beliefs. I don't believe I ever threatened them with public denunciation or tried to destroy their careers, but on a smaller scale, I had assumed the worst and spoken ill of people simply trying to find their way and live their truth. That realization truly amplified the pain of being thrown under the bus. I felt ashamed as I realized I had driven that very same bus in the past.

Along with considering this pattern repeating itself through history, I began to remember and look up people who had left the movement and embraced their authentic selves. I began to look at their lives. I started to ask questions of gay Christians and activists whom I had somewhat of a decent relationship with and realized they weren't "broken" or unhealthy. They hadn't "gone back" to sin. On the contrary, much of the "fruit" of their lives was healthy, honest, and thriving.

Then I began to look at the "fruit" of the lives of the people I had so highly esteemed for so long. I began to look at my own life and realized that those of us who were old-timers in the movement were myopic, selfish, narcissistic, vengeful, legalistic, ungracious, and unloving. I realized that the buses running over us kept doing so in a loop because they were trying to prevent us from exposing that their path had come to a dead, stagnant end with no exit ramp.

These realizations filled me with both despair and numbness. I found it hard to communicate with others, as I felt in a state of shock nearly all the time. In some ways, I was looking for answers to questions I didn't know how to ask. However, I knew that change was coming. I knew that change had to come and that it was a necessary step in healing for myself and so many others who had been the victims (and actors) in this close-minded ex-gay world. It felt like I was preparing for a Category 5 hurricane that was about to destroy everything, and I had to focus on both mitigating the impending damage while also realizing that everything could be destroyed and come to an end.

And Then Steven Left Us

All of that was happening in Exodus when Steven took his life. The searing pain I felt from losing him metaphorically nuked every last doubt out of my mind. I could not and would not be a part of Exodus. Just the month before, I began writing a report for the Exodus board explaining that we either needed to rebrand and consolidate Exodus or shut it down, based on both the turmoil happening in the ministries and the anecdotal data from survivors' stories that showed the ineffectiveness of reparative (now known as conversion) therapy. After Steven, I was committed to helping the board as best I could to decide on whether to shut Exodus down or not. However, I knew either way that I was done with Exodus regardless. After Steven, my only recommendation was to close Exodus down.

In the spring of 2013, it was clear that Exodus would not survive. Organizationally, it had failed in every aspect: staff, funds, vision, mission, and messaging. The primary decision to close it down was because of the harm and damage Exodus had caused; Exodus had not only not fulfilled its mission, but it had become an agent of destruction. I am proud of Roger and the board for not simply letting us go and hiring new staff to continue the work of Exodus. The death and damage needed to stop, and through closing Exodus, it did in a number of ways.

At the Exodus board meeting in June 2013, Roger did a fantastic job being professional and thorough and keeping his composure in explaining the reasons for closing Exodus. He invited me to the meeting because I had prepared the report recommending closure of the organization, which I helped him present. In the meeting, I also shared from my heart what I thought was best as well as Steven's story. The board unanimously voted to close down Exodus International, and Roger announced it from the stage at our international conference on its opening night.

A Profound Moment–Reflecting on the Exodus Closing Announcement

On June 19, 2013, during the opening night of the Exodus Freedom Conference, I sat in the front row with Roger's wife and the Exodus board. All of us were there to provide support for each other and Roger, as we knew that Roger was making one of the most important keynote speeches of his life as he announced that Exodus was closing.

It was excruciating—the tension, excitement, and knowledge of what was about to be said had my heart racing. Of course, I had known that night was coming for a while, but there is a difference between knowing and experiencing.

It was quite a profound experience.

You could have heard a pin drop in the room as the audience took in the news. However, if the internet could make its own social "noise," I think we might have heard a lit fuse extending toward a media explosion later that night and over the next two days.

When I opened my laptop in the front row to publish the announcement to the Exodus blog, I hovered over the publish button for about 30 seconds and just wept and wept. This was it, done, the end. I knew this would be both jeered and cheered around the world, which is what happened. As I hovered over the "publish" button, one of my friends close by said, "Go for it." As I wiped away the tears, I felt the Lord's peace, and hit publish.

While I know beyond a shadow of a doubt that closing Exodus was the right thing to do, hitting that publish button and being present for Roger's keynote is still one of the most important moments I have had in my life. It was a true act of leadership.

As always, the Lord has proven trustworthy and faithful. In hindsight, I could see His hand preparing Exodus for this moment for over 10 years—especially the last two. In opposition, some have said that we couldn't possibly have heard from the Lord in closing the organization. They are entitled to their opinion and false belief, of course. I, however, am confident it was His will and direction to close down Exodus and to use me for part of that process. We were brought into leadership for that ultimate purpose.

When we returned to the office, Roger, a few staff, and I began working out how we should close down many resources, equipment, administrative functions, and more. We did our best to manage it all in an efficient and appropriate order.

When I shut down some online resources and administrative paths that took years to build and maintain, significantly reducing the main Exodus website, I reflected on many moments and relationships. Though this was the necessary end of Exodus, I didn't feel glee over the matter, but I wasn't remorseful either. Closing Exodus was meant to be and because it was of the Lord, it was good. I have peace because the Divine provided clear direction at the time as well as a vision for the next adventure. I told a reporter that some people might have called it a bittersweet moment, but I don't. I had no "bitterness" over losing Exodus and nothing but confidence that we were doing the right thing and heading in the right direction.

Dancing Queen

When Roger issued an apology to the gay community and announced that we were closing Exodus International, we had a figurative global firestorm of media coverage. Of course, he did the bulk of the interviews, but I did quite a few myself. I don't want to minimize the importance of closing Exodus, but this next story happened as a result, and it is one of my favorite experiences to share.

One Christian network called and wanted us to be on two different shows, one late morning and the other mid-afternoon. Both of these call-in interviews were assigned to me.

The first show called, and it was not an easy interview. The host simply did not understand the need for an apology to the gay community. However, regardless of the disagreement, this guy was professional. He was asking good, substantive questions.

About halfway into the interview, when we were deep into the conversation, he asked me something that I don't remember today. However, I *do* remember using one of the talking points we had come up with in response: "That is a great question. What has happened is that Exodus has a mixed legacy. It is important to recognize others have had bad…" then suddenly, my mobile phone started ringing.

OUT LOUD.

The phone that I was on for the interview was next to my mobile phone, and the mobile phone was blaring music because I forgot to turn the ringer off. But that's not the best part.

The best part was that the ringtone was ABBA's "Dancing Queen."

I was answering a serious and profound question, very seriously and very profoundly, and out of the blue, these Swedish angels start singing,

> *YOU ARE THE DANCING QUEEN, YOUNG AND SWEET, ONLY SEVENTEEN*
>
> *DANCING QUEEN, FEEL THE BEAT FROM THE TAMBOURINE*
>
> *YOU CAN DANCE, YOU CAN JIVE, HAVING THE TIME OF YOUR LIFE*

SEE THAT GIRL, WATCH THAT SCENE, DIGGING THE DANCING QUEEN [8]

You would have thought lightning had hit me! In a fraction of a second, I said out loud, "OH no!…" I got flustered, dropped the landline phone and grabbed my mobile phone like a hot potato, fumbling as I tried to turn the ringer off. When I finally succeeded, I stared at the landline phone, open-mouthed and mortified.

"Dancing Queen"—the iconic gay power anthem—sound-bombed my nationally syndicated Christian radio program interview.

After what seemed like an eternity (maybe three or four seconds), I put the landline phone back to my ear and meekly said "…Hello?" The host had clearly muted me (you can tell by how it sounds when you are muted), and being the professional he was, I heard him talking about the muted Swedish angels. His producer, I'm hoping, muted me as soon as the song started when I said, "OH no!…" The host eventually came back to me to wrap things up. He thanked me for being on the show. I thanked him for having me on. There weren't any more questions after the "Dancing Queen" interlude.

Interestingly (or not, actually), the second show on that network never ended up calling me for their interview later in the day. I guess they didn't want "…THE BEAT FROM THE TAMBOURINE…"

I had a private joke with a friend about that song and had assigned that ringtone to them. As such, that ringtone ONLY plays for that particular friend, and they just decided to contact me at that specific time. So after walking around completely embarrassed for a couple of hours, I told a group of friends what happened, and in the retelling, I couldn't help but laugh with them until I snorted and cried and couldn't breathe.

Remember the earlier story about Aaron's Bible study where his friend called God "Abba," which confused me because I had only heard of ABBA, the "Dancing Queen" group? As I write this, I wonder if Abba (Father, heart of God) was telling me to lighten up at that moment.

Since I am laughing again as I type these words, I am pretty sure that is the case.

An Open Apology to the Gay Community

(This segment was originally published on my old blog on July 23, 2013. It is reprinted here exactly as originally published.)

---

8 ABBA. (1976). Dancing queen [Song]. On Arrival. Polar; Epic; Atlantic. No copyright infringement intended.

Today is the 21st Anniversary of attending my very first Exodus Member Ministry meeting. I didn't plan this apology to coincide with this date. I just realized the coincidence this morning. Regardless, I find it incredibly fitting that this apology is being published today.

When Roger Tompkins made his apology to the gay community, I couldn't have been more supportive. I am so proud of my friend and fully agree with what he shared.

I, too, have been taking a personal moral inventory. So many eye-opening experiences have occurred in the past 24 months—including the suicide of a beloved friend and former partner this past January. The loss of Steven forced me to face some issues I had not been willing to deal with until that time. And it's through this process that I've come to the conclusion that I need to apologize to the gay community.

Public Policy

My understanding of public policy at that time was limited to the talking points I was given to tailor my testimony around. I did not do much research beyond these talking points—and as a result, my perspective was limited and nearsighted. I am very sorry that my uncritical perspective contributed to the hurt that many LGBT persons were already feeling.

I participated in the hurtful echo chamber of condemnation. I gave lip service to the gay community but really did not exemplify compassion for them. I placed the battle over policy above my concern for real people. I sometimes valued the shoulder pats I was given by religious leaders more than Jesus' commandment to love and serve. That was wrong, and I'm disappointed in myself. Please forgive me.

I directly empowered people to co-opt my testimony and use it against the gay community. There were a few times I almost worked up the nerve to confront them, only to hear them invoke my name at an opportune moment. "Of course I love gay people," they would say. "Just look at my good friend Randy..." It was very selfish of me to back down in these situations. I apologize.

I was, in a sense, attracted to this kind of power and allowed my conscience to be numbed so I could have a seat at their table. In the name of trying to positively affect Christian leaders, I willingly became one of their pawns. Again, I was selfish and prideful. Please forgive me.

The only thing I don't regret about my past public policy efforts are some of the friends I made during that time. These few trusted Christians are in the public policy realm for all the right reasons.

Keeping the Peace—Putting Out Fires at Exodus

In 1992, I was part of an Exodus affiliated ministry in Texas that believed being in relationship with Jesus alone was our goal. I never felt pressured to change my same sex orientation. I saw my life greatly improved by having the freedom to question my sexuality and identity. I assumed this was what happened at every Exodus group, and I ended up idealizing the entire ministry based on my singular experience in Texas. However, after joining the Exodus staff, I was confronted with the reality that some methods used by some of our local ministries ended up bringing hurt and pain to the very people they were trying to comfort.

There are many good people in the broader Exodus movement that I didn't want to hurt by sharing the bad we'd uncovered. Other staff members and I dealt with some of these ills privately. But by keeping quiet and not even letting our own leaders know the depths of what concerned us, I contributed to the negative response surrounding Roger's recent apology. To protect some leaders, which was totally inappropriate, others didn't know how bad some things had gotten. Therefore, some have been shocked that Roger apologized and that I, among others, were supportive. In order to protect the reputation of some, I chose silence. I apologize for remaining silent and passive. Looking back on my time with Exodus, it seems I was always waiting for a convenient time to discuss some of my concerns publicly. But as Dr. Martin Luther King Jr. once said, "There is never a wrong time to do the right thing."

Past Teachings

When I look back at some of my old interviews, group meetings, and keynotes over the past 20 years, I realize there are many things I would communicate differently today. In the past, I taught quite a mixture of performance-based accomplishment along with God's grace. I taught that God is always present, but if we don't manage our sin properly, it could negatively impact our relationship with Him.

That's not grace. It doesn't take seriously the finished work of the Cross.

I look back on my time as a Oasis Mirage coordinator (eleven years ago) with the most remorse. Even though there is some good in this program, it often ripped open old wounds in the name of healing by attempting to manufacture an environment for the Lord to work in. I have to apologize for the times some people may have felt manipulated to bare their souls to a group full of strangers. I apologize for any pressure we, on the Oasis Mirage team I led, might have placed on group participants as we tried to help them cultivate "authentic experiences."

As a trained Oasis Mirage coordinator, I used to hang on to every word Jake Hautmess said. I even did some online consulting work for him. But today, over a year after leaving his employ as a consultant, I look back and recognize there were signs that something was wrong. In retrospect, I realize I helped build Jake Hautmess' online platforms—platforms which have increasingly gotten more vitriolic and stigmatizing toward the LGBT community. I regret that, and I'm sorry.

Conclusion

I apologize to the gay community for idealizing and reinforcing the institutional groupthink of Exodus. I apologize for remaining publicly silent about the hurt caused by some of Exodus' leaders and actions. I also apologize for my inexperienced participation in public policy, placing my personal ambition over truly serving the gay community as a Christian friend.

> *Moving forward, I pray the Lord helps keep me humble and reveals any issues/situations that require my consideration. I will keep an open heart and ear, and if and when action is necessary, I pray to find the grace and courage to quickly apologize and/or make amends.*

My current thoughts on this apology all these 10 years later is that, while earnest and sincere, it lacks the growth and revelations I have had since. There is a part of it that I no longer believe, which is, "The few trusted Christians are in the public policy realm for all the right reasons." I now know that I was trying to once again protect people who do not deserve to be protected. They are not to be trusted and are in public policy for all the wrong reasons.

Losing My Mind–Would I Follow Steven?

I call the fall of 2013 the great season of silence. For 11 years, there was a blizzard of noise and activity in my ears as I chased hundreds of ex-gay/conversion groups and counselors and tried to keep tabs on everyone, rallying them for certain things and leading them in other ways. It was part of my job to keep up with what everyone was saying, doing, thinking, and planning. Plus, I kept up with all the media and current events. People would contact me at all times of the day, and Exodus had become my life focus and what I thought would be my career/calling until I retired. People used to call for advice, encouragement, questions, training, speaking, crisis management, and friendship. There was never a dull (or quiet) moment.

But now that I was excommunicated, there was only silence. Dead silence. Not only that, any support I had previously received (and offered to others) just kept silently walking away (ghosting) or violently accusing me of the worst. I always thought it was weird how some Exodus leaders got so caught up in themselves that they couldn't see life beyond that ministry. So, I was broken-hearted and unable to get out of bed because I no longer knew who I was or what my purpose would be.

It's an awful feeling at 45 to know you had accomplished all of what you thought were your career goals, only to realize it was all based on flawed systems, religious stigma, learned helplessness, and lies. It was made even worse when all of the "friends" you thought you had disappeared and never tried to talk to you again. Some of the worst were those who gossiped and spoke to everyone about me instead of talking to me. I was morose, and at the end of 2013, I had suicidal ideations. Remembering the pain of

Steven kept me from actually doing it. I didn't have any hope for living, but I felt like I didn't have any reason to die either.

I cried out to God multiple times during my severe depression. One night in particular I felt like I was losing my mind as I heard myself say, "YOU KNOW I love You, and I want to be loved! YOU KNOW I need to know and be known by someone, to have a man to love and be loved by. YOU KNOW that I would choose that if I could, and I hate being alone! I've always felt alone."

As I stood in the living room wailing with grief in the early morning hours with the porch light shining through the window at the top of the door, I felt peace flood in and through me. I thought that instead of being run over by life and living in learned helplessness, I needed to fight for life, for myself. I needed to take the leap and trust that the vision I saw in my therapy session of the eagle soaring was, in fact, true. I needed to trust my true self in a way that would finally allow me to fly high—very high indeed.

So I did.

PART THREE

"How did it get so late so soon?"
–Dr. Seuss

"If life were predictable it would cease to be life, and be without flavor."
–Eleanor Roosevelt

"Never be bullied into silence. Never allow yourself to be made a victim.
Accept no one's definition of your life; define yourself."
–Harvey Fierstein

CHAPTER 10

Adventures in Gay Bar Time Travel

I'm Me. I Hated Me, But Now I Like Me.

I love communication. I am strong-willed and passionate. I also love and want to help people. When you add all these things together with vanity and a deadly belief system, you get the Exodus version of me that is no longer acceptable.

Unfortunately, while those qualities are my strengths, it also means when I put my foot in my mouth, it sometimes goes all the way up to my knee! And when I get passionate about something, you might want to hang on to the rail. The good news is I recognize that I might not have made it out of my teens if I wasn't strong-willed, passionate, and interested in others. So there's that.

Now, instead of embracing a dysfunctional and harmful ideology, I have embraced empathy and the beauty it brings to relationships. Today I use my superpowers for good to help end the Gospel According to Conversion Therapy, make amends, continue developing my new career as a corporate trainer, and provide for my family.

Of course, I know that being aware of your strengths isn't enough. I must be mindful of how easy it is to slip up and use those strengths for harm if I don't keep them in check. Being honest with both the good and the bad is my baseline for finding maturity and wisdom.

When honestly evaluated, I have learned that life experiences can lead to knowledge. But if I don't apply and test that knowledge, I miss out on wisdom. Knowledge and wisdom aren't the same thing. Many people run around with untested "knowledge," creating very polarized thinking. I fight for life, test knowledge by applying and challenging it, and then look for wisdom to raise Her voice, usually with a lesson just for me.

It was humbling to know that all the people throughout the years calling me naïve were correct. It's humbling to see that strengths and weaknesses are not always clear. But I have done the work, and while I am always open to learning, I embrace the good parts of myself and no longer feel disqualified to engage them for good purposes. I also embrace the weaknesses within me. They are there for a reason and help keep me in check. I don't think the path to wisdom can be traveled without embracing and intentionally stewarding all of the dark and light within.

Making Amends

The day after I came back out, Mr. Assume-WAY-Too-Much, who I only met once offline, contacted me and told me he should manage my making amends process. That I was to list everything I had written or said or done to hurt the gay community, and he would personally devise a plan for me to make amends. He would make a plan telling me what to do to make amends and hold me accountable to it.

I am sorry, sir, but that is not how making honest amends works.

Part of the amends process for me is figuring out what needs to be apologized or atoned for, figuring out if making amends would do more harm than good, and getting up the nerve to do it. My time of letting critics or anyone determine when and how I say things are long over.

Also, part of the amends process is taking what the universe arranges for me, which means that when someone comes to mind or comes to me and shares where I wronged them, I always listen. There have been times when people come to mind, and I think, "Wow, I was a major-not-fun-dick to that person," and I will reach out and apologize for specific things that I remember.

However, I don't initiate these conversations and plow right into such a potentially loaded conversation. I tell them they came to mind and invite them to discuss the past where I could apologize, but I don't want to make their thing my thing, so I understand if they do not want to talk. Some have said, "Nope, fuck off, you major-not-fun-dick." So I apologize for interrupting them and go on with my business. They know my door is open. Most others have been very welcoming to that kind of discussion, and it has been challenging but worth it each time.

At the same time, I am not a doormat either. One person contacted me about all the pain and suffering I caused him. He briefly went to a non-Exodus counselor and participated in a weekend retreat not endorsed by Exodus. Some of the referral agencies recommended these efforts against our advice not to do so. I knew when this incredibly angry man first started talking that I was symbolic of the people who had hurt him, so my coming out had triggered him. I did what I could to stay calm, hear him out, and apologize for promoting the same toxic beliefs that the people who hurt him used as a pretext for their bizarre approaches. But he didn't accept it and started personally attacking me, my family, and everything I hold dear publicly on every post I would create. I have extended several olive branches over the years, but he just slapped them out of my hand. Finally, it became apparent he simply wanted a public fight (he has done this with many people on all kinds of subjects), and I had to block him from all my social media.

Anyone who genuinely wants to talk about my part in promoting the Gospel According to Conversion Therapy and how it impacted them is more than welcome. I have always believed in honest and open discussion as a means to healing, provided it's just that: honest and open. If it's only a vehicle for venting and projecting trauma onto another, then I suggest therapy—which is what I did myself. As most therapists will tell you, trauma therapy is a unique practice that requires specific training. If you have been traumatized by conversion therapy, as so many have, I hope you will find a trauma therapist to help you. It really is the best path to healing and regaining your power in all areas of life.

Randy v. Other Former Ex-Gay Leaders

Over the years, I have seen many former ex-gay leaders try to pretend that that part of their lives is over and they can simply disappear and move on. I get it. I understand the desire to disavow a past that you are ashamed of and want to bury. But there are others who believe that when they do come out, somehow the LGBTQ+ community will accept and respect them as leaders now that they have abandoned ex-gay ideology.

No, that's not how this works.

We are no longer leaders. We do not deserve respect for *finally* doing the right thing. Any respect we gain has to be earned, deliberately and over time. We do not have a positive track record in establishing credibility; actually, we have proven to many that we are not credible, not to be trusted. That's not just going to disappear when we come out.

We do need to attempt to right wrongs. You can't just show up once, expect a seat at the leadership roundtable, and be applauded. You have to live your change of heart so the actions flow forth naturally. In my opinion, former ex-gay leaders should denounce their past lives publicly because it is the right thing to do.

At the *Pray Away* premiere at the Tribeca Film Festival, I said something to that effect during the after-film panel: "In the end, it doesn't matter what you think of me. What matters is that we end conversion therapy. What matters is we stop the abuse."

I believe that the only way conversion therapy in its pastoral form of ex-gay ministry will ever end is if all of us former leaders convince the current leaders to stop. I'm not going to drag former leaders out of the "it's part of my past" closet. But they know who they are, and they need to speak up. If they do, it will help save countless lives still trapped in that world.

After finding my way out of the post-Exodus depression at the end of 2013, I began to fight for life hard. "Fight for life and don't be run over by it" and "Don't be an asshole about your faith anymore" were my two mantras going into 2014. It was a new year, and I intended to make it count. As a result, I started doing things I hadn't done in years.

For starters, I was actually listening to LGBTQ+ people and other points of view. I was questioning everything. Putting every belief on the table and testing it with questions like: What kind of fruit does this tree (faith) bear? Is this life-giving or enslaving? Am I okay with admitting that I don't know everything? Am I going to be okay if I find out that I built my life as a house of cards super-glued together?

It helped that Momma Mella (George) came to town that August, as I was determined to see the Grand Ol' Gal of the South all these years later after she had helped me as a homeless teen.

Visiting George at the Local Gayopolis

Sunday, August 3, 2014 was the first time I had been in a gay bar in over 23 years. I went right after church to visit my friend Carmella Marcella Garcia, Girl! I hadn't seen her in 27 years. It was a trip.

We met where she was going to perform, the famous (infamous?) Parliament House (PH). It is now closed, but it was a world-renowned club because it was the largest in Orlando for decades. (Side note: When we met, we had lunch at the PH restaurant. The barely dressed man in the advert underneath the Plexiglas tabletop promoted an upcoming party. I couldn't help but notice all the muscles and the way he filled out those jeans! I even blushed. I didn't catch the details because I was busy chuckling, thinking, "This sure isn't Cracker Barrel.")

When I worked at Exodus, my face appeared on a billboard over the parking lot for about a week before the complaints took it down. The idea of a billboard seems so stupid/insulting now, and I apologize for being a poster boy, literally looking down on and insulting the P-House patrons.

Honestly, I truly apologize. I hate thinking about that.

Back to August 3rd. I got to the hotel before Mella arrived at check-in. Did I mention that this gay bar was also a resort? Yep, hotel rooms and everything. It had a pool area, a bar, and a restaurant, and I later joked with Mella, "This is like a Gayopolis!" I had heard PH had all these various amenities, but seeing it in real life was quite an experience.

As I sat in the lobby waiting on Mella, I admit I was nervous. It was partially about seeing Mella after so many years had passed, but it was mostly about wondering if someone in the bar might recognize me. I worried someone would start yelling at me or something. Of course, I realize that was a transference of my sadness over some of my past projects with Exodus. If someone did end up doing that, I probably deserved some or all of their ire. However, I now know my nervousness indicated my feelings of unease with some of the projects in which I had participated.

…Like those stupid billboards.

Conversely, I was not nervous about anyone I knew finding out I was there. Of course, my closest friends knew because I was excited to see George. No one else probably cared. When I posted pictures of George and me, I tagged her and "checked in" social-media-wise at the Parliament House. So I didn't have a problem with people I knew knowing I was there because I had nothing to hide.

At the time, I did wonder if going to a gay bar would feel nostalgic. I started going to gay bars when I was 17, and I stopped around the age of 23. As you now have read, bars, in general, were not a good scene for me. So not having been in a gay bar in a long time, I wondered if it would be like some odd homecoming.

Nope. Not really.

Our time together lasted a little over two hours, from 12:45 to 3:00 in the afternoon. I didn't see the club/resort with loud music, lights, and drag queens swinging from the disco balls, even though there were many disco balls over the main bar area, which I loved. Instead, it was just a big, empty bar with many middle-aged guys in speedos hanging out in the back by the Gayopolis pool.

If there is ever a movie about my life, this scene would be titled "Navigating the Sea of Speedo Bears." Fully clothed in my baggy blue jeans, red plaid short-sleeved shirt, and self-conscious insecurities about my not-so-past (at the time) right-wing activities, I felt a bit conspicuous.

In truth, I didn't feel nostalgic or at home until I heard George's voice.

She sounded like the Mella I knew. Her southern accent echoed my teenage home, and I loved talking with and hugging him after all these years. I know the Divine used him to save my life when I was a homeless/suicidal gay 19 year old, and seeing George put everything in a less self-focused perspective. At the Gayopolis that day, no one except Mella cared about how I felt or my past, and she loved me and was concerned with my welfare. I was not even a blip on anyone's radar. I am sure they were all much more concerned with what was happening in the Gayopolis pool.

Many people did come up to us, but it was to hug Momma Mella, not to start screaming at me. I wasn't the only one delighted to see him.

We spent our time catching up with each other. Mella shared about what was going on with her and her trip down to Florida, which was a bit of a mix between work and visiting friends. She asked me what was going on, and I shared a bit about my recent history in helping to shut down Exodus and the questions I was facing. As always, he was kind and supportive. I enjoyed watching his eyes light up with that great smile, as he shared his thoughts humbly and directly. I appreciated his input, insight, and willingness to share a meal with me.

Plus, he was hilarious. Mella is probably on a golden stage now, making the archangels blush. I am convinced she is one of my guardian angels; of course, in my case, I don't doubt the Divine would give that role to a drag queen named Mella.

Mella had a good heart and sought to do right by others. Of course, she had struggles, as we all do, but she was indeed a good person, and I am glad we had the chance to mend our friendship before she passed.

So yeah, going to a gay bar after all that time was a big deal to me. But grace opened doors, stripped bare my cluttered heart, and revived gratitude-based joy.

Post-Gayopolis Thoughts

As I read through the section above, I remember at the time, I still wouldn't call George "Mella." While George was Mella's off-stage name, I remember that I kept calling her George because I was trained not to affirm what we in the ex-gay world would have viewed as a false identity or a non-biological pronoun.

This was so ingrained that I didn't even realize I was doing it back then. At the time, I was profoundly conflicted. I longed to feel at home among my LGBTQ+ community, yet I felt like a complete foreigner and forever outcast. More than that, I felt like an enemy who didn't deserve to be in their presence.

But Mella was safe. Mella was home to me at that moment. Mella's warm eyes and welcoming embrace cast off the shadows. Her support showed me genuine grace from one Christ-follower to another in a way I have rarely experienced.

She would later tell me she knew during our visit together that I had to deal with being gay and that I would be coming back out of the closet soon, but she didn't bring it up or pressure me. She knew I would find my way. Eventually, I would share part of that journey in a blog, which follows.

A Peaceful Disclosure–I Am Gay

(The following was written for my blog on January 12, 2015, five months after meeting with Mella, and left as is. While edited for grammar, the content has not changed.)

> I have read many stories of people who have "come out again" or accepted they are gay after some time in the ex-gay world. Many of their stories are compelling and well-written. But, sometimes, I wish they would get to the point right off

the bat. Just say it, and then tell the story. So that is what I am going to do: I am gay.

Now take a deep breath (talking to myself here), and here is more of the story for those interested.

What Led to This Post?

The past six or so years have presented an opportunity to question my beliefs and evaluate my experiences without an idealized agenda. Then in 2011, as a result of all the turmoil that erupted at Exodus International (my former employer from 2002 to 2013), I began to dig deep and ask hard questions. Who am I? What do I make of my journey to date? How does God view me, my state of being? I questioned/pondered/re-examined all this and more again. Then in January of 2013, a man named Steven, someone I dated for a little while 24 years ago, committed suicide. We had remained good friends up until his death. His death was shocking, and I still mourn his passing. Steven had several complicated issues contributing to his suicide, and I know he also struggled with his faith and sexuality. His death shook me to my core and made all the questions I had been asking even more stark, consequential, and pressing. After being laid off from Exodus International (as a part of closing it down) in August of 2013, I began to have the personal space to think things through without distraction or filters.

Parallel to all this was a deepening and expanded understanding of God's grace. These factors get more specific and complicated, but I think that the above describes the gist of how I began to come to the conclusions that I present in this post. I could have written this post last summer but was discouraged by some feedback I received. Regardless, I needed to pray and think it through a bit longer. Now is the time to do this.

The Spectrum of Sexuality

To be honest and accurate, I would have to say that I am gay with some level of bisexual tendencies. The truth is that my primary sexual attraction is toward men. It is also true that to date, the love of my life has been a woman. I was attracted to her in every way. Many people won't believe me, but what I just shared is true. I would be lying by omission if I didn't share that side of myself. For me, developing strong sexual attractions is driven by emotional attachment more than anything else. My relational history has shown that I can indeed have attractions to either gender if the emotional attachment is there.

If that is confusing to you, welcome to my world.

Motivation, History/Post-Exodus

Some snapshots of my history. At the age of 10, I was "out" to myself. I came out to friends at 16 and out to everyone as a gay man at 19. At 19, I paid a heavy price for coming out. I was as liberal a Democrat as one could be, too. Then I became a Christian and moved toward being an ex-gay poster boy (the last executive vice president of Exodus International). At one point, I was featured in a full-page ad in the Los Angeles Times and featured in a book by Watergate figure Charles Colson called The Good Life. *For about five years of my time working for Exodus (2003 to 2008), I was a political activist on the religious right as well. I was vocal and open about my beliefs that I no longer identified as gay while in Exodus circles for 23 years.*

I share the preceding paragraph to illustrate that it is my nature to champion my personal beliefs. I've always believed what I have declared publicly to be true. Yes, those beliefs have been all over the map in 46 years, but I have always been a true believer in whatever I was professing.

Four or five times over the past five months, in offline social settings, I have been asked if I am gay. Each time I answered, without hesitation, "I am bisexual with a propensity toward dudes." That brought smiles each time, and I was told that if I was bi, gay… whatever, they wanted me to know they accepted me. But this is the first time in my life where I felt there were inconsistencies between what was happening in some circles as opposed to others. I started seeing the potential of a fragmented *life developing, and I *never* want that. There is nothing more torturous than feeling like you can't be consistently you wherever you are. These recent offline disclosures were leading to an issue of conscience for me. As I was thinking through and writing this post, it became clear that it is most accurate to say that I am gay with a bisexual propensity that I can't adequately describe :).*

Whether anyone cares, pays attention, approves, disapproves, friends, or unfriends me isn't the point. The point is that I need to stay true to how I am wired, be honest, and be consistent with what I believe to be true in this regard. Writing this post is something I need to do as a part of taking personal responsibility for my past journey and being honest in my present reality.

Faith

My love for Jesus and His finished work on the cross is unwavering and stronger than ever. I am as saved today as I was the moment I first believed in and received Him as my Lord and Savior. He rose from the dead to open the door to reconciliation with God and eternal life. I've already walked through that door. He is in my heart. None of that changes, regardless of my sexuality or my all-too-human musings. It doesn't change because it's all on Him, and He never changes. He loves me; I know it. He loves you and is not angry with you, and I hope you know that truth.

Dating

Currently, I am not dating. I have not been dating. I have not had a sexual partner in 24 years. I am in no hurry to change that reality. Plus, I have no doubt I would probably be a weird date *grin* I mean, seriously, how do you explain all... this? Being single has been a life-giving state of being for me and my place in the community. I am content. As a single gay man, I am relationally whole and at peace. There is love in my life, God, friends, family, and work. I'm in a good place.

About the Future

One thing I have learned is to stop declaring what tomorrow will be like or what the future will bring. Could I see myself with a man? Yes. Could I see myself with a woman? Yes. Could I see myself being celibate for the rest of my life? Yes. Today has its troubles, and I am not worrying about tomorrow. Instead, I rest in God's grace and trust Him to be the Good Shepherd He has proven, over and over, to be. Whatever happens, loving Jesus is at the core of who I am. Regardless of any relationship I have or will have, abiding in Christ will always be my "Home."

I found my first sense of identity and community as a gay youth/young man. I am not sure many will accept my apologies or this disclosure. I would understand some people's reluctance, given my history. While I care about what others think, I am doing this because I feel it is right.

I am gay. I am okay with who I am. I hope we can continue to journey together.

Afterthoughts on the "Peaceful Disclosure..."

My hopes to continue the journey together were quickly dashed in many cases. Almost all my remaining friends and the support I had after the Exodus implosion disappeared. All the old curses from that season came back from the same lips that had said them two years prior. Plus, a whole host of new critics came along.

I didn't think anyone would care, and while it wasn't breaking news on CNN, the gay blogs and quite a few big media outlets interviewed me. My church freaked out because I hadn't told them I would come out, and they said what I knew they would say if I had told them beforehand, which is why I didn't.

And my life group—people I had spent 10 years in fellowship with—all went to Roger to talk about me instead of talking directly to me. I also knew they would do that. They had been doing that for 10 years. I knew they were my friends via Roger. I loved them, but when Roger said, "You need to go talk to so and so..." I was like, "No. My door is and always has been open. They are going to you instead of walking up to me. That's the way it always has been. So if they want to talk to me and work this through, my door is open."

They never did walk through my door, and I never did go chase them down. It makes me sad to think of that, and maybe the gracious thing would have been to go chase my old "life" group down.

Nah. I'm tired of thinking I need others' approval to be at peace. If they don't dare to come to talk to me directly, they aren't friends I need in my life, if they were ever truly friends to begin with.

After coming out, I got a myriad of responses from the public. A great majority of it was very gracious and kind from the LGBTQ+ community and allies. Even some of the gay activists I had awful interactions with in the past were amazingly forgiving and wished me well. But unfortunately, the religious gay community sent a few very harsh and damning curses my way.

"You have sold out to the gay Hollywood agenda!"

"Go crawl back under the rock you came out from under; you have blood on your hands! We in the gay community will NEVER forgive you."

"You are an apostate leading people off a cliff. You are a false prophet and should have a millstone tied around your neck and dropped into the sea!"

"Randy is a Judas to those seeking freedom from sexual brokenness, don't listen to him!"

I never understood this next accusation: "Now that Exodus is closed, you need a paycheck and are just trying to manipulate people into giving you money and attention again."

After publishing my coming out post, the hyperbole and accusations were tough to get through, but I felt lighter than I ever had before. I was a hot emotional mess for two solid weeks because of a potent mix of fear, pain, and internal relief.

I Am the Gay Time Traveler

Though there has been a lot that is still the same, much has changed in the LGBTQ+ community from the first time I came out to the second time. However, I still have moments where I feel like an alien teleported in from the past instead of a native of the local and broader gay community today.

I am astounded at how far the LGBTQ+ community has come on every level. I don't mean just politically, even though that is major. I am talking in terms of: spirituality, financial resources, support systems/resources, cultural leaders, leadership in general, organizational vision, professional integration in business and personal integration in our communities, cohesion at every level, and more! Maybe it was because I was in Nashville in the

'80s, but I never would have thought that this modern gay world could ever exist back then.

As a community, I know that our quest is far from over. And yet I sit here amazed at how far the LGBTQ+ community has come. You inspire me, and I thank you for the grace, forgiveness, and acceptance you have shown me.

Some Things Haven't Changed. Many Things Have.

I previously talked about the bliss I experienced the first time I danced in a gay bar. I got attention, male attention, without any negativity, and poured my life out like water on a thirsty dancefloor. I felt at home, like I could find all the answers to life's problems in the swirling lights, thumping music, and men buying me free drinks. That's a big problem because gay bars are not designed to be a guiding light of parental concern and care, or a babysitter. At the time, yes, they were the only safe place for LGBTQ+ people, but gay bars aren't meant to be THE catalyst of self-actualization. I didn't know that the first time around.

I have found that many things are the same in the bars and our community years later. What's the same? Young drag queens channeling the current reigning pop divas through inches-thick makeup and doing amazing things in high heels. Old(er) drag queens channeling old(er) pop divas through inches-thick makeup in more sensible shoes. Back in the day, I got all excited when a queen would do that fresh, beautiful Whitney Houston, and I didn't understand the older gay men getting all misty-eyed when older queens would do love songs from the sixties or further back. Nowadays, I am not as amused with the high-heel high kicks, flips, and death drops to the modern songs, which must mean I am now the old gay man who gets all emotional when an old(er) drag queen does a throw-back… to Whitney Houston.

Age can be a real asshole sometimes. LOL

But then, of course, there is the same drag queen humor; young or old, ever since the first T-rex snatched a wig off of Lady Bunny, drag queens have been telling crass jokes for eons. They have been teasing women and straight *wink* men and oversharing their sexual exploits and preferences.

Drag queens, you vulgar bitches. God, I love you!

It should also be stated that the queens are brilliant and some of the most caring people at heart. They know their audience and would never take that kind of humor outside the bar. Even so, they are still fun and enjoyable to watch as they perform or do community service work.

Of course, we know that gay nightclubs are not just about drag shows. Since coming out of the church closet, I have reconnected with a group that I affectionately call The Youngins. I have called them that for years, and it first started with a few of them working at Exodus when I was their supervisor. Most of the rest of this group attended or supported Exodus. Now, thankfully, we are all out and gay affirming—living our lives as our true selves.

I don't call them "Youngins" to diminish the fine men they are. I do see them as peers and friends. I call them Youngins because I am separated from most of them by at least a decade. I have reconnected with them primarily by going out to the clubs. I love it when they are there. They don't freeze me out, and I always feel like I have a place with them. They are very welcoming. However, it is difficult for me to restrain myself in wanting to protect them when specific dynamics unfold.

For example, when one of them got drunk and was almost literally having sex on the dance floor with a stranger, everyone was slack-jaw shocked! He hadn't even accepted that he was gay. I didn't want to guffaw over it—I wanted to take a crowbar and peel him off the guy. I imagined taking his keys away, driving him home, walking him to the door, and saying, "NO! You are a treasure; wait for the right time and person." I didn't do any of that, thank goodness.

I know—paternalistic, overly protective, judgmental. I hadn't worked through a lot of my shit yet. But I truly worried about him on the way home and prayed he wouldn't do something to break his or the other guy's heart.

The above example isn't the only dynamic that unfolded when visiting The Youngins' at the bars. So far, I think I have been good about not overstepping my role as an acquaintance/friend. In this context, they have never asked me to be a protector or advice-giver, so I'm not. But their follies, silliness, grace, and triumphs have helped to clarify and reaffirm how different I have genuinely become since I was their age, out at the clubs in the '80s and doing the same stupid drama.

As the World Turns, Around the Youngins

Oh, the joy of a pack of 20- to 30-somethings and their gay bar drama. Back in the '80s, maybe it was because of my age, temperament, and inability to function socially without abusing substances, but I wasn't a true social butterfly—I was a social chameleon. My friends Stanley and Tye took me under their wing, and they used to say about me to others, "Girl, that Randy don't know who she is… just enjoy whatever gay little Randy puts out there." One week I was aggressive with the leather crowd. Next, I was doing cocaine with the drag queens, the next smoking pot with the punks, or drinking LOTS of beer and shooting pool with the gay rednecks, or flaming out on top of a box dancing to New Order. I tended to end up everywhere, and I was a mess at all of it.

So I got invited to just about everything. It didn't matter because I was going to show up anyway.

Then there were the Pool Room Kids (PRKs). They were the young, beautiful, trendy 20-somethings. They did things like hits of XTC and all-night parties that would often end up with piles of naked men or lots of sex in lots of nooks and crannies of whatever house we ended up in at 4 a.m.

I say "we." I just followed along. I wasn't a PRK. They liked me, though, I think.

But the thing about them is that there was always drama. Who was sleeping with whom, who had a crush on someone they could never have while treating the person who had a crush on them badly. The gossip, the meanness, the daylight crying jags that brought everyone back together, the nighttime club clique with an overly inflated, magnanimous sense of self that made others jealous or pissed off for being snubbed.

And you know what's different about today's young 20-something PRKs? Not a damn thing. Except now they can carry all that dramatic shit on via text message and passive aggressive status updates. Today's PRKs have the same snarky/exclusive dynamic, but they seem to have more reasons to snub you. It is a nonstop parade of selfies by themselves or with their besties. They are turning blue faced, not from holding their breath, but from the glare of staring at their smartphone to see where to meet up with the other PRKs next.

The abused substances are the same but stronger than back in the '80s. I don't do the hard drugs anymore, but I have heard from others my age that they are much stronger now. The lousy-decision sexcapade after-parties are the same. The danger is the same, but that also leads to what is different.

Today's PRKs are less afraid of everything than we were. Then, we had friends dropping like flies from AIDS; now, the drug combos and PREP can help prevent infection or cause the virus to retreat and let someone live a long life. We were terrified of AIDS in my day because so many of us died. Now, it's respected or seen as an "old" disease. For good and bad, it's not feared.

Today they seem less afraid of physical violence, harassment, and discrimination. This sense of confidence is good, but my Gen-X self who was in Nashville, Tennessee back in the '80s was miserable. Two guys violently attacked me at a Thanksgiving party (given what I shared earlier in the book, it's clear I didn't have a good history with Thanksgiving at that point). When the Davidson County police came, they laughed at me, sided with the attackers, and didn't even get my side of the story or my name. As mentioned earlier in the book, I was harassed at a job in Texas for being gay. I had guns pulled on me twice outside of gay bars where I thought I would die. Nowadays, these Youngins seem to have no underlying current of fear, but maybe I am just missing it—or they don't show it. I do think their confidence is a good thing, as long as people keep in mind that the homophobic people who want to hurt gay people are still around to do random violence and/or organized oppression.

Also, what is different now is that I know the PRKs aren't a manifestation exclusive to the gay community. That kind of social dynamic is in every community of every flavor. It's a human dynamic, not a specifically gay one.

All of that said, there is a sea of golden hearts flowing in and out of the clubs.

Time to Mend Fences, Come Together, and Come Home

Another thing that is better for us all today than back in the '80s is that there are some long-standing and newer discussions about what it means to be gay beyond the struggle for equal rights. For example, what does it mean for our community if "marriage" is the mainstreaming of gay couples into simply being a couple without the need to qualify their relationship as gay? In the '80s, in my experience, gay bars were the only social gathering places. Now, we have myriads of gay or gay-inclusive organizations. Of course, the gay communities have always been there. But today, they have exploded onto the scene and are thriving.

Progress = Beautiful

I love that the PRKs of today have less to worry about, but I am concerned they will lose our history. Those who are older need to share more of our stories and experiences and pass on our lessons learned and our shared points of connection.

PRKs, even the straight variety, will continue to do their stupid bar drama and make bad decisions, just like we did. Our brains aren't fully developed until our early to mid-twenties. PRKs of every generation operate with underdeveloped brains, so that is enough reason to have compassion. Yes, I laughed as I wrote that. Twenty-five years ago, I don't think we recognized an "eldership" in the gay community. I think it's time to humbly think about and create that type of resource for the younger and upcoming gay generations. At least, that is part of my goal and hope for the future.

In the '80s, the revolution for gay equality was starting to solidify and gain real impact and power. While I watched what was happening through the thick filter of shame and condemnation that formed my religious "closet," my self-loathing and subsequent indoctrination removed me from the daily unfolding of the gay community's struggles. Now it's like popping out of a time warp. Today, I see all the ground we have gained and all the achievements of the LGBTQ+ community. I see the remnants of prior battlefields and the raging new ones. Yet I see the enemies are still the same even as I take off the uniform of a traitor.

Yeah, okay, that last sentence... oof. Tough to say, but true.

But here I am, and now I look at a safer community, one that is becoming much more stable and integrated into the fabric of true equality—in most places, but obviously not everywhere (yes Florida, I'm looking at you). I also see very weary and worn LGBTQ+ boomers and GenX'ers, because cynicism and hyper-awareness were necessary survival tools and coping skills. Those were the thoughts I was having when I decided to try and volunteer with the local Human Rights Campaign (HRC) chapter here in Orlando.

"Oh... We Have Plans for Randy..."

After messaging HRC Orlando through their Facebook page, I met with an HRC Orlando representative over coffee at the Starbucks in Longwood. She was a lovely woman with brunette hair and one of those smiles that makes you feel completely comfortable. She asked many questions and was very gracious and present in the conversation. I rambled way too much and am incredibly grateful for her listening ear.

She invited me to their "Cheers to Equality" event, and I met more people from the group. I had two drinks, maybe a little too quickly, and felt like I was rambling even more there. Then the lovely representative introduced me to another leader, a tall man who had arrived about an hour into the event, and she said, "This is Randy."

He arched his eyebrows, looked at me, and said, "Oh… from Exodus?"

I said, "Formerly an Exodus leader, yes," and quick as a tack, he said, "Aren't they all formerly of Exodus, now?"

We both smiled, and I said, "Well, yes… that is true."

He went on to say, "Oh… we have plans for you, Randy."

That made me a little nervous but also excited. If I can help in any way, I stand ready to do so.

I have contacted other gay organizations on the local and national levels. I have offered to volunteer and help in any way I can. I haven't been pushy and am certainly in no hurry. I have talked with representatives for the Southern Poverty Law Center, The Tyler Clementi Foundation, the award-winning documentarian and the best storyteller on the planet, Daniel Karslake. I also was a part of the Emmy-nominated *Pray Away* documentary, and have had meetings with The Trevor Project. At each of these meetings, projects, or phone calls, I have shared that I only want to help if they think it would be impactful and truly helpful. They have all been very gracious, but most kept me at arm's length.

Maybe they don't trust me. I recognize that it takes about three seconds to google some ridiculous ex-gay talking point stuff I used to say about pro-gay legislation and similar issues. I am me—I can't hide that fact, nor do I want to. And yes, past me offends today me!

HOWEVER (in caps for a reason), while it's easy to search anybody's sins of the past (unless they deliberately try to bury them), it's important to factor in the deeds of the present, and present me only wants to contribute positively to the community I should have been calling home for many years. Sure, some of what I'm doing today is making amends, but that isn't what's important to the community. Amends really only matter to the person making them, the person they directly impacted and their close friends, and their God (or whatever represents a Higher Source for them). So yes, amends may be seen as part of the equation, but the focus is on contributing positively to our LGBTQ+ community because I love them. I love us. I want to serve selflessly and sacrificially, if need be. I want to use my talents, experience, strengths, hope, lessons learned, and expertise to serve the common good. In my situation, that translates to continuing to call for the end of conversion therapy and expose ex-gay ministry for what it is: a toxic, corrosive ideology.

Some Would Call It a Crisis. I Call It a Mid-Life "Evaluation" of a Lifelong Crisis

Mid-life crisis is the commonly held belief that we hit middle-age and suddenly need to create drastic change to feel relevant again. For me, my whole mid-life "evaluation" worked itself out by ending my almost 20-year career because it was based on a foundational, multi-generational, religiously institutionalized lie. In addition, it then took every single belief I had regarding identity, my "calling," spirituality, culture, politics, and relationships and raked these beliefs over the coals. Then I lost all my savings after helping shut down Exodus, before also losing a friend to suicide alongside losing 97% of my friends and church support. Then, ultimately, I came out again before finally losing 80 pounds and buying a brand-new car.

Well, okay, in hindsight, maybe it was a fricking crisis! I see many mid-life evaluations when I look at other 40 and 50 year olds. I also see many chubby, hairy men posing like 20-year-old sports models on Instagram.

Yet one more example of things that haven't changed. LOL.

I am encouraged to see that many LGBTQ+ people my age are trying to figure it all out in ways that are true and honest to who they are.

How did we go from the trauma of the '80s to the perseverance of the '90s and '00s to arrive at a very different world our younger selves could have only imagined?

I've seen many, and I mean many, of my peers hit bottom on substance abuse and join 12-step programs or go into rehab. Many finally leave the church closet not to "go back to a 'lifestyle' of sin" but to move into a healthy life we never thought possible.

Unfortunately, there is also a lot of pessimism, cynicism, and just a general belief that gay men are terrible when it comes to commitment, emotional maturity, selflessness, and faith.

I believe every gay man (and the people who love gay men) should read Alan Downs' book *The Velvet Rage: Overcoming the Pain of Growing Up Gay in a Straight Man's World*. While I believe every gay man will get something out of it, I especially think that my middle-aged brothers would be significantly helped by reading it.

Phrases like, "OH, my WORD!... That is so fucking true!" could be heard as I read every page in the book.

The wisdom found in that book—along with meeting other men my age who are healthy, whole, and seeking to take better care of themselves and the world around them—helped remove a huge stack of weights on my shoulders that I didn't even know I was carrying.

Plus, even though I know *Velvet Rage* was written with gay men in mind, Downs' ideas easily translate to an entire ex-gay movement. I found this book very liberating personally. It makes so much sense, so read it. Well, after you finish reading this book. :)

Gay Bar, Early 2016

I picked up the rough draft of this chapter the day after I had gone out to Southern Nights to watch Mella perform. She was funny and incredibly, I mean INCREDIBLY, raunchy. I loved it. But what I loved the most was watching her enjoy herself.

Before and after the show, I ran into one of the Youngins, his roommate, and one of their friends. I also ran into another former Christian leader from another big organization (not Exodus), and we chatted for a bit. Of course, when I first got to the club, I had my usual Jack and Diet Coke.

I am a middle-aged man, so when I (rarely) head out, I show up early when there is no cover (and nobody there) and the drink specials are still going. Not so I can drink more for less, just so that what I drink costs less. How's that for adulting! I caught up with my favorite bartender and finished my drink during the drag show. I got a fireball shot with a Diet Coke right after and talked to the Youngin about all the joys, trials, and travails in his life.

We veered into oversharing about sexual escapades that had us both laughing loudly at one point. The fireball shot was dedicated to the potential of multiple male orgasms! After only kind of knowing about them and how they work, when I started dating after coming out the second time, I quickly learned that in fact they exist! No, seriously, they do! And they are glorious.

I guess I am much more sex positive now, LOL.

Then at about midnight, I was done with the drinking. I wasn't even buzzed. The Youngin and his crew left, and I stood near the now-packed dance floor as I drank my unadulterated, plain ol' Diet Coke.

I looked down into the bubbly brown liquid and thought, *That shit's toxic. I should have gotten water instead.* But I also felt at peace. I didn't care what people thought of how I was dressed or if I was too old. I watched a couple dancing on one of the elevated platforms, a lesbian couple who were getting married that weekend (which I found out during the drag show), and I smiled.

There was also another young man bionic twerking to the right. Goodness! You could have dropped him in a tub of water, put in some suds, and had an instant clothes washer! I would have been that guy back in the day, but I probably would have been a little more naked and doing the whole bop-slinky "underground" house-type dancing thing.

Then this thought came to mind: *I am so glad I am older, responsibly sober, and comfortable with my connection to the Divine… and ready to go home.* But before I left, I took a moment to capture memorable snapshots in my mind of the packed nightclub. I looked through the front door at the wide variety of people present, their myriad of smiles and joyful expressions while listening to the loud and good music. This might be odd to say, but I also prayed for their safety and for all the modern young people who are hurting and trying to escape difficult situations.

When I walked to my car around 12:20 a.m., it was lightly raining. It felt refreshing. I looked back at the club and, with genuine appreciation, said, "It is what it is, and it's okay."

CHAPTER 11

Life Post Exodus

It's funny how some themes that I would always hit on are still valid. Whenever I spoke or taught workshops at Exodus events, I would say this one thing repeatedly throughout regardless of the subject: "There is more to life than this one issue. Do not limit the totality of life to what you believe about sexuality. It is not the entire context of your life."

I still completely agree with that statement. Yes, I am more than okay with the label of "gay" describing my life. Labels inform, but they unfairly limit a person's perspective when they become the full—or only— context. I am Randy; I am a Christ-follower, gay man, artist, Uncle Silly, asshole in the morning before coffee, socially liberal yet fiscally conservative, husband, bonus dad, etc. There is much more to me than being gay, but being gay is an accurate descriptor.

It was interesting to learn how much "not being gay" or "ex-gay" had confined my worldview. It was all in the name of becoming more spiritually mature, but in truth, it was a formulaic behavioral modification that only served to stunt my growth, not make me more spiritually mature. It was a system of belief that was lacking in integrity and accountability. The ex-gay/conversion world was a complete denial of my physical/relational reality and a rejection of the reality that the finished work of the cross, the Divine's grace personified in Jesus, is for God's gay children, too. By trying to conform to someone else's image of God, I dishonored the one They had already given me to reflect.

So much of my life had become about "not being gay" that it saturated my relational life to the point that I thought God called me to live a celibate life. I lived that way for over 23 years as a result. It became my career to not only "not be gay" but also to teach others how to deny an intrinsic part of themselves. I was a true believer, and I thought I was free during the entire time I was actually shackled and caged. It was nice in a numbing, "don't think about it too much" way.

Initially, After Leaving Exodus, I Was Crestfallen, Isolated, and Then Pissed

As I wrote in Chapter 8, 2013 was a horrible year. At Exodus, life was running at 900 mph and FULL of noise for years. When it all fell apart, everything went silent, and depression kicked in. So, when I went on my "fight for life, don't get run over by it" kick, I got furious.

As in super-duper pissed off, head exploding, inner-drag-queen-snark-monster fury!

In the aftermath of an entire movement and all the relationships that came with it writing me off, I was finally able to process the past few years' events personally. I didn't have to worry about Exodus or helping my boss think through the issues and responses. I wasn't being distracted by the next ex-gay leader tantrum and the incessant "need to talk" phone calls and emails. It was just me, a shit-load of questions, and God. It very well could be God that had me reread this paragraph and realize that with all the cussing I just wrote, I am still quite angry.

Yes, there is more to life than this one issue. I always told myself never to believe that I would be in ex-gay ministry for the rest of my life. Yet the void of not being at Exodus left a huge, gaping hole in my life. The feeling of isolation was potent and deeply surprising. I was 45 years old, questioning everything, and at a complete loss as to who I was and what to do next.

However, as I write this, I am remembering my eagle vision from my time in therapy. I am imagining my wings are unfurled, and I am flying but not used to turbulence.

Celebr8ing the NOH8 Campaign

On May 9, 2015, I got up early and went to Target to find a plain white t-shirt. As dull as shopping for a simple white t-shirt sounds, I was nervous as I browsed through the various displays. My mind was full of thoughts about going to get my photo taken at the NOH8 campaign's Orlando photo shoot. NOH8 was a photo and marketing campaign originally created to counter Prop 8 rhetoric. It would be a symbolic culmination of ending years of estrangement from myself, my heart, and a community I truly love.

Symbolic in the sense that it was one of the first—if not *the* first—times that I made a plan to partake in and support a gay cause, and going to Target to buy a t-shirt just for that photo shoot was something that would have been seen as spending money to promote sin while I was part of the ex-gay world. But that was no longer true. Spending money on a simple white t-shirt was about promoting equality, and it was especially important for me because the NOH8 campaign was an integral piece of my turning away from the ex-gay movement and Exodus and finally accepting and embracing who I was—and then making the decision to express that publicly through my support. The irony that it was a *white* t-shirt was not lost on me. In the religious context, my former colleagues would have seen wearing white being symbolic of the scripture that states, "Come now, and let us reason together, saith the Lord: though your sins be as scarlet, they shall be as white as snow; though they be red like crimson, they shall be as wool" (Isaiah 1:18).

That scripture is why many Christian faith traditions have people wearing white robes when they get baptized. For my former colleagues, I was committing a sin by participating in this campaign. For me, I was taking a first step toward cleansing the sins of my past.

The Importance of People Like Scottie

My friend Scottie Thompson and I started following each other online during the ongoing Prop 8 battle. I caught wind that he was an activist within the LGBTQ+ community and just started following him online. At the time, one friend said to me, "You only follow that Scottie guy because he's always naked and HOT!" (To be clear, Scottie is only sometimes naked, and most of that is only half-naked. And well, even clothed, he— maybe I should stop there.)

In response to this friend at the time, I said, "Oh no, no… He's just an interesting person who does the gay activist thing differently—a way that will work to their benefit."

Now, gurrrrrl, you know part of me was following him hoping the next post would be another temptation to think naughty things, but I was still in the "I'm just here to minister God's love" denial game.

So, the first time I messaged Scottie while I was still at Exodus, I wrote some weird little greeting, to which he replied, and I loved his response! It's still my favorite response from a gay activist ever. With a very gracious intro, he went on to say something along the lines of, "I have nothing but antipathy for what you are doing at Exodus and what Exodus stands for." He then, of course, being him, ended the message graciously.

Being a word person, I can't tell you how happy I was that he used the word antipathy, and I was ecstatic he used it correctly! Of course, it wasn't so fun to be a part of the receiving end of Scottie's "antipathy," but this is indicative of why I am drawn to follow his life online. He is fair, purposeful, eloquent, and thoughtful. But instead of consuming and regurgitating it as infotainment activism, he contributes to the overall discussion.

Plus, you get all that AND his chiseled frame is allergic to wearing shirts.

I spent quite a bit of time talking with Scottie before and after coming out again in January 2015. During that time, we talked a lot about Prop 8. After hearing his heart, my own stirred with deep emotion as years of questioning turned into a change of heart about marriage equality. Not only that, my conversations with him (and a couple of others) sent another lightning bolt through my hard heart of stone, and I found myself yearning for my future husband—NOT lust, not self-focused, not selfishly need-based, but to genuinely love and adore another man as my spouse. I began to open to that possibility for myself in a way that may not have ever been so passionate and deep before.

Of H8 and Prop8

When anti-gay marriage Prop 8 passed, I was boasting online that what we, the religious activists, had done was the right thing to do. I was so cheerful that it and other anti-gay marriage amendments I had lobbied for had passed that evening. I talked a good game online, but when the gay community, including Scottie, took to the streets in protest, my big mouth was forcibly shut by my stunned heart. I didn't say anything at the time, but looking at the grief and anguish on their faces took me by surprise. It was a moment that made me question if what we had just done was wrong for the first time in years. While watching the protests that night, the Spirit asked, "How could you do that to your community?"

I met many conservative leaders during my anti-gay lobbying days. I went on numerous trips to various states to lobby against marriage equality and made visits to Capitol Hill and the White House in DC for a myriad of interviews. I had to shove the potential impacts out of my head at the time. It was too much and didn't fit the legalistic culture-vulture framework I had willfully forced myself into.

Do you know what happens when you try to channel a force of nature through a weakly constructed framework? The flimsy framework, like wet cardboard, will erode and break. The power of nature and the reality of that force is that it WILL take its natural course and place among creation. So as the unnatural walls—developed and embraced by weak men like I was— came crumbling and crashing down in light of God's grace and love, my repentant sorrow poured out and eventually helped me back to the course I was created for as a gay man.

My house of cards may have been held together by super glue, but even that was no match for the truth that set the whole fucking thing on fire.

Many events, people, and I believe God worked to erode the ex-gay ideology/theology I had worked myself into believing. The gay community being honest, forceful, non-violent, and direct was incredibly important for marriage equality. What lodged in my heart and stayed there were the humanizing opportunities that most LGBTQ+ communities took.

Two examples:

1. Personal: Scottie is honest yet approachable and gracious.

2. As a community: The NOH8 campaign put a face to the issue. Many beautiful faces, in fact.

I love people. I love words. Being an artist, I love art and symbolism. I can't tell you how many times I have privately welled up with emotions looking at various NOH8 portraits. The beautiful lighting and the simple, innocent symbolism of white shirts bring the viewer's eyes into focus. But the grieved/angered faces and the duct tape over people's mouths rip my heart out. The thought that I contributed to silencing the gay community on such a heart level is a deep regret, a shame I carry. I have apologized to the gay community, but I don't think I have fully forgiven myself for my anti-gay lobbying. I can understand why some won't and will never forgive me. It hurts, but it is a hurt I inflicted. I'll leave it at that for now.

Mr. Future Husband–NOH8 Becomes Personal

Early on, when dating in the spring of 2015, a romantic interest I had dated for around five weeks let me know that he was going to pursue a relationship with someone else. Someone he had been upfront about from the beginning, a man he had met about a month before me.

I was heartbroken. This guy was a great guy. He handled everything very well. He was and is honest, above reproach, humble, and a man of integrity.

After coming out again, it took me almost three months to be willing to date. I had been on a few dates, but this guy was the first person I had been on more than two dates with. During this time, LOADS of insecurity and fear came rushing back. It was overwhelming and excessive. After much journaling and talking with a few friends, I remembered that I hadn't dated men in over 25 years. I had only seriously dated two women during that time, so my dating experience was pretty much reset to zero.

Plus, 25 years prior, I didn't date so much as I just partied. The three men I fell in love with as a teen/young adult were:[9]

- Ralph—I was 17 and he was 36 when we first "got together." That should be enough said. But he also passed away from AIDS a year after we stopped hooking up. How I am HIV-negative is a mystery to me. His death was severely shocking. He didn't even know he was HIV-positive until two weeks before he died. He was among those who were taken in the first horrible waves of the AIDS pandemic. And, as I edit this and reflect on my history, I can finally admit to myself that this is the man who raped me. It's been almost four decades, and I've just gotten to the place of being able to acknowledge that there is a difference between hooking up and what this man did the last time we had sex.

- Todd—I was with him for 18 months until the brawl in Atlanta, and he was incredibly abusive. We were constantly drinking and doing drugs as well. Looking back, I see why I thought abuse was love, but it still saddens me.

- Steven—We were romantically together for just a few months, but he was a very kind and healthy person. After deciding we were better as friends than boyfriends, we remained friends for 23 years. Sadly, as I wrote earlier, he took his own life in January of 2013.

---

9 As a reminder, names have been changed.

So the three men I had believed myself to love and be in relationships with had all ended tragically. Those were my only experiences of trying to have real "relationships" with men. No wonder there was an undercurrent of fear to overcome.

Other than these three men, my "dating" experience was random party dudes discovered via the magic of bar light. It wasn't a huge, long list, but because my relational history with men had been so terrible, it was easy to project my hurt, fear, and disappointment on the gay community as a whole. Then, when I found myself in the ex-gay conversion therapy world, who were encouraging me to objectify and transfer all my hurt and personal dysfunction onto the gay community, my dysfunction felt validated, so I did. In other words, the church found a hurt, dejected, and scared man wandering the desert alone and searching for a place of belonging and love, and instead of offering me sanctuary and love, they offered me lies that only reinforced my pain and fear. They met me where I was at and took advantage of my situation to their benefit. Yes, I was a willing participant, but a willing participant who was damaged, blind, broken, and searching for anything that would make it better.

Today, I know that God created me to be who I am. And as a personal force of nature, that shame-fueled ideology could not stand against God's grace and love for me as Their son in Christ. A son who happens to be a gay man, among many other attributes. That weak ideology of cultural stigmatization cannot possibly stand in the light of God's love and grace for the gay community.

Today, my emotional maturity and coping skills are age appropriate. I humbly assert, "I got this." However, in 2015, my heart and my mind were still catching up. I had shut off the dream and joy of looking for my future husband from 1992 until I came out again in 2015.

I will never shut down my heart again.

The first inkling I had at wanting the dream of marriage was at the NOH8 photo shoot that I started writing about in this section. On that day, I ran across Dan, who mentioned being so in love with this little young 20-something man, and well, I found myself jealous. I sent well wishes but wondered when that would end. The spark of curiosity was lit. It was about a year and a half before we started dating, even though his relationship with the young man would end soon after that day at NOH8.

Later in the book, I will share more about the man of my dreams.

Common + Unity = Community

As I stood in line at the NOH8 photo shoot event pulling the "inspected by" sticker off my new white t-shirt, which somehow survived the laundry, I experienced many heart-tugging moments:

- Watching a smiling lesbian mom chase after her rambunctious toddler who grabbed my pant leg, wanting me to pick him up.

- Seeing a group of friends on the stage (where the photo shoot was set up) support each other with a clever group photo.

- Witnessing a moment where an older gay male couple with emotion in their eyes held each other's hands.

I even marveled as I listened to an obnoxious queen complaining about everything. I was so glad to be there, and I felt my nervousness evaporate.

I had texted Scottie the night before about a friend being concerned that the NOH8 folks might not appreciate me being there. I wasn't too concerned, but I thought I should check with him, just in case. Scottie was on the board of directors for the NOH8 campaign, so he knew NOH8's leadership and texted them. He said they would be welcoming, and they were. They were incredibly kind, gave me hugs, and seemed genuinely glad for my change of heart. They both said, "This is why we do what we do. It's about changing hearts and minds, so you are welcome here."

As the flash went off on the camera, I followed their instructions for posing. I felt the duct tape on my mouth and was humbled by God's grace in liberating my heart and leading me to this symbolic (to me) act of repentance. I was also proudly conscious of the NOH8 temporary tattoo on my cheek and felt incredibly positive about everything in that moment, including who I am and where I was.

The symbolic duct tape made me realize how I had silenced myself for years, living a lie and encouraging others to do the same, all for the love of a God who loved me anyway. The ex-gay ministry does its best to behave like duct tape, silencing those who are living their truth. Ultimately, they will never succeed, because God, however you understand Them, will always be greater, and God's love will always be greater than cultural hatred. In that moment, I finally started to realize just how loved I had always been. Gratefully, I am finally living and speaking an unhindered truth from my heart.

My heart is an open book and door for my entire community (LGBTQ+, church… anyone willing to be "family"), but it was also reserved for the man I ran into at that photo shoot and would eventually marry, Dan. He makes me feel safe when we embrace. When I look into his eyes, I know I am home.

We had met briefly once before and had become friends on Facebook the day I came out again. Little did I know that a year and a few months after bumping into each other at the photo shoot, he would find me at Orlando Pride 2016 and ask me out for coffee, and we have been together ever since.

Respecting Each Other's Journey and Process

Since I started speaking out against ex-gay conversion ministries, many productive and essential conversations have happened online and off. Today, I want to clarify that I have total respect for someone's personal journey. However, I don't respect organizations that feel the need to perpetuate cultural bias and stigma in the name of spiritual growth, relational healing, and "biblical truth."

I still have a few (not many, by their own choice) conservative Christian friends that I love dearly. Some of whom are ex-gay, same-gender attracted, and married to people of the opposite sex, or gay and celibate because of their spiritual beliefs. Some of these friends have been my friends since my early 20s. I would do anything to help them and make no apologies for supporting them in any way I can. I love them, and they love me. Mutual love and respect matter.

If someone tells me I am wrong and that they can't live with the "gay" label—okay, thanks for your opinion. I am more interested in you than labels, too. Suppose they believe that same-gender sexual expressions and identity are sinful; well, I think you're wrong, but you are entitled to your opinion. If they want my thoughts, which isn't always the case, I have no problem sharing them in genuine, life-giving conversation.

However, what I won't do is judge them in my heart and try to ma-nipulate my way into changing their mind. When appropriate or asked, I will share my experience but not try to impose it as a template for anyone else to follow. Imposing our will on others is exactly what ex-gay ministry is all about. When I left that harmful ideology, I made the decision not to impose my will or beliefs on anyone again. Instead, I share my story and invite conversation and thoughtful discussion.

For example, if someone believes they are "called" to celibacy, I don't try to persuade them otherwise. I lived it myself for 23 years. I learned MANY things about celibacy scripturally and in a real, practical application sense. Living that way helped me think through things, have *extraordinary* spiritual intimacy with God, and develop natural, lasting character strengths. But unfortunately, I also lived that way because of overwhelming fear, brainwashing, and idealization. So my motivation and experience were a mixed bag because they weren't rooted in a true "calling"—they were rooted in shame and conversion therapy.

In the ex-gay conversion therapy world, celibacy becomes the only option when you are attracted to others of the same gender. That's not a "calling." It's oppressive manipulation resulting from religious stigma. In order to rationalize this, a person can work themselves up into a goose-bumpy, "I heard from the LORD, I am His Bride!" kind of tizzy to "confirm their calling" and resolve the cognitive dissonance they are experiencing. However, in truth, that's using your imagination to reconcile the irreconcilable. As a gay man, you are probably a sexual creature who will not know your whole, authentic self if you do not accept yourself as who you are. In truth, sex is a gift, regardless of your sexual orientation. Having a relational state of being as a whole LGBTQ+ person is a gift. Embrace that truth, and you will find your own relational fulfillment, whatever that means for you. A true calling to celibacy is a gift, but embracing a call to celibacy out of stigma, fear, and brainwashing is a prison—a gilded cage.

I say this knowing the heartbreak it may cause some. I learned these lessons the hard way, and that part of my journey broke my heart in very sensitive ways. I share this so that you don't repeat my mistakes. If you are considering a life of celibacy in order to avoid the truth of being who you are, I believe your season of celibacy will end one day so you can meet your true relational needs as befits you as a queer person. You can and will find love. You can have sex, and it is a good, genuine, God-given gift.

The problem with ex-gay groups is that they make a career out of repeating the cultural bigotry against gay people of faith and distorting reality by saying celibacy and opposite-sex marriage are the ONLY way gay people of faith can adequately live in relationship to God. They say that if you are not happy, healthy, and whole living as a celibate or married to the opposite sex, you still need the group to help fix whatever else they can determine is still "broken" in you. Because in their world, you wouldn't desire "sexual sin" if you were genuinely healthy and in a relationship with Christ.

And the treadmill of shame and condemnation keeps going and going.

Here's the truth. Gay people aren't broken because they are gay. Like the rest of humanity, we have issues, but being gay is not a negative—it is a gift. Gay people of faith don't need to be fixed or restrained through behavioral modification to be "right with God." We need the same respect, opportunities, and resources straight people and couples have. That's it.

When I was suicidal after the close of Exodus, it was because I realized I had been living a legalistic lie on many levels. I couldn't see the good of the past (and there is plenty) and was spiraling into despair. Living a celibate life was no longer life-giving to me. Intimacy with God was still there, as it is now, and I felt Him guiding me to question everything. He's always made it very clear that I could trust the Divine; He loved me for who I am. I knew in my heart and soul that the season of living a celibate life had ended, and initially, I was deathly afraid of what that meant. I was taught for over two decades that all I could do was be celibate or find a wife. Now that I was free of those false shackles, in my heart, my desire for my future husband was more vital than ever before.

I fought it tooth and nail, but I fell in love with my husband long before knowing who he would be. I found my eyes constantly drawn to the horizon in search of him. Then the Spirit removed my blinders and showed that the yearning and desire I had in my heart was a beautiful expression of love… one that I was afraid to look at, honestly. Instead of being scared and alone, I could see it as a healthy natural extension of the whole person in Christ I had grown to be.

My encounters with the Divine have been comprehensive and, across the board, amazing. This includes being set free to love as God created me to love. To serve as God created me to serve. To move from one finished season of life to the next fantastic chapter, still in love with and trusting the Divine and my Guardian Angel Squad.

I can also trust the Divine to take care, protect, and shepherd my marriage to Dan and our little family. When I look to the horizon of my future now, Jesus is there, pointing us in the right direction.

My process and journey are my own, and I have zero interest in trying to make my life a template for someone else to follow. I only seek to be the best friend I can be as others seek to live in a manner they feel compelled to live. I trust in a God who is the author of every single breath. I trust in the Divine's gift of you and me to the world.

Let's look for the beauty of God in every person's face and spirit without being distracted by the perceived faults of others.

CHAPTER 12

#OrlandoStrong

Pulse – June 2016

(These are my social media posts from June 10 through June 19, 2016—before, during, and after the Pulse shooting in Orlando.)

June 10, 2016, at 9:47 p.m.—Instagram. I just left the HRC Orlando/Central Florida Federal Club event, where I shared my story. It was a great experience, and I met so many amazing people! I am blessed and humbled! And exhausted! Such a great night!

June 11, 2016, at 9:09 a.m.—Facebook. Good Saturday morning! It was so great to sleep in and just shuffle around the house drinking coffee, reading this, remembering that, dreaming about the future, and checking out your Facebook shenanigans. You all are highly entertaining with your Facebook shenanigans :). I am headed back out at noon to a steering committee meeting for HRC Orlando (yes, another post about them!). It's a planning meeting that will last the afternoon, and guess what? I am going because I joined their steering committee! I'm not sure what I signed up for about that, but I feel I will figure that all out today. I'm excited and definitely in #HappaRanda mode. Have a fantastic day!

June 11, 2016, at 7:42 p.m.—Sanford—Facebook. I am feeling all the feels tonight. I am excited for last night's and today's meetings, angry about a friend being poorly treated (in my opinion), grateful for being free, loving, and missing someone very dear, laughing at an Instagram post, and emotionally pooped from being immersed in a whole new world last and this weekend! What is needed now is to just lay here on the couch and play a round of expert-level Sudoku.

June 12, 2016, at 7:34 a.m.—Facebook. I woke up early to learn about the mass shooting at Pulse Orlando. I am texting and messaging all my friends to find out if they are okay. I know one person who works there and any of my friends who go out may have been there. My heart is shattered. Please pray, and whether you pray or not, we all must do something to stop this. I'm so incredibly upset/angry/concerned. #PulseOrlando #StopTheHate #PrayForOrlando

June 12, 2016, at 2:42 p.m.—Sanford—Facebook. The Orlando area community (and especially the Orlando LGBTQ community) is fantastic and strong. On the one hand, I keep weeping over the tragedy and the victims; on the other, I get deeply emotional over the strength and courage of the family, friends, and neighbors. The outpouring of love and support personally and from around the world for our community is overwhelming. Cowardly, murderous terrorists horrify at the moment, but love wins the day and forever. #LGBTQ #PrayForOrlando #OrlandoStrong

June 12, 2016, at 9:02 p.m.—Instagram. I know it is a small thing, but I have put a gay pride/equality sticker on my car for the first time. I hadn't done so before because I didn't want any negativity drawn to my vehicle. It seems silly to think about that concern now. And, after today, it is a small way to show that I love and care for our #LGBTQ+ community. This #Equality logo (which I love) is the only gay-themed bumper sticker I have. After today, if I had others, there is a good chance they would have all ended up in the car. So yes,

Hubert the Handsome Humble Hybrid is an ally. I think he wears it well.

June 13, 2016, at 8:28 a.m.—Facebook. It's Monday, and while I am having a hard time saying good morning like I usually do on Mondays, I will say that I will do my best to find good, or do good, this morning. Orlando has asked that there be no large vigils yet (safety concerns, police resources), but several smaller ones are happening. I will be going to one today hosted by First Congregational Church of Winter Park, United Church of Christ (LGBTQ+ affirming), at Rollins College with Roger and his wife. It will be good to be with family (of the chosen variety). So, my Facebook friendlies, regardless of the status of your morning, I hope you find the good in and do good for others today.

June 13, 2016, at 6:54 p.m.—Instagram. Crowds are gathering for tonight's vigil in Orlando.

June 13, 2016, at 9:31 p.m.—Instagram—Orlando. "The City Beautiful" lives up to its name. Walking back to my car, I am overwhelmed with emotion. I love my community. I will be posting more pics to my Facebook page later tonight or tomorrow morning.

June 14, 2016, at 1:04 p.m.—Facebook. Last night driving home from the vigil, and today, I am so furious. I know it is from not sleeping much because of PTSD-triggered nightmares the past two nights. It would be unfair and unhelpful to go into full-on rant mode in this state. But yes, I am tempted to do just that. It is very hard not to go crazy when I read posts by opportunistic, attention-seeking manipulators trying to force this terrible situation into a false context. What happened at Pulse is a hate crime against the Latinx and LGBTQ+ communities as it is a domestic terrorist act against all US citizens and freedom-loving people worldwide. To leave out those first two basic, essential facts is to bear false witness. That, in turn, and in my opinion, dishonors the victims and their families. Now that my blood pressure has risen to an excellent moderate boil, I will stop there. <--That was hard to do. You should have seen the first three drafts of this post! I need to take some Excedrin now.

June 14, 2016, at 6:13 p.m.—Facebook. The social media streams I monitor (for clients, news, and personally) just refilled with a higher level of really ugly hatred and anger (justified anger and not). I am back to struggling with trying to find the words. More than a few friends and acquaintances have said that this is a life-changing moment. I feel the same way. I am going to choose to make it a positive life-changing moment. Careful confrontation is essential, but reverse stigmatization, hatred, and insults aren't ever acceptable and perpetuate a toxic cycle. I want to confront when necessary, carefully, but always seek grace/peace and try my best to facilitate some level of unity. We will get through this. #WeAreOrlando #OrlandoStrong

June 15, 2016, at 11:19 a.m.—Facebook. It's Wednesday morning. I want to share something that I feel is important. I got a message from a conservative evangelical Christian acquaintance saying that this is an "opportunity" for "the church" to rise and be of love and support to our community. She generalized "community," so there is no acknowledgment of the Latinx and LGBTQ+ communities. Then she quoted an Old Testament scripture saying that if God's people didn't rise to help, He would bring help from somewhere else.

Here's the truth: God's people have already "risen." The victims who prayed "rose up" while being caught in that horrible moment. God's people have already risen with ongoing prayers by and for the families and the friends, partners, and loved ones. God's people sprang into action minutes after the horrible tragedy unfolded via the friends who did what they could to protect and help. God's people sprang into action through the first responders who ran into harm's way. God's people have already risen through Latinx and LGBTQ+ affirming clergy selflessly and sacrificially serving. God's people have been in action at every point of need, at every resource, and every vigil.

God's people of all faiths and not religious people have all equally "risen up" since those first awful moments until now and on into the future. We all have manifested a beauty and healing that can only be brought about by a truly loving, unified, and selfless community.

I believe that God has been present in every tear shed and every memory shared; His image is present in every picture wet with tears, every spontaneous song, every message of love and support from around the world, and with every hand extended in comfort and service. Wherever there is mourning with those who mourn, comfort given to the grieving, provisions made for the need, and champions giving voice to grace and justice. God's beauty manifests, and the Divine through us *all* conquers hatred and darkness.

I am glad this acquaintance has a desire in her heart to love and serve. If she and other conservatives in her world want to love, help, and support our Latinx, LGBTQ+, and Orlando community at large, they are more than welcome to join those of us who are already doing what we can to help and serve.

While I can only speak for myself, I believe our community would take sincere, honest, and selfless help from anyone. But God's help is already at work. His people have already risen to the task. Join us?

June 16, 2016, at 9:11 a.m.—Facebook. It's Thursday morning. My priority is the Pulse shooting victims, survivors, and their families and loved ones. I am also consumed with thoughts of Orlando and our local LGBTQ+ family. As I was typing, my mind intended to write "local LGBTQ+ *community*" but my heart took over my fingers and typed "local LGBTQ+ family" instead.

Today, I want to focus on these beautiful people and not policy. Not federal policy, not state policy, not church policy. Those conversations are necessary and need to happen. Today, though, family first.

June 16, 2016, at 7:53 p.m.—Facebook. I went to a new barber tonight, and we had SUCH a powerful conversation. A bustling, hole-in-the-wall-off-to-the-side shop, I ended up in this guy's chair. We talked about the tragedy, and then he honored me by saying how it impacted his brother, who is trans, and one of their cousins was one of the victims. I am blown away and speechless. Please pray for this new friend and their family. #WeAreOrlando #OrlandoStrong

June 17, 2016, at 9:44 a.m.—Facebook. It is Friday morning, and I want to share something that has been of great comfort. Even though it has been incredibly stressful this week, I have been humbled and blessed to see how amazing our local community is. These folks have HUGE, selfless, service-oriented, and sacrificial hearts. They also have the brains, expertise, experience, and organizational structures to get people mobilized while staying on point. They can withstand the pressure and keep focused on serving the victims' families and survivors first while seeking justice, unifying, and protecting the community. From the very first moments, watching from my limited vantage point, I received comfort that I belong to a community with heart, wisdom, and perseverance. This is a family that does understand true grace and embodies genuine love in both intent and action.

And while I am an emotive, burn-through-the-Kleenex kind of guy, you know what else I like about this beautiful community? They know how to get shit done! My goodness! Never in my life have I seen people act in "one accord" this beautifully! Common + Unity = Community, and in Orlando, it also means family. I <3 Orlando

June 17, 2016, at 5:18 p.m.—Sanford—Facebook. Why yes, I am going out tonight. I am going to enjoy my friends; I will dance with and laugh with my community. Then, of course, I will raise a glass in remembrance and process with everyone where we are and where we're going. Then I will meet new friends and listen to them as they share their stories. And you know what else? I will celebrate freedom, life, love, and the Orlando LGBTQ+ community. Of course, I will be safe, and I will NOT be afraid.

If you are local and going out tonight, message me if you want to say howdy.

June 18, 2016, at 11:10 a.m.—Sanford—Facebook. Hello, my friends! I had a wonderful time visiting with loved ones and meeting new friends last night. There were, of course, lots more hugs than usual, a few tears, and harrowing stories. But I have to tell you, I am so stinking proud of our community. Seeing the beautiful souls and loving hearts last night was a treasure.

That said, this old man is plum tuckered out! I boogie oogie oogied till I just can't boogie anymore! So I will be taking it easy today.

June 19, 2016, at 7:25 a.m.—Sanford—Facebook. I woke up, and it was cloudy, darker than usual. Listening to a soft rain shower hit the roof and weeping with the skies and remembered it is one week later. #OrlandoUnited #OneOrlando #OrlandoPulse

After Orlando Pulse Shooting—A New Era Has Begun

I will never forget waking up Sunday, June 12, 2016 and shuffling over to my phone. I saw an alert pop up from a friend's nephew messaging me, "Did you see what happened in Orlando?… Holy shit! At Pulse!" I flew to my computer, and between that and my phone, I was messaging, checking social media profiles, and emailing any friends who might have been there or who I knew worked there.

It's hard to describe the power of the mixed feelings that happen when one by one, you find your friends are alive, but the death toll climbs to a staggering 49 people. I did not know any of the people murdered. However, the devastation rippled outward further and further, deeper and deeper, as the week went on. I know two friends who lost cousins in the attack. Another friend lost a good friend and had a co-worker wounded as she fled the scene. I also learned of many other friends and acquaintances who lost someone or knew someone who was injured and trying to heal. Two of the Youngins were planning on going that night but changed their minds. Thank God. I met a man at one of the vigils who lost three of his friends, and another one of his friends was in the hospital fighting for his life. And at every event and meeting I went to, I saw the haunted eyes of people who had seen horror and felt loss in ways that words cannot encapsulate.

Plus, we are still learning the details and hearing the stories. These are my neighbors, people I may have danced next to at one time or another on a crowded dance floor or seen at various events. The ripples and pain from the stories and aftermath keep flowing.

As I left the big downtown vigil on Monday night, June 13th, I took a picture of the enormous memorial area where everyone was leaving flowers. While I was there, a young man and his boyfriend walked up with tears pouring down their faces. Then, the taller of the two peeked up over the crowd to see and immediately collapsed to the ground in mourning. He couldn't be consoled, and his boyfriend joined him on the ground, scooped him up, and held him tight.

Those of us around them gathered and placed our hands on their shoulders and arms. While spiritual in energy, it wasn't a religious act. It was humans mourning with those who mourn. It was an act of communal support that transcended words. Smartphones and cameras disappeared, the unfiltered beauty of humanity emerged, and our tears fell as whispered words of comfort and love eventually flowed forward to the grieving couple.

One Orlando, One World, One Voice

Within 24–48 hours, it was evident that the impact had devastated Orlando, and the ripples created virtual tsunamis through the internet and social media. I couldn't stop crying at all the videos and messages streaming in from around the world. Paris lighting up the Eiffel Tower in rainbow colors. Tel Aviv's city hall was doing the same, and tens of thousands were in the streets of London, singing. Then there was LA Pride and London Pride (and many others) stopping the parades for moments of silence. All the major cities across the world did magnificent memorials—an outpouring of love.

Earlier that year, I started trying to learn more about, engage with, and serve the local community. I had done some volunteer work for HRC Orlando (Human Rights Campaign), and eventually they asked me to share my story at an event for them the Friday night before the Pulse tragedy. All that to say, I was a newbie in that world and didn't know all that I needed to know at the time, and I still don't know what I don't know yet. Even so, I was able to join my HRC Orlando friends at one of their houses that horrible Sunday morning. There were tears, and that is when I learned that the death toll had jumped from 20 to 49, it was crushing news, and I am glad I was not alone, and we had each other at that moment.

Later in the morning, there was a conference call of many different leaders, local and national, and I listened in. It was comforting, listening to these folks keeping proper perspective and priorities while operating in selflessness and wisdom. I was deeply touched and inspired by the heart of our community leaders and volunteers. I am amazed that they knew how to get mobilized rapidly, efficiently, and comprehensively. It was indeed a community, at every level, in "one accord," and it was beautiful. Even though I had been in community-based organizations for over two decades, I have never seen anything like what unfolded that day. It is a comfort that there is a genuinely loving community we can turn to and rely on.

As Momma Mella once said to me when I was a homeless gay 19 year old, "When the world mistreats us, we have to love each other. WE have to be there for each other. We are family."

Catalyst

Many in the local LGBTQ+ community are saying Pulse was a historic turning point for us. Many—and I do mean many—of my personal friends and acquaintances were saying that it was a personal turning point for them as well. I agree. Of course, we all have our processes, so I will be interested to see how they adapt and grow beyond this. I know for me, it became an unbridled passion for our community. To do what I can to carefully confront and hopefully end destructive religious bias and bigotry against God's gay children. That last sentence encompasses a lot.

While I can only speak for myself, I believe the LGBTQ+ community has had enough. We have been beaten, bullied, and abused as children, mocked and abused as teens, pressured, discriminated against, turned away, disenfranchised, and violently attacked as adults. We face widespread discrimination in every sector of society, and most LGBTQ+ people still live in secrecy and fear. All because of our natural relational state of being—who we are.

No more. Simply put, no more.

This will end. It will stop. Love is winning and will overcome hatred. There is no other option. Others may choose to be silent. Their silence is noted but will not discourage us. Some will decide to oppose full LGBTQ+ equality like I once did. Still, as they seek to reinforce institutionalized/

generationally reinforced closets of shame and condemnation, we will be selflessly serving. We will be sacrificially giving toward the good of all and not lost in the myopic concerns of a few. Hearts and minds will change along the way.

Mine did.

Shortly after the Pulse tragedy, I joined 19 other LGBTQ+ siblings as we took part in the Orlando City Soccer Club pregame show. We were lifting the massive, circular Orlando Lions logo flag. As we walked on the field in five lines of four, we proudly held each other's hands. At the end of the fourth row, I held Jagger's hand (another former Exodus staff person). When the crowd roared as they noticed our group, the volume tripled as we then raised our held hands in the air. I looked around at our crew's huge, broad smiles, lots of emotion in our eyes.

We will always grieve the loss of our brothers and sisters killed. We will take care of their families. We will unite as a city and nation. We are here with the rest of the world's love pouring in and echoing through our hearts and streets. Love is winning, as it always does.

The Tone-Deaf, Heartless Culture Vulture Reaction to Pulse

The following story led to my outburst on Facebook posted on June 14th around 1 p.m., mentioned earlier in this chapter.

"Randy, hold on…" was what I heard when I picked up my phone. Then there was shuffling and the closing of a door in the background. My heart was racing because of the name I had seen on the caller ID. We will call him Mr. Gorgeous, or Mr. G for short. He worked for Focus on the Family, a right-wing organization. He is a man who at heart is very loving. We really hadn't talked since the closing of Exodus and my coming back out of the closet in 2015. At the time of the call, we were on entirely different sides on any issue, but even so, I have always liked the guy. And Mr. G, if you are reading this, yes, I've always thought you are gorgeous.

"You there?" he asked.

"Yes, what's up?"

"For starters, I am so sorry for all that has happened in Orlando and am so glad you are safe. I have a situation here at work. I am hiding in one of the conference rooms so I can talk freely…"

And as he explained the situation, my blood began to boil, but because this man had done nothing but try to be a friend during all the hubbub at the end of Exodus, I kept my cool and didn't cut him off.

He had been asked if he would be a spokesperson for Focus regarding the Pulse tragedy. Mr. G was being advised to only contextualize the event as a domestic terror incident at a nightclub. He asked how that would come off. I knew he already knew the answer, or he wouldn't have called. Calmly, I said, "While those two details are true, you will be lying by omission if you do not include that it was a domestic terror incident against the Latinx LGBTQ+ community. To leave those last two important details out is to bear false witness about the event and, in my opinion, dishonor the fallen and survivors."

"I don't think they will be on board with that."

"Then don't do it."

I haven't heard from Mr. G again except for brief comments on Facebook. That's okay; we weren't incredibly close even though we were friends. In truth, I was honored he reached out to me, as it showed the extent of the friendship between us. In the end, I didn't see him on any cable news or large media outlets (right-wing or not), so I am assuming he stood his ground with them, because I know he agreed with me, or he wouldn't have called.

The "just say it was a domestic terror incident at a nightclub" crowd cares so much about not affirming LGBTQ+ people in any way that they are willing to lie about such a tragedy. They (the primarily religious-right organizations) cared more about reframing the public narrative than sending financial support to the organizations set up to help families of the fallen and survivors with their hospital, mental health, and everyday bills. These culture vultures were more interested in securing camera time to bolster their confirmation bias and drum up support from their base than mourning with those who were mourning and providing essential resources for the hungry and vulnerable. Instead of simply telling the truth and expressing broken hearts over the hate followed by acts of love of service, they wanted to gloss it over in a way that made them feel better about "showing support" when that was the last thing they ever intended on giving. Paying lip service in the face of the horror of what happened that night was not loving. It was a mockery of love. Repeating manipulative talking points in an interview is selfish, indulgent, empowers a glossed-over hatred, and isn't anywhere near the heart of the Divine or the teachings of Christ.

The Exit Door Is This Way

The following is full of emotion, but it is not written with contempt. It's my honest opinion born out of experience. It is direct and to the point, so it would be easy to read it as harsh, but please don't. It is written from a broken heart and an abuse survivor's passion, not a vengeful one.

Religious legalism is of immense harm to LGBTQ+ people.

First, I believe the bastardized version of religion—which was taught to the man who shot the beautiful souls at Pulse Nightclub—is an evil ideology. This corrupt system of thought led him to think it was a divinely blessed mandate to murder 49 and wound 53 Latinx LGBTQ+ people in a mass shooting.

Second, the bastardized version of the religion I am associated with (Christianity) teaches LGBTQ+ people an evil ideology that says to be divinely blessed and okay with God's will and people, we must kill our core relational sense of being, identity, and expressions of love.

Both of these twisted versions of spiritual teachings are abusive and deadly.

Systemic bigotry and bias have been passed down for generations. So much so that many LGBTQ+ Christians feel our only option is to become something we are not. We are forced to conform to misguided and stigmatizing church teachings based on cultural conditioning, not the life-giving and affirming teachings of Christ. Shame and condemnation are repackaged as smiling promises of "liberation from brokenness" and "freedom from homosexuality." To make things worse, if we do not conform to what is presented as our only option (a false projection of self), we are disenfranchised, abandoned, often punished, and routinely stigmatized.

We become the scapegoat. Somehow, we are made out to be a villain when all we are trying to do is be ourselves.

As a result, unfortunately, too many LGBTQ+ people die slowly through self-loathing, destructive addictions, and unhealthy relational patterns. Even worse, some choose the horror of suicide.

The overarching point I am trying to make is this: I believe that every single day, the Pulse tragedy is repeated when LGBTQ+ persons around the world are thrown out of their homes, violently attacked, persecuted, murdered, or take their lives because of the shame-driven toxic stigmatization of LGBTQ+ people.

Stop the abuse.

Stop demonizing us for who we are and how we love.

Stop the killings.

If I could put down the lies and open my eyes to the beauty, not brokenness, of the LGBTQ+ community, anyone can. Dear conservative religious reader, will you?

People can choose to live however they want, but after over 20 years in a conversion ministry movement, I know it doesn't work. I no longer believe that building bridges to non-affirming and non-accepting churches is the fitting metaphor or action to take. Instead, I believe in finding the exit door to those non-affirming churches and inviting others to come outside of its confines. Sometimes the most gracious, brave, and life-giving thing is to walk away from a non-affirming church and live an honest life.

A Summer of #OrlandoUnited and #OrlandoStrong Turns to Rally Together at #OrlandoPride.

On November 12, 2016, I popped out of bed around 5:30 a.m. That is evidence of a miracle because I never pop out of bed at 5:30 a.m. on a Saturday. As I was preparing my coffee, I said, "I can't WAIT to go to Pride!" I got to Lake Eola around 9:30 that morning.

Early on, a friend asked, "Are you excited? Do you have high expectations for the day?" I said that yes, I was excited, but I had no idea what to expect. Of course, there would be a huge crowd of LGBTQ+ and affirming people and a parade, but I didn't know what that would look like or how I would react. In the end, though, it went way beyond anything I could have imagined. I will never forget my first Pride parade and festival.

What Didn't Happen

For so long, watching from afar, I had believed that "Gay Pride" was simply hedonism on display. The right-wing activists I used to work with only posted incredibly racy and licentious photos of men dressed in leather and drag queens sneering and prancing their way down the double yellow line in the middle of the streets. Then, of course, these same activists described the parade as ungodly and a horrible influence on kids and the community. Back then, I knew they were exaggerating but expected that this description was probably accurate for a lot of what happens at these events.

Nope.

I couldn't have been more wrong.

I realize I can't have seen all 130,000 people (estimated) at the 2016 Orlando Pride, but I was ALL over the festival and the parade. I saw maybe a dozen barely clothed muscle men who were not doing drugs and hanging from harnesses. Instead, they handed out water and took photos with all kinds of folks.

I wished for more barely-clothed muscle men and Daniel Craig to parachute in and rescue me from a sneering, mean, Villainous Street Preacher, but the reality is a lot more fun because it's the truth :).

I don't think I saw a single drunk person at that Pride. No drugs, no hedonistic sex in the streets. The drag queens were incredibly gracious and kind. Still a little prancy, but if you looked that fierce, you would prance too!

Everything I had been told to expect for the years that I was back in the (church) closet was a lie. In order to serve their narrative, the ex-gay ministries' deliberately chose to focus on the smallest percentage available and create their own story. I was so happy to be at Orlando Pride in 2016, as it was one of the most fun, engaging, and embracing events I had ever been to… and I haven't missed an event since.

Welcome!

"I'm 'out' for the day, and it is the best day of my life!" This lovely woman in her sixties said with a hushed voice in my ear. I was standing in the HRC booth, and she was a friend of a new friend of mine I met through HRC. She had come around the table to meet me, and within minutes she was sharing her story about being bi, that she had never really been "out" except when she was much younger. But now, with the LGBTQ+ community having been attacked over the summer and being backed into a corner politically with the election of Trump just days before, she felt it was time to tell her husband, very clearly, about who she was and to be more public about it.

With tears in her eyes, she said, "Not sure what tomorrow will bring, but I am 'out' today. I am among my community, and it feels SO good!" I encouraged her to take the steps she needed to prepare first and then courageously follow what her heart and mind led her to do. She hugged me and was reluctant to let go. Her hug reminded me that while I have always been interested in politics, my primary passion is for people.

Getting Tested

"Randy, we got the result. You can see by the one blue dot that you are HIV-negative. Did you expect this result? Are you surprised in any way?" I said that I had expected it to be negative. However, I didn't go into the fact that at that point, the only sexual activity I had had with another person in 25 years was a guy I'd dated last year. He and I had intense conversations/preparation, so by the time we did come together, we knew neither of us had STDs, and we were both HIV-negative. So no, I wasn't surprised by the result, yet a part of me was relieved.

I was astonished at how simple and fast the test was. I was tested a few times in the '80s, which was a horrible experience. Because the onset of HIV/AIDS was taking away so many friends, there was tremendous fear and stigma about the whole process and situation. Add that to the fact that we had to wait months and months to get accurately tested after the risky behavior, and then weeks to months to get the results, getting tested was traumatizing in and of itself. At the 2016 "Come Out With Pride" event, I went into a mobile testing vehicle, and five minutes later had my test results and a free hand fan I gave to my friend Jagger. I was amazed by the experience.

I'm A Hug Ho and Chat Addict

At the HRC booth at the parade, I said to the fun person signing up as a new member, "If you increase your donation by $5, I will hug you!"

They said, "Well, I will increase it by $10, so I can get two hugs!"

So I said, "Deal!" And they got their two hugs with a bonus hug.

I think I set a personal best for my HPH (Hugs Per Hour) rate! I was hugging friends, strangers, strange friends, a statue of Mickey Mouse, people at booths, in the parade, puppies (lots of dogs around), an unappreciative street preacher, and many others.

Also, I talked to everyone about everything all day. I was in extrovert utopia!

Then this particular guy, The WonderDan, fought off the Zombie Apocalypse, survived raging rivers full of alligators, traversed thousands of miles, and searched through 130,000 Proud Orlando LGBTQ+ Pride revelers to find the HRC booth. I had posted on Facebook that I would be there and to say hello if my friends were going to be there.

"Is Randy here?" I heard over my shoulder. I was facing the back of the HRC tent. We had just finished marching in the parade, and I had a Jack and Coke and was winding down from a long, fun, and exciting day.

I looked around, and that silver fox smiled big with his bright blue eyes.

"How are you?" he said as his smile grew bigger.

So let's back up for a minute.

Earlier that day, my friend Nadine, an HRC supporter and volunteer, had decided to bust my chops as we walked around the various exhibit booths picking up free swag like little pride flags and lanyards from different LGBTQ+ organizations. Nadine is pretty with her cute, asymmetrical bob haircut and South Carolinian drawl. She said, "Randy, you need to let go of that past relationship (a man I'd dated who I was STILL pining for) and get rid of your "list" of things you want in a man and just be open to various possibilities. Just say yes to being open to going out with someone new. You just need to let go of the past and enjoy your present."

I was like, "Yes, ma'am, Ms. Nadine ma'am!" She cracked me up with how matter-of-fact she was. She wasn't playing either.

So, at that moment, God sent a chops buster named Nadine to prepare my heart for...

"Randy, if you are open to it, I would like to go on a coffee date, or like a "date" date, with you sometime." That question came after Dan and I had talked for about an hour. We'd had a couple of drinks, and we had a wonderful conversation about the day, as well as remembering running into each other at the NOH8 photo shoot. He shared a bit about his life, and then he let me debrief about attending my first Pride, after which he popped the coffee date, or "date" date, question.

I said, "I would love to have coffee with you. When?"

"Tomorrow night?"

"Sounds good."

And we have pretty much been together almost every day doing something since. In fact, at the time of this writing, we are married! Legally and in front of God and everything! AND OH MY gosh, what a unique and beautiful challenge it has been! (But there's more about all of that in the next chapter.)

Coming Home

At the beginning of this chapter, I shared my social media posts about having the opportunity to tell my story, for the first time, as an out gay man with the local gay community at an HRC function less than 36 hours before the Pulse tragedy.

I talked for far too long at that event, but I got nothing but support and encouragement. Of course, there were some tears in the crowd as well. Especially when, at the two darkest moments of my life, I believe God used gracious LGBTQ+ people to help me 1) stay alive and 2) see heavenly grace personified on Earth.

However, I will never forget this man, a very successful realtor, who commented on how my story impacted him. He said, "There is one thing you need to stop doing. Stop apologizing."

At the beginning of what I shared, I apologized to them because I was literally on the opposite side of many issues almost the whole time I had been in Orlando to that point.

"Yeah, you don't need to apologize to us. You know better now, and as they say, 'once you know better, do better.' So I don't want, and we don't need, your apology. Just do better." The people standing around us nodded in agreement, and one woman put her hand on my shoulder with a supportive squeeze.

Two more people during that evening said almost the same thing. "Honey, you didn't have to apologize. We all have our journeys, and we have to go through shit to get where we are. You don't have to apologize. We understand."

"Randy, it's so sweet you felt like you needed to apologize, but don't worry! We are so glad to have you with us now!"

Since then, I have had at least four other people from that evening, at other events, say something similar. "Your past is your past. We have a lot of important work to do and are glad you are here to lend your talents to the effort," and so on.

I share this because, for the first time in my life, I am experiencing a cohesive, forgiving, gracious, and unified community on a level that far surpasses the myopic church bubbles I was accustomed to. Of course, there are plenty of quarrels, and of course, we are human, so we share all the same frailties as any other community. But I know that I am home for the first time. I know my place among my peers, and I am at peace.

CHAPTER 13

Being Gay on Sunday

It has been my joy and honor to know Reverend Tammi Fierce, who leads an MCC Church in Orlando. When we first met to get acquainted, I shared my story. I also shared how I wanted to reclaim my spiritual calling and gifts and use them for good.

We talked for 90 minutes and covered plenty of ground—including the potential of working together to help others heal from and find their way out of religious stigma and legalistic Christianity in all its forms, specifically in how it manifests in ex-gay/conversion ideology.

An unexpected blessing occurred while talking to her. When I was sharing all the feedback I got when I first came back out, I mentioned that a vast majority of the LGBTQ+ community was incredibly supportive and gracious. On the other hand, alongside many in the conservative religious community saying I was a heretic, a few gay folks said they would never forgive me. I was told a few times, "You have blood on your hands! We will never forgive or accept you."

In response to someone who was incredibly hurt by conversion therapy, I said, "You say I have blood on my hands. All I can say is I am afraid to look down at my hands. I can understand if you never forgive me; it's hard for me to forgive myself."

Now, I know I have never literally killed someone. However, I was in an essential position at Exodus. I honestly believed an ex-gay worldview was the good and right thing to live out. I walked my talk. But now it is evident that I was also in deep denial, self-loathing, suffering from PTSD from my own traumatic experiences with abuse, and frankly naïvely ignorant. The only thing my efforts and beliefs to help people "change" their sexual orientation or "find freedom from homosexuality" did was to support and empower systemic homophobia. The homophobia that ripped apart families solidified non-lifegiving marriages, confused many singles into a life of loneliness and pain in the name of celibacy, and led many to feel their only option was to self-destruct through dysfunctional behavior and or suicide.

After meeting with Tammi, the thought of my past contribution to that systemic hurt and pain went deeper. This time, however, I didn't shut it down. I took a long, hard look.

As a result, in a metaphorical sense, I feel that my past self is somewhat like the Apostle Paul (when he was the Pharisee of Pharisees, Saul), who the scriptures reveal as never picking up a stone to throw at Stephen (the first Christian martyr). Still, instead, he held the cloaks of those who did. He cared enough about them to keep their clothes clean and yet approved of the horrendous murder of Stephen because he thought it was the right and godly thing to do. For years, I heard reports of ex-gay theology/ideology's damage and destruction. I refused to believe the horrible accounts were the result of what I believed and promoted. I was great at blame-shifting—an "I am so sorry, but that hasn't been my experience" kind of attitude. I was in denial of my misery. I was much more interested in protecting the appearance (cloaks) of being a "success story" and our other leaders being seen as experts. I believed the ex-gay hype that what we were doing was the right and godly thing to do instead of looking at how horrible we were acting in the name of "love and truth." Plus, my brainwashing was so complete that I honestly and truly believed there wasn't any other option than to believe the way I did.

Until Steven.

Steven's death revealed the symbolic blood on my hands and the various cloaks (excuses, appearances, lies) I was trying to keep clean during my Exodus years. I hate to admit to succumbing to cult-like indoctrination, but it's true. I was tone-deaf to others' pain until it ripped through my heart. I wish I had listened—truly listened—to others' pain. I am deeply sorrowful that I didn't until it was too late.

In my talk with Tammi, I shared that my passion and vision are to help the LGBTQ+ community carefully confront, heal from, and leave stigma and religious legalism behind. But until that meeting, I hadn't recognized that there was a large part of me that still felt like I didn't deserve to do so.

That was all exposed when Rev. Tammi said, "Isn't it just like Jesus to take the very man (Paul) who participated in the murder of God's people to be the guy to minister to and serve God's people? Isn't it just like Jesus to take a guy like you, someone who did all THAT in opposition to gay people, turn you around, and send you back to serve the same people? That sounds like Jesus to me, and I think you will help many specifically because of your experience. I look forward to seeing what happens."

I often feel before I know why I feel what I feel. When Tammi said that, it was like a lightning bolt went through me and my perspective (and hope) completely changed in a moment. A heavy burden I didn't realize was weighing me down just fell off.

I have found my authentic voice over the past nine years, and I have known what I have to offer as a gay man of faith and as a leader for quite a while. But today, my "hands" aren't frozen with guilt and shame. Nor are they bloodied. Now that I am free from the shackles of learned helplessness from my past, I am ready to share my story and help others thrive and find help. This book is a significant step on that journey.

Guilt can be sneaky and often prefers to remain hidden so that it can immobilize the good and creative. However, when shame is exposed and owned, stagnant pools can become life-giving and free-flowing rivers.

Thanks, Rev. Tammi, for the personal joy and freedom you helped bring forth in our meeting.

Self-Confidence and Acceptance

In the '80s and beyond, a favorite LGBTQ+ protest chant has been, "We're here, we're queer! Get used to it!" I love that—very to the point and easy to understand. For this book, though, I will echo it with a slight modification: "We're here. We're queer. Whether you get used to it *or not*." Some opponents say "tolerance is a two-way street," and "if you want us to affirm you, you have to affirm us."

Except that's not how either tolerance or affirmation works.

Tolerance isn't a two-way street; it's a passive way to not do anything. Also, I am not asking for affirmation. You either affirm or you don't. While I love people and would never want to insult them for the sake of insulting, I will not encourage or accommodate stigmatized views that damage God's queer children. I want LGBTQ+ people to find the courage and be empowered to embrace and affirm themselves, and if others want to come along, great. Either way, we will assert our lives, loves, and relationships as equals. We will continue to press for simple human dignity and decency afforded to everyone else in public policy, culture, and our places of worship.

It's not, or shouldn't be, that difficult to see that, in essence, we are the same as all humans and in the eyes of the Divine.

I Am the Luckiest Fairy Godmother/Bonus Dad Ever

I love my husband, Dan. I do. We have been together for over seven years and married for two years at the time of this writing. Dan is loyal, patient, long-suffering, and other-centered. I love holding his strong hands, and I feel the same profoundly when he tells me he loves me. We are meant to be together. The fact that he kisses me every time we go our different ways in the morning and every time we come back together again in the evening is a dream come true. I love that he loves rom-coms and tolerates my sci-fi and monster movies addiction. I also love that while vampires are my favorite monster-human hybrid and I would always choose them over rom-coms, he thinks J-Lo is a great actress and that I have underestimated her acting abilities.

Dan isn't the only heavenly blessing in this relationship; he brings his daughter, The Diva. She's a treasure in and of her own. And yes, she knows it.

Granted, while in the moment it felt a little irritating, I love remembering the ten-year-old girl jumping on the bed as she excitedly said, "Hey Randy! Daddy said he would think about letting us have fish!"

Or

"Randy, can I have some of your A&W Root Beer?"

Or

"I like waffles but not pancakes. Pancakes are DISGUSTING."

Or

"So what if I want to stay up all night? It's the weekend."

In between her pushing back on and questioning everything, we get to hear—I mean, we are incredibly blessed to listen to—her non-stop karaoke versions of the choruses to Taylor Dayne, Mariah Carey, or Jennifer Hudson songs.

She is now 17. God help us.

I didn't even like teens when I was one, yet I love her with my life. This is a whole new experience for me. One that has revealed how incredibly selfish I can be in new ways. It has also shown how old tapes in my head from childhood can be confronted when trying to learn what's best to relate to our resident Diva.

I love her. I love teasing her about her crushes on boys at school. I loved her smile when we determined that it was okay to call me her Bonus Dad (aka Fairy Godmother) at this point in our relationship. I love it when she brings her teenage reasoning to politics. It was cute to blow her mind when I answered (after being asked) that my opinion of Donald Trump is, "Trump is a national disaster." Her first response to my not-a-Trump-fan statement was cute indignation (her mom and other stepdad are big Trump supporters), but she gets to learn how to deal with liberal Fairy Godmothers, which is good.

Yes, there are times when I need to watch *Star Trek Discovery* in one room while The Diva watches her 700th episode of *Glee* in another or belts out parts of songs. But who could ever get tired of Taylor Dayne's karaoke?

No one, ever.

Yes, I love her father, The WonderDan, and in doing so, I fell in love with a little girl with strong pop-song diva tendencies and became her Bonus Dad, her Fairy Godmother. I am the luckiest Fairy Godmother ever.

Unexpected Grace Comes to Visit: The Parents

His knock on the door was surprising. It was the middle of the day during the work week. Of course, I was in the back of the house, so I couldn't see who was at the door through the living room windows, but I expected it to be Jehovah's Witnesses or maybe the postman dropping off a package from Dan's mom. She likes to send care packages.

I was in my huge, baggy shorts, Chewbacca-style hair, and "Straight Outta the Closet" super gay t-shirt.

I opened the door, and there stood my mom and stepfather, Harry. My once socially conservative mom. My mom, who I hadn't talked to in a while because of her reluctance to want to see or acknowledge Dan and that I am gay. My stepfather who was now looking peaceful and happy, not anything like his past.

Her beautiful brown eyes and his honest smile conveyed unconditional love. "Hi honey! Surprise!"

I was astonished, and the house was a four-alarm wreck. Plus, I had just greeted my mom while wearing a super gay t-shirt. So I told them to come in, forgive the mess, and I would change my t-shirt.

"Don't you worry about it, honey," was her response. "We didn't call, so don't you worry about a thing."

I refused the temptation to flip over the photo on the table by the door, which was of Dan and me kissing. But I did change my t-shirt.

They visited, asked me about work, and we talked about Dan and The Diva a bit. They spent a *lot* of time telling me how great my paintings were and how much they liked my large painting, "Life Flow." Then they took me to Jeremiah's Bar and Grill for lunch. Over not-the-healthiest-but-excellent food, we caught up with their health, hobbies, and family. The most awkward thing was how not uncomfortable it was.

I *never* expected them to visit. Ever. Let alone to visit mine and Dan's home, yet there they were, sitting in the living room talking about how lovely the house was. I almost pinched myself to make sure I wasn't dreaming.

Unexpected grace, indeed.

As they pulled out of the driveway to head back home, it was my turn to stand on the porch, waving as they left. I was holding Mom's other half of her French dip sandwich she gave me to have for lunch the next day. It was a warm feeling that accompanied my walk back into the house; it empowered the smile on my face.

It's tempting to want to analyze the visit. To read something into what happened and figure out "what it means…" Maybe it's my age and experience, but I just want to enjoy it. To store it away as a charming visit. When they said they loved and were proud of me, I chose to believe them.

Maybe next time I won't change my super gay t-shirt.

Being Gay on Sunday

We walked into the gay-affirming church near downtown Orlando seven minutes late. The Diva was in the middle, with one hand holding Dan's hand and the other mine. We always seem to be a little late to events in

Orlando, and I always seem to be the only one to notice. I was raised that if you are 10 minutes early, you are already five minutes late. That's another echo from the past I struggle to "let go" of.

Since coming back out, I quit going to my church of 10 years after an awful public shaming incident with my life group. I had "liked" a racy photo on Facebook (not porn but racy) and left a silly comment. That made the post show up in one of my life group's daughter's (who was an adult at the time) newsfeed, and all of a sudden, a friendship of 10 years turned into me "endangering" their children and the need to text shame me in front of our entire life group.

Yeah, okay. Bye now.

Since then, I have visited my old church twice and a few gay-affirming churches along the way. However, the gay-affirming church we walked into that morning was the first fully "LGBTQ+ and allies" church I may have ever seen since I lived in Texas. I suppose the Texas one doesn't count, though, because when I went there, it was on a weekday evening and it was to sneak up to the building with my friend William to "lay hands" on the structure to drive out the demons.

I was not kidding. We thought we were some spiritual ninjas or something.

We thought we were being "wise as serpents, innocent as doves," when in hindsight, we were being judgmental and trying to make ourselves feel better about what we feared. We were co-directors of the group I led in Texas at the time and wanted to be able to say that we did "spiritual warfare" for the lost, sexually broken souls at that church.

We truly believed that to be the case, but I look back on it now and feel like an idiot.

I have been reluctant to go to any church, but over the past year or so I have missed worship time. I miss regular life group meetings and hearing an occasional sermon blow my mind. I want to be in church right now, I don't want to be in church right now—that's the great ambivalence.

Many people, myself included, detest the institutionalized and "branded" church for many good reasons. But it's the treasure within those churches that I yearn for. I am not talking about the personal bank accounts funding the budget, beautiful modern or ornate fixtures, or trappings of this or that program or amenity.

I am talking about the real treasure within the church: you. I miss being with you on Sunday.

It's worth repeating for emphasis: The treasure is you. You are the treasure. You are a treasure to me.

Jesus didn't die on the cross and rise from the dead to create a standardized fan club of alienated members singing in harmony while their hearts are in discord. His atonement didn't clear the way to the father yet call us to obstruct fellowship, objectify heartache with clichéd answers, and judge each other with worldly "us vs. them" thinking.

That's why I, as an openly gay man, am not with you this morning. I cannot get beyond the label of being one of "them" today. My hurt and anger have led me to respond in kind in some ways, making it all the more hurtful. I am not proud of that.

However, the treasure I see is in you, as a peer. Your worth transcends estimation. If I were looking you right in the eyes, I would say, with full belief and conviction, I *know* you are a treasure to this world and the people you are in a relationship with. I love the song of your life. You are a treasure regardless of what any of us, or maybe even you, see. Even favorable judgments of you aren't enough; you are a magnificent mystery, a person God fell in love with.

You.

I am not Jesus. Thank God, literally, or we would have been doomed during my first three-year-old tantrum. If we had made it past that, we would have seen hellfire and brimstone the first time I tried to drive in Los Angeles traffic! I am not anywhere close to the suffering and pain Christ went through. Not anywhere near that, but the hurt and suffering that keeps me from wanting to sit next to you in a church today are something I need to work on. My past is full of trying to live out something I wasn't. Still, when I fell in love with the real treasure within, my higher and authentic self, I realized the greatest miracle of all time is to be open to the Divine and dignity found in everyone that draws breath. Even jerks like me.

The Path Out of Fear–Come Soar with Me

As mentioned earlier in the book, I was part of a 12-step program for a little while. I learned many lessons from that experience that I still carry with me today. One of those is the necessary exercise of conducting a fearless moral inventory and acknowledging the actual "fruit" of your beliefs and the impact they have genuinely had on yourself and others.

Luke 6:43–Luke 6:45 NIV: "No good tree bears bad fruit, nor does a bad tree bear good fruit. Each tree is recognized by its fruit. People do not pick figs from thorn bushes, or grapes from briers. A good man brings good things out of the good stored up in his heart, and an evil man brings evil things out of the evil stored up in his heart. For the mouth speaks what the heart is full of."[10]

It is evident that all of my beliefs sounded nice on paper and helped empower an entire movement of people. Yet everything about those beliefs fell apart in destructive ways when even slightly challenged. The long-timers in the ex-gay world were more concerned about self-preservation and being "right" than being accurate, gracious, or even truthful about their experiences and our relationships.

The fruit of my life was being alone, constantly frustrated, and depressed. For a while, I thought I had it all with the excellent salary, condo, car, traveling, a high profile in the movement, and the acknowledgement that I could see myself in a relationship with a woman. However, the effects of the beliefs and life I had ascribed to ripped apart families, reinforced the stigma and oppression of LGBTQ+ people, and drove others to incredibly destructive patterns of behavior, including, at its worst, suicide.

My beliefs were making me suicidal. Those same beliefs killed Steven.

And it was all gone in the blink of an eye. Divine fruit doesn't create temporary earthly gains that are wiped out in the blink of an eye. The fruit of the Spirit, life-giving fruit, doesn't rip apart families or contribute to religious, social, and political oppression.

The ex-gay/conversion ministry world lives in a state of oppositional bias affirmation. They know that they are as attracted to the same sex as they ever were, but the more they can state how "not gay" they are, the more convinced they are that the bitter fruit that comes from their tree is a sweet, juicy apple instead of cyanide for the soul.

For me, listing my beliefs one by one and questioning the true fruit, both positive and negative, of what they produced was the first step. Then, busting through legalistic fear, I believe God gave me the grace to say it was okay to question everything. As a result, I am out today and still a Christ-follower (again, of the Universalist flair).

The path out of fear also recognizes that not all was or is a loss. I have seen many people in the ex-gay/conversion ministry world leave it behind,

---

10 Luke 6:43–Luke 6:45 NIV

embrace their authentic selves, and joyfully retain certain aspects of their past journey.

For me personally, I "inventoried" the true and good lessons that happened during my time in the ex-gay/conversion world. I did learn how not to abuse substances and how to stand on my own two feet among other Christians. While the environment wasn't exactly healthy, my leadership, creativity, and communication skills were also manifest during that time. My fear and hatred of conservative Christians fell away. I had many incredibly spiritual moments, a lot of growth, and good times to store in my soul's treasure chest as authentic experiences.

I learned to take personal responsibility and gained emotional maturity during that time. I had life-changing experiences and relationships. It's so easy to forget that God is good, loving, and benevolent at every single stage of our life. The Creator's fingerprints of grace and loving guidance are all over everything. We have to look and ask Him to reveal Themself as brighter than the dark filter of experience.

Another truth I stumbled across is that true joy in life is not based on what you have or even what you can do. There can be manifestations of joy, but the true, joyful life is the ability to be content regardless of circumstance by being intentionally grateful.

Some would say I have had a fucked-up life. My PTSD counselor said my life could be a rated R horror movie that somehow makes you chuckle here and there. And if I wanted to live my life as a victim, I could acknowledge the truth that I have had many messed-up experiences and live there.

Uh… No thanks.

This book, in fact, is a summary of how a person can somehow survive horrific things (for decades), live out of alignment with who they are (for decades), and *still* finally find freedom, joy, and peace to live out the rest of their life authentically.

Again, I fight for life and refuse to be run over by it. I am grateful God gave me a black Pomeranian guard dog named Teddy Bear to stand guard by my crib. I am thankful for a positive experience with a gay babysitter in my younger years who let my brother and I discover the transcendent wonder of dancing in a rain shower and marveling at the brilliant pink and orange light in the sky. It is a joy to remember outwitting Baptist deacons and having funny church stories about sitting on a Baptist preacher's throne, of experiencing the love of God many times before I ever knew His name or that He is, actually, They.

I love the awkward but true stories of when I first developed crushes on Bo and Luke Duke. I love that even though my parents and I have had a rocky relationship over time, I can remember my mother's laughter as she taught us the bump, and Granny Grunt always having an ice cream sandwich and a "Cokey Coley" ready for me when I came to visit.

I love that I survived the blurry years, learned my lessons from them, and never went back. I am grateful for experiencing gay life and culture in the '80s before going into the church closet in '92. I will always be thankful for Baptist spaghetti potlucks and a God who made Themself known through angelic guys in Daytona while I passed out on top of a "party barge" bus looking at the stars.

I am grateful for a pistol of an aunt who gave me a one-way ticket to Dallas, for my lifelong friend Daphne, and for Steven's influence and legacy on my life.

I am grateful for a God who is not offended by garage sale chic living rooms or my desire to love another man. I love that the two times I came out were due to Jesus placing loving, safe, and gracious LGBTQ+ people around me.

As weird as it might sound, I am grateful for Exodus International, and I am also thankful I was given the opportunity to help shut it down. My path led me through that world, and it was there that my true self finally found its voice, where I walked away from the false prison of learned helplessness created by legalism, condemnation, and shame.

During those years, the Divine showed me that I was so much more than I had ever imagined. So much so that I am now living for a genuine purpose and not out of fear of others or myself.

The false shackles of ex-gay/conversion ideology fall away as my wings unfurl and the wind of the Spirit lifts me higher and higher.

And I soar.

Join me.

EPILOGUE

You know it's a good party when only one ambulance shows up. I would have preferred zero ambulances, but I can't control others, nor can I control the recipe for one of my relative's special medicinal brownies.

I did not partake of the brownies myself, and the person who ended up in the ambulance was warned by multiple people to *not* eat a whole one. In fact, he was advised to only eat a quarter of one—or, if brave, a half, but not a whole. Unfortunately, he (the man I will now refer to as The Gnome because he became a lawn ornament about two hours later) recklessly thought he would prove his badassery to all of us. Out of rebellion against wise advice, he ate one whole brownie and tried to eat two before someone stopped him.

He certainly fucked around and found out.

So when I noticed he was out front wandering around our yard like a zombie, I ran out there, only to find his date was already there trying to calm him down. The Gnome was demanding an ambulance. We had a registered nurse at the party who checked him out and said he was fine, but The Gnome wouldn't believe him. So… if the man wants an ambulance, the man gets an ambulance.

Of course, our neighbors loved all the commotion, and they still bring up the collective memory from time to time.

I stood out there with The Gnome and his date until the ambulance arrived. Even the EMT ambulance driver, after checking him out for a few minutes, was like, "Man, you probably just partied too hard and need to sleep it off." But The Gnome wouldn't respond, so he got carted away to sleep the brownie off in an emergency room.

Nothing like a $5k bill to sober you up the next day. That was a helluva expensive nap, buddy.

He called the next afternoon and apologized for being a downer at the party. I told him that while we missed his presence, no one had missed a beat, and the party carried on till about 1 a.m. However, I did say that he probably wanted to apologize to his much younger date, who was stranded at our house overnight because he couldn't drive The Gnome's old-but-very-cool stick shift car.

His date, who we will call Blondie, looked terrified as the ambulance drove away. He was socially awkward and barely talked beyond one-word answers. After we walked back inside, I asked if he wanted a drink to steady his nerves. He said, "No, I can't drink alcohol."

I said, "Well good for you. A coke? Juice?"

Blondie didn't want something to drink, but instead asked, "How old do you think I am?"

I replied, "Mid to late twenties?"

He said, "No, guess again, lower."

I was excited to hear complete sentences coming out of his mouth so I guessed, "Twenty-three?"

He was like, "No, a lot lower."

At that point, I was no longer happy with the guessing game. Clearly registering my shift in emotion, Blondie said with a big grin, "I'm only nineteen, so I can't drink alcohol or eat those brownies."

My immediate thought was to tell my family members to get the friggin' medicinal brownies out of range and for no one to fix Blondie a cocktail, just in case he changed his mind. I didn't do that, but I did ask a few friends to keep an eye on him. More surprisingly, perhaps, my second thought was: *I wish I had that kind of self-awareness and control when I was 19.*

BOOM.

Fuck.

The Universe set me up again! I can't tell you how many times I ended up almost blacking out, or fully blacking out, drunk-stranded at afterparties when I was this young man's age. Nineteen. Just nineteen. Then I realized this 19 year old was a sober version of me 36 years ago.

He was scared, awkward, and stranded, and he didn't know anyone. His date had just been taken away in an ambulance, and while he thought it was funny to see my face when he said he was 19, you could tell he was frightened. So I sat with him for a while and chit-chatted to let him know he was safe and welcome. I reassured him that The Gnome was going to be fine according to the nurse and the ambulance crew (I asked) and just needed to sleep it off. I said that I didn't think anyone was headed to Blondie's neck of the woods (about 90 minutes away), so he could stay at our house and sleep on our big comfy couch until The Gnome came to collect him. We had family staying that night as well, so we were all ready with fresh bedding and blankets. I told him that The Gnome would probably wake up early in the morning, and until then, he was welcome to have all the good food (except the brownies) and Sprite he wanted. He smiled, relaxed, and seemed to enjoy himself while watching the other 30-ish guests have a great time.

Around 1 a.m., I got emotional. After I said goodbye to a beautiful friend and her wife, I walked back in and saw Blondie with an almost cherubic face snoring like a freight train, curled up in my great-granny's quilt (yes, we still use it) on our couch.

At that moment, I reflected on the memory of my 19 year old self: stranded at a roach motel, overdosing in Louisville, throwing up over overpasses, and so on. I wished I had a maternally-minded 55 year old look out for me instead of the nightmare I had been through.

Then I remembered Momma Mella. Mella had done that for me, and instead of taking anything from me, she had simply asked me to "pay it forward." I realized I was doing exactly that as Blondie slept safely in our living room. He was literally wrapped in a quilt made from another incredible example of unconditional love, my great-grandmother.

And that same love and heart from both Mella and my Great Granny live on... *in me.*

The next morning, I slept in until 9 a.m. or so. It was the actual day of my birthday (May 14th), and I decided there was no rush to get up. When I finally got out of bed, I realized that Dan and two of our family members were out taking stuff to the dump (from work that was being done at our family member's house). Blondie and a female family member made a fine breakfast of sausage links and croissants. We didn't have anything else except leftover potato salad and ranch dressing from the night before.

Shortly thereafter, The Gnome sheepishly came to get his car and date, and all was well in the world again. My female family member left to go set up a Mother's Day celebration for her soon-to-be mother-in-law, and for a little while, I was alone in the house.

Our house, our home.

No one except our dogs could see the happy tears as I realized I was finally at home with who I truly am, and literally in a home that love built and protects. I looked at all the gifts and fun birthday cards, roses, and balloons, and I realized my inner child had a huge smile on his face. After all those birthdays where I believed I was forgotten and intentionally abandoned, I was finally having a birthday party as birthday parties were meant to be: celebrations and not just another day. I was finally in the community I was meant to be in all along... and I am finally among the family I should have always belonged to.

I am now the man I was created to be.

Beautiful.

AFTERWORD

Afterword by Yvette Schneider[11]

I met Randy at an Exodus conference in Chicago when he worked for the ex-gay group in Arlington, Texas, and I worked for Family Research Council. We chatted for several minutes in the corridor of a campus building at Wheaton and formed an instant bond. From that point on, we called ourselves siblings separated at birth. Years later, when we worked together at Exodus, we would talk about how dedicated we were to serving God, meaning that we were obedient to what we believed God expected of us. We weren't the ones "falling" into sexual "sin." We were the holy ones, the pure ones, the ones who followed the rules, and wondered why everyone couldn't be like us. We were true believers, convinced that everything we had been taught about the Bible and Christianity was an irrefutable fact.

But there were doubts, cracks in our convictions, questions for which there were no answers. For years, we saw firsthand that people who were participating in Exodus ministries and coming to the annual conference were not changing. It was heady to speak onstage before hundreds about how God had changed us, to have the audience cheer their approval,

---

11 Names used in the Afterword by Yvette Schneider are the same pseudonyms used in the rest of the book.

hoping God would change them next. But the reality behind closed doors was much different. Those who remained single struggled with loneliness and the temptation to form romantic relationships with someone of the same sex. Those who married someone of the opposite sex clung to their ministry groups for dear life, worrying about their ongoing desires for a gay partnership. To imagine that God was behind the relentless struggle of every gay Christian, and the fruitless efforts to change, became untenable.

Still, many of us clung to the belief that at least some people changed from gay to straight, despite the dearth of evidence. Roger Tompkins, the executive director of Exodus, when speaking at the Gay Christian Network conference in 2013, said that 99.99% of gay people do not change to straight. He later revealed that the .01% he was referring to was me. Because being "ex-gay" was a God-given calling and career, it was essential to keep my same-sex attractions locked down and tucked away, so no one knew I hadn't changed either, including myself. This is how the misguided notion that gay people could change continued; 1 Corinthians 6:11 ("Such were some of you; but you were washed, but you were sanctified..." NASB) was offered as proof that God could and would change gay people. Believing the only way to be accepted by the church, family, and friends was to be straight, gay people pursued change and conformed by suppressing and sacrificing their true selves. "Ex-gay" leaders assured gay Christians that they, too, could change.

As we came to terms with our lack of change—as well as everyone else's—we had to step away and say, "This is not working." But we couldn't say it only to each other; we had to say it publicly. For this reason, Randy has had to summon the courage to tell the stories only he knows, the ones that were hidden and covered up to protect the illusion of change the church so desperately wants to believe. The only way to end this emotionally and spiritually devastating practice of shaming gay people into the closet is for those of us who know the truth to speak up and tell the world what we saw. As Randy has demonstrated his commitment to see full inclusion of LGBTQ+ people in the body of Christ, as well as in society as whole, and an end to the dangerous practice of sexual orientation change efforts (SOCE), so we all need to lift our voices and tell our stories. Our LGBTQ+ brethren still caught in the clutches of an overbearing and controlling church community, and in families whose church communities influence their views on gay Christians, need our voices in books and movies, on social media and TV shows, in private and public conversations, to say enough is enough. We are perfect as we are.

HELPFUL RESOURCES

The resources listed here are current as of the publication of this book and descriptions have been taken directly from their respective websites in accordance with their copyright. Please practice discernment concerning your own needs and values as you do your own research to find the resources and help you need. —Randy

Helpful Resources

The *Pray Away* film website has a discussion guide to go with the film on Netflix and also has various social media accounts where they post updates and announcements on film screening and Q&A panels: www.prayawayfilm.com

To reach Randy, please visit www.randyscobey.com. He would love to hear from you.

Orlando Resources

Zebra Youth® is a network of organizations that provide services to lesbian, gay, bisexual, transgender, and all youth (LGBTQ+) ages 13–24. The coalition assists young people facing homelessness, bullying, isolation from their families, and physical, sexual, and drug abuse with individualized programs to guide them to recovery and stability: www.zebrayouth.org

Joy MCC is the spiritual home to a multi-cultural, inclusive, and diverse community of faith. We are rooted in the life, ministry, and teachings of Jesus. We experience a vibrant spirituality that is positive, practical, and progressive:
www.joymcc.com

One Orlando Alliance is a vital support network for LGBTQ+ organizations in Central Florida. We lower barriers, provide critical communication, and promote effective, influential, and sustainable opportunities for transforming the culture of the region. We understand transformative change in attitudes and behaviors begins with an unwavering commitment to bettering the welfare of all. We will achieve this by fostering a deep respect for one another and ensuring inclusiveness within our diverse population:
www.oneorlandoalliance.org

The mission of *The LGBT+ Center Orlando, Inc.* is to promote and empower the LGBT community and its allies through information, education, advocacy, and support. We have locations in downtown Orlando and Kissimmee:
www.thecenterorlando.org

Free Mom Hugs has chapters in all 50 states and other initiatives forming globally. The group's growing force of more than 14,000 volunteers is a national groundswell dedicated to empowering the world to celebrate the LGBTQIA+ community through visibility, conversation, and education:
www.freemomhugs.org

Hotlines

Trevor Lifeline is a crisis intervention and suicide prevention phone service available 24/7/365 offered through the Trevor Project. If you or someone you love is seeking help, please call 1-866-488-7386 or text "START" to 678678.

Trans Lifeline is a trans-led organization that connects trans people to the community, support, and resources they need to survive and thrive. Available 7am–1am PST / 9am-3am CST / 10am–4am EST.
Call 877-565-8860.

Advocacy

Tyler Clementi Foundation exists to honor Tyler Clementi by sharing his story to help raise awareness around the issues that impacted Tyler and led to his death. The Tyler Clementi Foundation seeks to find actions and solutions to those issues based on research because we wanted to make sure that no one else ever suffered the same pain, shame, and humiliation that Tyler experienced.
www.tylerclementi.org

Born Perfect is a campaign of the National Center for Lesbian Rights focused on passing laws across the country to protect LGBT children and young people from the harm of sexual orientation and gender identity change efforts. Born Perfect drafts, introduces, and passes legislation, spreads awareness through public education, media, and advocacy, and empowers conversion therapy survivors and their families. If you'd like to get involved or share your story, you can sign up here:
www.nclrights.org/our-work/bornperfect

The Trevor Project provides 24/7 life-saving support via phone, text, and chat, as well as a safe space social networking site for LGBTQ youth, as well as creates and runs research, education, and advocacy programs. In the effort to protect LGBTQ youth from conversion therapy in every state of the nation and countries around the world, The Trevor Project has launched 50 Bills, 50 States:
www.thetrevorproject.org

Truth Wins Out is a 501 (c)3 non-profit organization that educates the world on the harm caused by destructive "ex-gay" conversion programs, while fighting to eliminate anti-LGBTQ prejudice and discrimination. We believe that genuine freedom and contentment derive from authenticity and living one's truth.
www.truthwinsout.org

PFLAG is the first and largest organization for LGBTQ+ people, their parents and families, and allies. You can find PFLAG's webinars and their free training toolkit to assist people looking to take action in the effort to protect LGBTQ+ people from conversion therapy in all its forms here:
www.pflag.org

GLAAD is a non-profit media organization that works through entertainment, news, and digital platforms to share stories from the LGBTQ community that accelerate acceptance and provoke dialogue that leads to cultural change:
www.glaad.org

MAP's mission is to provide independent and rigorous research, insight, and communications that help speed equality and opportunity for all. Their website includes up-to-date Equality Maps, which include a state-by-state assessment on the current status of conversion therapy bans across the U.S: www.lgbtmap.org/equality-maps/conversion_therapy

GLSEN is an American education organization working to end discrimination, harassment, and bullying based on sexual orientation, gender identity, and gender expression and to prompt LGBT cultural inclusion and awareness in K–12 schools.
www.glsen.org

LGBTQ Faith Organizations

At *Canyonwalker Connections*, faith and scholarship intersect to repair the division that exists between social and Christian conservative and the lesbian, gay, bisexual, and transgender (LGBT) community through education, training, and dialogue in both secular and religious environments:
www.canyonwalkerconnections.com

The National LGBTQ Task Force's Institute for Welcoming resources is an ecumenical group that aims to provide resources to facilitate a paradigm shift in multiple denominations whereby churches become welcoming and affirming of all congregants regardless of sexual orientation and gender identity:
www.welcomingresources.org

Q Christian Fellowship is an ecumenical Christian ministry focused on serving lesbian, bisexual, gay, transgender, queer, and straight ally Christians. QCF seeks to cultivate radical belonging among LGBTQ+ people and allies through a commitment to growth, community, and relational justice. In keeping with its mission, QCF has launched the UNCHANGED campaign as an affirmative counter to the damage wrought in the name of God through ex-gay theologies and conversion therapy. You can read the stories, submit your own, or join the community here. Additionally, QCF has partnered with The Trevor Project to launch The Good Fruit Project, a comprehensive educational resource that presents a faith and researched-based case against LGBTQ+ change efforts:
www.qchristian.org

Transmission Ministry Collective is an online community dedicated to the spiritual care, faith formation, and leadership potential of transgender, nonbinary, genderqueer, and gender-expansive Christians. If you are looking for support or are in need of virtual community, you will be able to find that through TMC's text-based chat servers and video-based support groups as well as their online Bible studies:
www.transmissionministry.com

The Reformation Project is a Bible-based, Christian organization that works to promote inclusion of LGBTQ people by reforming church teaching on sexual orientation and gender identity through national conferences, local chapters, and digital resources:
www.reformationproject.org

Support for Conversion Therapy Survivors

The Naming Project is a Christian ministry serving youth of all sexual and gender identities. They provide a safe place for youth who are gay, lesbian, bisexual, transgender, queer, questioning, or allied to learn, grow, and share their experiences. The Naming Project is a space in which youth can comfortably discuss faith and who they understand themselves to be and how they relate to God and the rest of the world:
www.thenamingproject.org

Conversion Therapy Survivors is an online group of people who have experienced reparative therapy, 'ex-gay' ministries, sexual orientation change efforts (SOCE), aversion therapy, and other methods to understand or change our sexual orientation or gender identity. CTS exists to affirm our lesbian, gay, bisexual, transgender, or queer identity as psychologically, spiritually, and relationally whole:
www.conversiontherapysurvivors.org

Beyond Ex-Gay is an affirming online community and resource for those of us who have survived ex-gay experiences:
www.beyondex-gay.com

ABOUT THE AUTHOR

Randy Scobey is currently a writer and corporate trainer. In his former career, Randy served as the last Executive Vice President and lead spokesperson for Exodus International—the ex-gay organization he would eventually help shut down. Since its closure, Randy's unique perspective and experience has led to him being featured in the award-winning documentaries *Pray Away* and *For They Know Not What They Do*.

After coming to terms with being a gay man of faith, Randy has (re) embraced his life and his truth. Today, Randy serves as an activist and volunteer to help denounce conversion therapy and its harmful effects. He works passionately against this toxic ideology—especially in its "pastoral" form of ex-gay ministry. Ultimately, by sharing his extraordinary story, Randy hopes to further prove that the abuse must end and that the proverbial "stained glass closet" is no match for authentic love.

Randy lives with his husband Dan, their daughter, and two fur babies in the suburbs of Orlando.